U0627283

《暨南外语博士文库》

主 编／宫 齐
副主编／王 琢／蒲若茜

视访谈中话语缓和的语用研究

ATIC STUDY OF MITIGATION IN TELEVISION INTERVIEW TALKS

李海辉 著

中国出版集团
世界图书出版公司

**图书在版编目（CIP）数据**

电视访谈中话语缓和的语用研究：英文/李海辉著.
—广州：世界图书出版广东有限公司，2014.1
ISBN 978-7-5100-5542-3

Ⅰ.①电… Ⅱ.①李… Ⅲ.①电视—语言艺术—研究—英文 Ⅳ.①G222.2

中国版本图书馆CIP数据核字（2014）第005003号

## 电视访谈中话语缓和的语用研究

**策划编辑**：刘正武
**责任编辑**：程 静
**出版发行**：世界图书出版广东有限公司
　　　　　（广州市新港西路大江冲25号 邮编：510300）
**电　　话**：（020）84451969 84453623 84184026
http://www.gdst.com.cn　E-mail：pub@gdst.com.cn
**经　　销**：各地新华书店
**印　　刷**：广东天鑫源印刷有限责任公司
**版　　次**：2014年1月第1版
**印　　次**：2014年1月第1次印刷
**开　　本**：880mm×1 230mm 1/32
**字　　数**：240千
**印　　张**：8.5
ISBN 978-7-5100-5542-3/H·0842
**定　　价**：35.00元

**版权所有　侵权必究**
咨询、投稿：020-84460251　gzlzw@126.com

# 项目基金

1. "广东省高等学校高层次人才项目——当代话语冲突与话语缓和的语用研究"（122-GK120002）。

2. 国家社科基金一般项目"分析哲学视域下感觉词汇的认知语义研究"（12BYY119）。

3. 广东省哲学社会科学"十二五"规划项目"话语和谐—不和谐取向的社交语用研究"（GD12CWW08）。

# 总　序

　　暨南大学创办于1906年，是我国第一所由国家创办的华侨高等学府，是目前在全国招收港澳台和海外华侨学生最多的高校，是国家"211工程"重点综合性大学。"暨南"二字出自《尚书·禹贡》篇："东渐于海，西被于流沙，朔南暨，声教讫于四海。"意即面向南洋，将中华文化远播到五洲四海。

　　暨南大学外国语学院的前身是创办于1927年的外国语言文学系，历史上曾有许多著名专家、学者在该系任教，如叶公超、梁实秋、钱钟书、许国璋等。1978年复办后，外语系在曾昭科教授、翁显良教授的主持下，教学与科研成绩斐然，1981年外国语言文学系获国家第一批硕士学位授予权，成为暨南大学最早拥有硕士授予权的单位之一。当时的英语语言文学硕士点以文学为主、专长翻译，翁显良、曾昭科、张鸾铃、谭时霖、黄均、黄锡祥等一大批优秀学者先后担任硕士研究生导师，他们治学严谨，成绩卓著，为我们今天的发展奠定了坚实的基础。

　　如今，外国语学院已拥有专任教师138人，其中教授10人，副教授46人，讲师70余人。教授中有博士生导师2人，硕士生导师37人。学院教师中获博士学位者36人，在读博士20余人。现有英语语言文学系、商务英语系、日语系、法语系和大学英语教学部等5个教学单位，有外国文学研究所、应用语言学研究所、跨文化及翻译研究所、日本语言文化研究所及外语教学研究中心等5个专门的研究机构。学院现有外国语言文学硕士学位一级学科授权点，有英语语言文学、外国语言学及应用语言学、日语语言文学3个二级学科，以及翻译硕士专业（MTI）学位授权点。英美文学方向主要为华裔美国文学研究、英美女性文学和英美后现代文学研究；外国语言学及应用语言学方向以理论语言学、功能语言学和音系学为研究特色；日语语言文学方向侧重现当代日本文学、日中比较文学、日语语言及中日文化研究；翻译方向从语言学、文学和文化等多个层面探讨翻译理论与实践，突出翻译的实践性。研究生导师大多数具有海外大学或学术机构从事教学、科研和进修的经历。目前，学院教师主持国家社科基金项目6项，教育部、广东省社科规划项目数十项。

《暨南外语博士文库》丛书（以下简称《文库》）是暨南大学外国语学院部分获博士学位教师的研究成果，它的编纂主要基于以下目的：首先，是对近十几年来我校外语学科获博士学位教师研究成果的梳理；其次，为我校中、青年外语学人搭建展示团队科研成果的平台，以显示本学科发展的集群效应；第三，旨在激励暨南外语学人不断进取，勇攀教学、科研的新高峰，再创新辉煌。《文库》主要收录了2000年以后我校外语学科博士学位获得者尚未正式出版的博士论文，这些论文均经本人反复修改和校对，再经相关方向博士生导师的认真审阅后提交出版社排版付梓。《文库》涵盖了语言学、外国文学、翻译、文化及其他相关学科，涉及语种包括汉语、英语、日语、法语、西班牙语等。《文库》第一批拟出版8部，其他教师的博士论文将在此后陆续编排、出版。

《文库》的成果是新一代暨南外语学人孜孜不倦、努力奋进的结晶，是他们宁静致远、潜心治学的象征。这些成果代表了暨南外语学科的进步与发展，预示着我们的未来和希望，这也是我们献给暨南大学110周年校庆和外国语学院90周年华诞的一份厚礼。

《文库》的出版得到了广东省优势重点学科建设项目和我校重点学科建设项目的支持，此外世界图书出版公司在本套丛书的编辑、设计等方面付出了大量心血，在此我们一并表示衷心感谢！

编 者

2013年12月16日

# 序

那是上世纪90年代末的一段日子。李海辉从暨南大学赶来广东外语外贸大学，旁听我主讲的硕士学位课程"语用学"，每周一次，风雨无阻，他求知的坚毅与努力给我留下了深刻印象。此后，到了本世纪初，他就以优异的成绩被广东外语外贸大学的外国语言学及应用语言学研究中心录取，在我名下攻读语用学方向的博士学位。李海辉有很好的外语基础，他在博览群书，特别是研读国外话语研究成果的基础上，结合汉语话语实际，选定"话语缓和语"作为自己的论题，开始过着一段兼顾日常教学与学位论文写作的艰苦、漫长的日子。

那时，冉永平教授和我都在语言学及应用语言学研究中心工作，我特意请他作为博士生副导师，协助我指导李海辉的论文写作。当我退离工作岗位后，李海辉最终在冉永平教授的指导下完成了现在付梓的博士论文——《电视访谈中话语缓和的语用研究》，顺利通过了答辩，取得博士学位。

对话语缓和语进行专题研究是很有意义的。我们知道，冲突与缓和是人际交往中普遍存在的两种状态，也是语言使用中言语行为、话语、词汇等选择及其语境制约下语力博弈的两种常态；同时，化解冲突，实现语言缓和与人际关系和谐是交际主体意在努力实现的永恒主题，这是人类社会发展的内在需要，也是人类理性的重要表现。为此，受制于人际之间的社交语用目的，缓和手段（mitigating devices）、缓和语（mitigators）等广泛存在于语言交际之中。自20世纪80年代以来，以Bruce Fraser, Claudia Caffi等为代表的国际学者将语言使用中的缓和现象（mitigation）引入现代语用学研究，使其成为了语用学的研究对象。

近年来，国内学者对该现象的研究成果日益增多，尤其是基于汉语交际中的缓和语言研究，出现了一些从语用学的角度探究汉语文化语境下缓和现象的成果。比如，李海辉的这本博士论文《电视访谈中话语缓和的语用研究》以中央电视台节目《实话实说》为语料，在语用学理论的指导下，探讨实现语用缓和的策略类型、语境制约因素以及语用缓和的功能等，这属于动态语境下媒体话语的语用学研究，其中的话语选择既受制于说话人之间的人际语用关系，也体现了媒体交际语境下话语使用的机构性特征。也就是说，类似研究不完全等同于日常交际中话语缓和的语用学研究。

李海辉认为，缓和就是言语交际中说话人刻意降低其施为力度，以减缓话语负面效果的一种语用策略。在话语内容可能造成对听话人的面子损伤、情感伤害或心理打击时，说话人往往设法阻滞此类效果的产生，这就是话语缓和。它是言语行为的施为力度与成事效果的同步弱化。根据施为力度的发生层面以及言语行为的三分法，话语缓和策略包括命题缓和、施为缓和与成事缓和三种主要形式，其表现特征为说话人弱化自身话语的认知、道义背书，亦即说话人拥有的话语权利与义务，这些不同于现有文献中的研究发现。在言语交际中，它们可以消除听话人对交际的抵触心理，实施面子维护、情感安抚等人际功能与规劝、说服等交际功能。从 Jef Verschueren 的语言顺应论的角度来说，无论是策略的选择还是功能的实现，均为语言顺应的结果。

基于语料分析，李海辉在本论文中认为，从利益取向看，话语缓和是既利他也利己、先利他而后利己的。顺应本质上是利己的，但也可以是利他的，而移情是纯利他的。移情涵盖了顺应，但顺应并非总是移情。故此，制约话语缓和的机制是一种特殊的顺应机制——移情顺应。与非移情顺应相比，移情顺应遏制了说话人采取话语加强以及听话人选择交际规避。移情顺应的主要特征是相互性。话语缓和的策略选择源于说话人对听话人的面子、情感、心理需求的趋同、认同，而其功能的实现取决于听话人对说话人交际意图的协同、配合，这就是相互移情顺应。这是语言顺应论视角下的话语缓和功能。

移情顺应可以为话语缓和与礼貌之间的关系提供如下解释。缓和并非总是礼貌，礼貌也并非总是缓和，二者之间不存在谁蕴含谁的问题，不是子母集或并集关系。缓和与礼貌的关系是交集关系，其共核是利他，而利他也是移情顺应的本质特征。这些都是这本博士论文中富有启发性的见解，令人欣喜。

可以说，李海辉的研究进一步拓展了话语缓和的探索范围，特别是对媒体话语的语用学研究。人际交往中的缓和语、弱势语等有助于减弱所在话语的驱使性，或维护交际主体的面子、身份地位等，是维护人际关系的有效手段，更是人际和谐管理的需要与表现，否则可能出现冲突性话语，引发人际之间的不和谐。为此，话语缓和的系统研究是十分必要的。

话语研究是宏观语用学研究中的一个重要项目。人际交往的语用问题涉及话语的表达和理解，它在社会、文化、心理、认知等方面与人们有着千丝万缕的复杂关系，汉语话语的语用研究还有一大片未开垦的处女地，值得我们从跨学科的角度去探索话语语用的方方面面，丰富语用学研究。李海辉博士在本论文中取得的成果正好表明他在这方面迈出了可喜的一步。

何自然
冉永平
2013 年 10 月 8 日
于广州白云山

# Abstract

Mitigation is a pervasive phenomenon of language use that inherits much theoretical importance from the indispensability of the illocutionary force of a speech act to doing things with words. It involves a breaching of the Gricean maxims of conversation and generates nonconventional implicatures, which makes it an interesting topic of research. Mitigation is also a pragmatic strategy which the speaker uses in various ways in adaptation of different contextual factors to perform diverse functions at the interpersonal and the communicative dimensions. Despite its importance, it has been understudied in that more attention has been given to classifying its strategies than to describing its functions and explaining its mechanism. As a partial response to such limitations, the present study aims to make an integrative study of mitigation in ordinary language use. Based on Chinese data obtained from television interview talks and adopting a qualitative research methodology, it attempts to answer the following questions: 1) What are the mitigating strategies? 2) What contextual factors constrain the use of mitigation? 3) What functions does mitigation perform? 4) What is the general mechanism of mitigation?

Mitigation is defined in the present study as a pragmatic strategy whereby the speaker reduces the illocutionary force of his speech act in order to soften an unpleasant effect that is detrimental to the achievement of his communicative goal. By illocutionary force is meant the justifiability of the speaker's illocution and the determination with which the speaker goes on record performing the illocution. By unpleasant effect is meant one of the perlocutionary sequels of the ensuing speech act. This definition involves two criteria, a reduction of the illocutionary force and a softening of an unpleasant effect, in comparison to previous definitions which take only one criterion. The adoption of this strict definition is justified to the extent to which it isolates prototypical instances of mitigation to the exclusion of peripheral cases and makes the present study more systematic and manageable. However, although both criteria are indispensable to the qualification of mitigation, the satisfactions of them do not have to be simultaneously manifested in the semantic meaning or the explicatures of the mitigator. In fact, in most cases only the satisfaction of one of them is made explicit while that of the other is left implicit and takes inference to be recovered.

Mitigation can be classified into propositional mitigation, illocutionary mitigation and perlocutionary mitigation. Propositional mitigation explicitly operates on illocutionary vagueness, illocutionary mitigation on illocutionary non-endorsement while perlocutionary mitigation works on the speaker's concern or control over a perlocutionary sequel. All these trigger off a negotiation or a reshuffling of rights and obligations between the speaker and the hearer, and, by the principle of synchronic weakening, succeed in softening a negative effect of the speech act that is detrimental to the achievement of the speaker's communicative goal. Through a detailed analysis of the data, the present study has found that there is sufficient regularity in the manner in which the illocutionary force is reduced or the unpleasant effect is softened to further classify mitigation into several subcategories. Thus, propositional mitigation subsumes under it strategies such as understaters, evidentials, tag questions, epistemic modals and subjectivizers, among which understaters work on propositional fuzziness while the others work on the uncertainty of the speaker's propositional attitude. Illocutionary mitigation incorporates disclaimers, deprecators, truth claimers and hesitators, among which disclaimers encode the speaker's illocutionary non-endorsement more explicitly than the others. Perlocutionary mitigation includes strategies such as simple anticipation, concern showing, penalty taking and direct dissuasion, among which direct dissuasion represents the most explicit effort of control. Such findings contribute to a better understanding of mitigation than is provided by earlier studies, which directed their attention overwhelmingly to propositional mitigation.

Like other phenomena of language use, mitigation is subject to the constraint of various contextual factors. It has been found that mitigation is interadaptable with powers, negative emotions, controversies, taboo topics and social values. These factors are highly relevant to the interview talks in which mitigation occurs, so there is self-evident correlation between the two. In addition, there are social norms related to these factors that require the speaker to mitigate his illocutionary force so as to be socially and communicatively rewarded rather than sanctioned. Mitigation is seen in this light as the result of linguistic adaptation to these factors and their corresponding norms. Moreover, when mitigation occurs, there is often a linguistic description of a social factor or the social norm related to it which constitutes the background for the use of mitigation and serves as the standard by which the illocution is characterized in the light suggested in the mitigator. In other words, the characterization is made with reference to the social norm. Thus, mitigation only makes sense when seen as a faithful representation of social norms, as an apology for a violation of the social norms and as an attempt to downplay the seriousness and the consequences of the violation. By analyzing examples extensively, the present study has found that different contextual factors constrain language use in their unique ways and are correlated with specific mitigating strategies. Thus, power in the hearer entitles him to more speaking rights and obligations and constrain the speaker into using tag questions and disclaimers typically to limit his own speaking rights and obligations. Negative emotions in the hearer call for the speaker's understanding and sympathy and constrain him into using deprecators, disclaimers and the strategy of concern showing predominantly. Controversies require the speaker to respect and acknowledge others' different views and lead the speaker to employ subjectivizers, epistemic modals more frequently than other strategies. Taboo topics motivate the speaker to use disclaimers to avoid violating them or to use deprecators to apologize for an inevitable violation. Social values such as modesty, honesty and restraint require the speaker to present himself as upholding these values by means of subjectivizers and disclaimers. It has also been found that these contextual factors are especially relevant to specific participants in the interview and lead to the clustering of different mitigating strategies around different participants. The host, for example, has to constantly adapt to the power in the guest or the honored guest and to the negative emotions in the guest, therefore his mitigating style is characterized by a combination of tag questions, deprecators and disclaimers. Controversy and the value of modesty are especially relevant to the honored guest, who overwhelmingly uses subjectivizers to adapt to the different views held by other honored guests and to present themselves as being modest. The guest has little to adapt to, his concern being to recount his experience or feelings as accurately as possible. The audience have only to adapt to the competition for the speaking floor and guest's negative emotions, so they mostly use subjectivizers to take and keep the floor and use the truth claimer "实话实说" to pacify the guest while making unreserved outpourings.

Mitigation is used to perform various functions in specific contexts in accordance with the speaker's communicative goal. Mitigating functions include interpersonal functions and communicative functions. Interpersonal functions refer to the contribution made by mitigation to the maintenance or improvement of the relationship between the speaker and the hearer while communicative functions refer to the role played by mitigation in heightening communicative involvement or effectiveness. At the interpersonal level, mitigation performs the functions of image management, pacification and solidarity building. At the communicative level, it performs the functions of invitations, floor manipulations and persuasions. Through a detailed analysis, the present study has found that these functions are regularly associated with specific participants who use different strategies to adapt to specific contextual constraints. Thus, image management is especially relevant to the host and the honored guests, who use deprecators, subjectivizers and disclaimers to adapt to social values and taboo topics to avoid being negatively evaluated. Pacifications are the result of the host's adaptation to the guest's negative emotions by means of concern showing and disclaimers. Solidarity building occurs between the host and the guest who feels ill at ease at the beginning of the interview. The inviting functions result from the host's adaptation to the guest's experience or negative emotions or to the honored guest's expertise by means of tag questions, disclaimers, and concern showing. Floor manipulations are realized due to the mitigator's performativity, negotiability and by creating psychological expectations in the hearer, mostly through the use of subjectivizers by the audience. Persuasions are the ultimate goal of communication aimed to be reached through all forms of mitigation.

Four patterns emerge from a summary of the findings concerning the mitigating strategies, the contextual constraints on mitigation and the mitigating functions. Firstly, tag questions are almost exclusively used by the host, who adapts to the power in the guest or the honored guest in order to perform inviting functions. This is consistent with the observation that the host is mainly concerned with securing a maximal degree of participation in the interview to make it run smoothly. Secondly, the subjectivizer "个人认为" is surprisingly monopolized by the honored guests whose power entitles them to speak more assertively. This is explained by one honored guest's empathic adaptation to the controversial views held by another in order not to impose and not to be imposed upon, as well as to appear modest. Thirdly, subjectivizers such as "我认为" and "我有个观点" are favored by the audience, who adapt to the strong competition for the speaking floor in order to seize and keep the floor. Fourthly, the truth claimer "实话实说" is favored by all participants partly because it justifies an unreserved outpouring while mitigating resentment and partly because it has come into vogue due to the popularity of the TV program.

It has further been found that mitigation is inherently related to empathy. On the one hand, it involves an incongruence, such as underrepresentation, irrelevance, redundancy or contradiction, between the semantic meaning of the mitigator and the speaker's illocutionary intention. This semantic incongruence can only be reconciled by assuming that in the use of mitigation the speaker is taking the hearer's perspective, showing affective convergence to the hearer and being altruistic to him. On the other hand, despite being aware of the problematic nature of his illocution and despite his wish to empathize with the hearer, the speaker goes on record performing the illocution. This seeming irrationality can only be explained away by assuming that the speaker is bidding for the hearer's empathy on the ground of reciprocity. In other words, by the use of mitigation the speaker is also attempting to get the hearer to take his perspective, converge to his affect and make an altruistic interpretation of his utterance. These constitute the speaker's empathic intention in engaging in mitigated communication. Metapragmatically speaking, through the use of mitigation the speaker explicitly communicates his empathic intention to the hearer and hopes thereby to realize various mitigating functions. Mitigation conveys the metapragmatic message that in general or in other contexts the speaker would agree with the hearer, but in the present context he would expect the hearer to agree with him. In terms of interpretational constraints, the speaker discourages the hearer from making a conventional interpretation of the utterance but constrains him into making a novel and altruistic interpretation based on the adoption of the speaker's perspective.

In order to account for mitigation, the present study proposes the notion of empathic adaptation. Adaptation is egoistically oriented, empathy is altruistically oriented while mitigation is both altruistic and egoistic. Thus empathic adaptation captures the very nature of mitigation, namely that it is egoistic via being altruistic. The explanatory power of this notion is manifested in its account of the motivation of mitigating strategies and the realization of mitigatingfunctions. On the one hand, the use of mitigation can be viewed as resulting from the speaker's empathic adaptation to various contextual constraints. That is, the speaker does not only have to take his communicative goal into account, but also has to adopt the hearer's perspective and affect with regard to the corresponding constraint. Given the egoistic orientation of adaptation, the speaker would probably opt for reinforcement rather than mitigation if he were not empathic with the hearer. Conversely, if the speaker empathizes with the hearer while adapting to the contextual constraint to reach his communicative goal, he will naturally choose mitigation as it takes care of both needs. On the other hand, the realization of mitigating functions can be viewed as resulting from the hearer's empathic adaptation to the speaker's mitigating strategy. If the hearer adapted to the speaker's use of mitigation, but were not empathic with the speaker, he would be stuck in his own perspective or preoccupied with his own affect, so much so that he would fail to see the speaker's perspective and mitigation would fail to realize its functions. But if he empathizes with the speaker while adapting to his use of mitigation, he will interpret the utterance in a way that is advantageous to the speaker. If and only if this happens can the mitigating functions be realized.

In sum, mitigation is a multidimensional and multifunctional phenomenon that takes a multiperspectival research paradigm to reveal its intricacies. The present study has explored the mitigating strategies, the contextual constraints on mitigation, the mitigating functions and the mechanism of mitigation, yet it is more extensive than intensive, more rudimentary than systematic and more tentative than conclusive. It has only revealed the tip of the iceberg, which awaits more penetrating studies to come.

**Key words:** mitigation, mitigating strategies, contextual constraints, mitigating functions, empathic adaptation

# 摘 要

话语缓和（mitigation）是一种常见的语用现象，涉及对格莱斯会话原则的违背以及非常规会话含意的产生，因此它是一个有趣的、值得深入研究的课题。话语缓和也是一种形式多样的语用策略，其目的是通过顺应各种语境因素及相关社会规约对话语内容和方式的制约，实现人际及交际功能。尽管如此，话语缓和现象没有得到足够的重视，体现在它的众多功能没有被发现，工作机制没有得到有力的解释。鉴于此，我们有必要对日常交际中的话语缓和现象进行多维度综合考察。本研究以中央电视台《实话实说》节目的转写文本为语料，采用定性研究方法，尝试回答以下问题：一、话语缓和有哪些策略？二、话语缓和受什么语境因素的制约？三、话语缓和可以实施什么功能？四、话语缓和的工作机制是什么？

本研究将话语缓和定义为**说话人为了达到其交际目的而采取的弱化施为力度、减缓负面效果的策略**。这是一个涉及双重标准的严式定义，一方面要求满足弱化施为力度的条件，另一方面要求能够淡化某个负面效果，只有这样才可称为话语缓和。与以往众多定义相比，严式定义可以分离出典型的话语缓和实例，使研究更趋系统，易于驾驭。严式定义的双重标准不必同时显现，多数情况下只显现一个标准，另一个隐含其中。

受Austin（1962）言语行为三分法的启发，我们首先将话语缓和分为命题型缓和、施为用意型缓及成事效果型缓和。命题型缓和与施为用意型缓和直接作用于施为力度的弱化而间接导致负面效果的减缓，成事效果型缓和则直接作用于负面效果的减缓而间接表达施为力度的弱化。话语缓和是一个调整、优化交际双方权利、义务分配的动态过程，其结果必然是消除、淡化负面因素的影响，加强正面因素的作用，使交际走向成功。可见，凭借同步弱化的工作原理，施为力度的弱化导致负面效果的消除，从而满足严式定义的双重标准。通过对语料的分析，本研究发现施为力度弱化的方式或负面效果淡化的方式有一定的规律性，据此可将话语缓和进一步分为若干子类。例如命题型缓和下辖弱陈语、理据语、附加问句、模态词及主观语，其中弱陈语作用于命题内容的模糊性，其余的作用于说话人命题态度的不确定性；施为用意型缓和包括放弃申明语、自贬语、事实声称语及犹豫话语，其中放弃申明语最明确地表示放弃施为用意，余者次之；成事效果型缓和策略包括简单预测、显露担忧、认罚及劝阻，其中劝阻最直接体现说话人对成事效果的控制，余者次之。这些发现有助于克服以往研究偏重命题型缓和策略的局限，加深我们对话语缓和现象的认识与理解。

语言使用是不断做出语言选择以顺应语境因素变化的动态过程，话语缓和作为一种语言现象乃顺应权势、负面情感、争议、禁忌及价值理念等语境因素的结果。一方面，这些因素时常伴随着话语缓和现象的发生，说明他们之间有着某种自然的联系，甚至有些因素（例如负面情感）是话语缓和的直接作用对象。另一方面，许多社会规约要求说话人在面临以上因素时必须弱化己方话语力度，以维持人际、交际层面的语用均衡，否则说话人将被视为另类，遭到社会拒斥。这种利弊关系是说话人采取话语缓和以顺应社会规约的理据。再者，话语缓和常常以话语定性的形式出现，而定性标准常常是与之相关的社会规约，这说明话语缓和是社会规约在语言现实中的折射，是社会规约即将被违背时的预防措施或事后补救措施。通过大量的例证分析，本研究发现不同的语境因素以其特有的方式制约语言交际，导致特定话语缓和策略的使用。譬如听话人的权势使他享

有更多的话语权限，承担更多的话语义务，这就使得说话人采用附
加问句、放弃申明语等策略限制自己的话语权限与义务；听话人的
负面情感常常得到说话人的同情与理解，从而使说话人采用自贬语、
放弃申明语及显露担忧等策略；争议迫使争议的一方尊重另一方的
不同意见，导致他更多地使用主观语与模态词；禁忌是不容随意违
背的，说话人应尽量避免它，如不然则需申明、致歉，因而说话人
多采用放弃申明语或者自贬语；像谦虚、诚实与内敛等价值理念要
求说话人采用主观语或放弃申明语以表明自己崇尚这些价值理念。
本研究还发现，不同的访谈参与者使用话语缓和来顺应不同语境因
素的制约。主持人主要以附加问句、放弃申明语来顺应嘉宾或客人
的权势，以自贬、放弃申明、显露担忧来顺应客人的负面情感；嘉宾
主要以主观语来顺应观点分歧，以自贬语、放弃申明语来顺应禁忌话
题与价值理念；现场观众主要顺应客人的负面情感及自身吐露心声的
愿望，他们采用的策略多为主观语和事实声称语"实话实说"。

　　话语缓和的功能包括人际功能与交际功能。所谓人际功能是指话
语缓和在维持、改善人际关系方面发挥的积极作用，交际功能指它
对提高参与度与交际效果所产生的正面影响。在人际层面上，话语
缓和发挥着维护形象、安抚情绪、增进感情的作用，在交际层面上
可以实施邀约、话轮操控、说服等功能。大量的例证表明这些功能是
不同的参与者以不同的缓和策略顺应不同语境因素制约的结果。譬
如，形象维护功能是主持人或者嘉宾以自贬语、放弃申明语、主观语
等策略顺应禁忌话题与价值理念的结果；情绪安抚功能集中体现于主
持人以自贬语、放弃申明语及显露担忧等策略对客人负面情感的顺
应;感情增进功能主要源于主持人以附加问句对客人拘谨心理的顺应；
邀约功能则源于主持人以附加问句、放弃申明语等对嘉宾或客人的权
势进行的顺应；话轮操控功能借助话语缓和的施为性、商讨性，特别
是通过制造心理期待得以实施，体现现场观众对有限发言机会的顺

应；说服功能是一切缓和策略旨在达到的终极交际目标。

综合诸方面的发现可以总结出如下规律。第一，由于主持人主要关心嘉宾和客人的参与度，而附加问句是实施邀约功能的主要手段，因此它成为主持人的专用缓和策略。第二，主观语"个人认为"主要为嘉宾所用，这是嘉宾之间意见差异很大但是他们力求互不干涉的结果，同时显示嘉宾意欲保持谦虚的姿态。第三，诸如"我认为"、"我有个观点"等主观语是观众喜用的策略，其动因是抢占发言的机会。第四，事实声明语"实话实说"是参与者通用的策略，原因可能是节目的成功已使它成为时尚。

话语缓和与移情有着密不可分的联系。一方面，缓和语在语义上与说话人的意图存在明显的反差（话不尽意、不关联、冗余、矛盾），这意味着说话人正站在听话人的角度替他道出心声，反映出说话人对听话人的情感趋同以及说话人的利他情怀，即说话人对听话人的移情。另一方面，说话人意识到己方施为用意不合时宜，但"明知不可言而言之"，旨在让听话人也能够对说话人移情，亦即站在说话人的角度看待事物，情感趋向说话人，对话语作有利于说话人的解读。两相结合构成说话人的移情意图。从元语用的角度看，说话人通过话语缓和明确地向说话人传递这个移情意图，希望听话人能识别并配合这个意图，以实现话语缓和的各项功能。通俗地说，说话人向听话人传递一个元语用信息，表明说话人在一般情况下或其他语境下会同意听话人的看法，但是在当前语境下他希望听话人能同意他的看法。换句话说，说话人利用话语缓和阻止听话人从自己的角度对话语作常规解读，同时敦促他从说话人的角度作移情解读。为了更好地揭示话语缓和的机制，本研究提出"移情顺应"的概念。顺应是以利己为取向的，移情是利他的，话语缓和则是利他、利己的综合体，因此移情顺应揭示了话语缓和先利他后利己、利他为手段利己为目的的本质。这个概念比较充分地解释了话语缓和策略的使用及其功能的实现。从策略的角度讲，话语缓和的使用是说话人移情顺应语境因素的结果，也就是说话语缓和反映出说话人在面临语境因素的制约时不仅要考虑如何达到自己的交际目的，还要考虑听话人对该因素的视角与情感。如果说话人只是顺应语境制约而不对听话人移情，鉴于顺应的利己取向，他可能会选择语用加强而不是话语缓和，可见非移情顺应不能解释话语缓和现象的发生。从另一个角度看，功能的实现是听话人移情顺应说话人缓和策略的结果，也就是说听话人要站在说话人的角度来看问题才有可能使设身处地感受说话人的话语，才有可能相信他的话语或实现其他功能，可见移情顺应的作用也是明显的。如果听话人只顺应缓和策略而不对说话人移情，他可能受制于己方视角，不可能对话语作出有利于说话人的非常规解读，因而使话语缓和的功能无法实现。

　　总之，话语缓和是一种多维度现象与多功能语用策略，值得我们对它作全方位的深入研究。本研究从策略，语境制约、功能、机制等方面对话语缓和作了一些探索性的研究，其发现是有限的，可谓"冰山一角"。我们期待着更多的、更深入的研究成果问世。

**关键词**：话语缓和现象；话语缓和策略；语境制约；话语缓和功能；移情顺应

# Contents

# Chapter 1
# Introduction

## 1.0 A General Introduction

In the study of meaning, Austin (1962) represents a break away from the logico-empiricist tradition by envisaging the speaker's doing something in saying something instead of expressing a proposition that is true or false. Ever since, much attention has been given to the various kinds of doings, i.e., to making classifications of illocutionary acts (Searle, 1969, 1976). Searle (1976) categorizes illocutionary acts by the criteria of illocutionary point, direction of fit and psychological state. Yet such criteria are not sufficiently discriminating. For example, suggesting and ordering are both grouped into the category of directives on the ground that they both constitute an attempt on the speaker's part to get the hearer to do something and involve a fit from the world to words. However, there is a big difference between the two: while a suggestion gives some options to the hearer an order leaves no room for negotiation. Intuitively, the issue at hand is a divergence in the degree of imposition that the speaker intends to exert on the hearer, or in the illocutionary force of the speech act. Thus illocutions falling into the same broad category can have different degrees of force.

Apart from such cross-illocution variations of forces, there are cross-situation variations. Indeed, there are different ways of performing the same illocutionary act with different degrees of explicitness and directness, which are appropriate in different contexts. The question then arises as to who suggests to whom or who orders whom in what situations. Furthermore, there is the possibility of strategic variation: it is possible for someone entitled to giving orders to opt for a suggestion, for example. In such a case, the question is even more intricate with regard to the motivation and possible benefits of strategically varying the illocutionary force of the speech act.

The variation of the illocutionary forces of speech acts is an inherent property of language use, as argued by Caffi (2007:1):

...style is inherent in the use of language. However useful heuristically, the neutral, grey expressions used as examples in linguistics, including pragmatics, do not exist but in the minds of linguists. In real life, our utterances are usually modulated, i.e., stylistically 'colored' in order to fit different contexts and express our feelings.

Thus, the variation in illocutionary force is another dimension which contributes to the characterization of a speech act beyond its illocutionary point, direction of fit and psychological state. If saying is doing, the variation of illocutionary force, either mitigation or reinforcement, is a modification of what is done in saying and thus merits investigation.

## 1.1 The Rationale of the Present Study

The choice of mitigation as the object of the present study is motivated by the following considerations.

First of all, mitigation derives much theoretical significance from the illocutionary force of a speech act. As noted above, although each speech act can be attributed with an illocutionary point, a direction of fit and a psychological state, these do not exhaust the meaning conveyed in the performance of the speech act. The intricacy of meaning can only be captured by the illocutionary force of the speech act, which is inherently subject to variations. At the face of it, a variation of the illocutionary force of a speech act is complementary to the illocutionary point, but in actuality it often plays a more important role in shaping human communication. Very often it is the strength of the illocution, rather than the type of illocution itself, that makes the difference. Mitigation assumes an important role due to the indispensability of the illocutionary force to the performing of a speech act. Thus a study of mitigation (and reinforcement, too, for that matter) is highly relevant to the development of the speech act theory.

Second, mitigation is pervasive in language use. Practically, given that the communicators are rational and want to achieve their communicative goals, they would attempt to remove any obstacle that may impede the achievement of the goal or to reduce its impact, therefore mitigation in the sense of weakening some negative effect that is detrimental to the communicative goal would naturally result. Intuitively, mitigation pervades non-confrontational interactions where the communicators are not emotionally opposed to each other and carry on the communication in a detached, rational way. It also pervades the situations where radical viewpoints are attempted at, in which case there is the need to negotiate the common ground and pave the way for meaning expression. Indeed, as observed by Stubbs (1983:185), mitigation is the basic interactive dimension of spoken language. The study of such a pervasive phenomenon will enrich the academics of pragmatics and inform ordinary language use.

Third, mitigation as a phenomenon of language use is an intriguing research topic, in that it breaches the Gricean maxims of quantity, quality, relevance and manner. In terms of quantity, mitigation provides insufficient or redundant information. In terms of quality, it provides information that is untrue of the speaker's illocutionary point or that underrepresents the speaker's epistemic and/or deontic certainty. Concerning relevance, the mitigator is semantically irrelevant to the propositional development or the pragmatic progression involved in the interaction. With regard to manner, mitigation is verbose. Such violations of the Gricean maxims tend to generate nonconventional conversational implicatures that constitute the core of the communicated meaning. A study of the implicatures generated and the mechanisms therein involved can shed light on the dynamic process of communication and thus bears immediate relevance to pragmatic theorizing. Mitigation is also a marked form of language use, which requires a motivation. What lies behind mitigation is not only of theoretical importance but also of practical pertinence. The knowledge of what factors motivate the use of mitigation sensitizes the language user to this strategy either in language production or language comprehension, which in no small measure determines the success of communication.

Fourth, mitigation is a multifaceted phenomenon that combines elements of semantics, pragmatics and metapragmatics in such a way as to allow active interplays between those elements. A systematic study of its many facets can reveal the mutual influences of those elements and contribute to our understanding of what happens at the semantics-pragmatics and the pragmatics-metapragmatics interfaces. For example, when semantics gives in to pragmatics and when metapragmatics takes over from pragmatics will be partly answered by such a study. Further, how metapragmatics exerts its manipulative effects on pragmatics and semantics can also be tackled.

Last, the ability to successfully use and interpret mitigation is part of the language user's pragmatic competence. Studies have shown that it is the part of competence that is resistant to development in the second language learner. A study of the patterns of mitigation in the Chinese context may help pave the way for studies of the acquisition of mitigation by Chinese learners of English or other languages. Studies have also shown that mitigation is an area most prone to negative transfers from the first language to the second. An analysis of the cross-cultural variations in the mitigation patterns not only highlights the areas that demands explicit instruction in language teaching but also guards against cultural prejudices by raising our cross-cultural awareness.

In sum, the aforementioned considerations have combined to arouse my sustained interest in the linguistic phenomenon of mitigation and lead to its choice as the topic of the present study.

## 1.2   Problems with Previous Studies

Problems with previous studies of mitigation, as can be revealed by a review of the literature, include descriptive problems and explanatory problems.

First, previous studies suffer from a definitional problem. Up to the present, no commonly-agreed-upon definition has been given. In fact, some of the definitions offered in previous studies are greatly divergent from one another owing to the different definitional criteria adopted and the research foci chosen. Fraser's (1980) is based on the unwelcome effect of the current speech act and can be seen as end result-oriented. The definition adopted by Holmes (1984) and Sbisà(2001) is based on the illocutionary force of the speech act and can be seen as means-oriented. The one proposed by Caffi (1999, 2007) and elaborated on by Huo (2004), which is based on interactional parameters, can also be seen as means-oriented. Such definitions, interesting as they are, are just too broad to leave out marginal cases of mitigation and to foreground the prototypical ones. A narrower definition based on a stricter criterion is desirable but still lacking.

Second, previous studies are inadequate in their descriptions of mitigating strategies. Even though wide and near-exhaustive taxonomies of mitigating devices have been attempted (Holmes,1984; Blum-Kulka et al., 1989), they are restricted to the epistemic dimension, i.e., they focus on the speaker's commitment to the validity or truth of the proposition. The deontic dimension has largely been ignored so that some of the mitigating strategies operating on the illocutionary level and all those operating on the perlocutionary level have escaped systematic attention. Especially, some of the Chinese-specific mitigating strategies revealed by my pilot study have been left out of the domain of mitigation.

Third, most of the previous studies have taken a unifunctional view to mitigation. In describing the functions of mitigation, these studies have exclusively concentrated on interpersonal functions, much at the expense of the communicative functions. To this trend, Caffi (1999, 2007) and Huo (2004) are the only exceptions, as they highlight interactional management and thus extend to the communicative level. Even at the interpersonal level, most previous studies have attributed to mitigation only the function of face-based politeness.

Fourth, concerning the issue of explanation, no comprehensive and systematic account has been given of the strategies, the functions, the contextual constraints and the working mechanism of mitigation. Although a few attempts have been made in this direction, they are inadequate in their explanatory power either because of their limited orientation or because of the particularity of their data. The felicity-condition account and the distancing account only explain the semantic working mechanism of mitigation in a decontextualized manner, largely ignoring the socio-cultural and psychological motivations of mitigation. The deresponsibilization account represented by Caffi (1999, 2007) is convincing, but her data are obtained from schizophrenic discourses, which makes the account ungeneralizable to other types of data. Huo's (2004) regulation account is more integrative and acceptable, but more efforts are needed to test its applicability to other activity types than the traditional Chinese medicine clinical interviews he was interested in.

Last, the bulk of academic research of mitigation has been conducted in English or other European languages like Italian. Thus western cultures are overrepresented while eastern cultures are underrepresented. In such a situation, the research findings and related theorizing are bound to be Anglocentric. To redress this imbalance, studies based on eastern languages like Chinese are highly desirable. Huo (2004) represents a response to the gap, but studies from other approaches and based on other data types are still badly needed.

Such problems with the previous studies of mitigation constitute the background for the present study.

## 1.3  The Object of the Present Study

Given the problems with the earlier studies of mitigation, the overall objective of the present study is to attempt to provide a comprehensive account of mitigation. More specifically, it is to attempt to achieve the following sub-objectives.

First, based on the assumption that linguistic meaning cannot be exhausted unless the locution, the illocution and the perlocution dimensions of the speech act have all been examined, the present study will explore mitigating strategies that have recourse to these dimensions.

In other words, it will be concerned not only with propositional mitigation, but also with illocutionary mitigation and perlocutionary mitigation. In fact, it will pay special attention to illocutionary and perlocutionary mitigations since they have largely been ignored by earlier studies. Following Sbisà(2001), Holmes (1984) and a few others, the present study will appeal to the semantic features of linguistic items and the pragmatic inferences they warrant as criteria for qualifying the items as mitigators or mitigating strategies. The pragmatic inferences will be explored in terms of rights and obligations, a term borrowed from Sbisà(2001) but to be extended in the present study to include deontic modality related to social/moral appropriateness. Thus, the present study will attempt to offer a taxonomy of mitigating strategies based not only on epistemic modality but also, and more importantly, on deontic modality.

Second, communication takes place in contexts, which means that it is subject to the constraint of various contextual factors. With this in mind, the present study will explore the psychological and socio-cultural factors that have a bearing on the use of mitigation in verbal communication. For the identification of such factors, the criteria to be adopted are linguistic evidence, contextual inferability, cross-contextual consistency of correlation and communicative sense making. On the strength of these criteria, the present study will attempt to bring to light the major factors that motivate the use of mitigation in TV interviews in particular and in language use in general.

Third, it can be assumed that language users engaged in verbal communication are equally concerned with the interpersonal relationships between themselves and the smoothness and effectiveness of their communication. Whereas earlier studies have mostly focused on the interpersonal functions of mitigation, the present study will pay equal attention to its communicative functions. The criteria to be adopted for the identification and testing of the functions of mitigation are linguistic evidence, local coherence and pragmatic progression.

Furthermore, the present study will be concerned with the metapragmatic dimension of mitigation, i.e., the metapragmatic constraint on the interpretation process exercised by the speaker through the use of mitigation. It will be hypothesized that the speaker, by using mitigation, communicates an empathic intention and expects the hearer to recognize it and accommodate it in order to realize the various mitigating functions. Based on this hypothesis, the present study proposes the notion of empathic adaptation, in terms of which the use of mitigation and the realization of mitigating functions will be accounted for.

In sum, the present study will attempt to answer the following research questions: 1) what are the strategies and substrategies of mitigation in Chinese in the area of TV interview talks? 2) what are the constraining factors that motivate the employment of specific mitigating strategies in specific contexts? 3) what functions can be performed by mitigation at the interpersonal and the communicative dimensions? 4) why can these functions be realized by mitigation?

## 1.4   A Description of the Data

The data on which the present study is based are the transcripts of the CCTV interview program *Tell It As It Is*(中央电视台"实话实说"访谈节目)hosted by Cui Yongyuan(崔永元). They were downloaded at *www.cctv.shss.com* in July 2004 , cover 110 interviews, and contain 900,000 Chinese characters (computer estimated). The play time for the interviews was 55 hours.

The data are characterized by the following features. First, since the topics of the program are mostly novel ones that have never been openly discussed before, the data thus produced strongly appeal to me. Second, there is an agreement, as implied in the title of the program, for the participants to be frank and sincere in what they say (the term "实话实说" can be interpreted as meaning that the participants should have no reservations and open up their hearts in expressing their personal views and that they should take no offense at what is about them), so that there is an element of genuineness that suggests its desirability. Third, as the talking at the interview was unprescribed and unrehearsed beforehand, the spontaneity lends much naturalness and validity to the data.

In case the reader is not familiar with the interview program, a few remarks about the participants, the process and the participants' concerns are in order. The participants in the interview include the host, the guest (whose personal experience has been chosen as the topic of the interview), the honored guest (who is an expert in a field related to the topic), and the audience (who have been more randomly selected). The process of the interview runs as follows: first the host introduces the topic of the interview by engaging the guest in a narration of his experience, then he hands the matter over to the honored guest who is to give an authoritative analysis of the issue at hand, and at last he encourages the audience to interact with the guest and the honored guest by raising questions and offering viewpoints. The concerns of the participants are also obvious. The guest is mainly concerned with narrating his experience and relating his feelings about it, the honored guest is concerned with giving a detached, thorough and objective analysis of the matter, while the audience can be more emotionally involved since they are mainly concerned with getting a chance to have their say. Most interesting of all, the host plays a triple role: he is the organizer and facilitator of the interview, a representative of the central TV station and an ordinary participant like the audience members. Thus the host is first and foremost concerned with the smooth running of the interview, especially the full involvement of the guest and the audience in the interview. However, he is also concerned with the reputation of the interview program and with expressing his own views. These distinctions in the participants' concerns offer much assistance in analyzing the mitigating functions.

In a word, the data were chosen out of the consideration of their richness, novelty, validity and analyzability. Thus the examples to be used for illustrative purposes in chapters 4, 5 and 6 are exclusively taken from this data source and the title of the specific program will be given in quotation marks in the embedded reference for each example.

## 1.5   Outline of the Thesis

The present thesis consists of seven chapters, each with its own major concern, to be specified as follows.

Chapter 1 is the introduction to the present study. It deals with the rationale of the present study, the problems with previous studies of mitigation, the object of the present study, a description of the data and an outline of the thesis.

Chapter 2 presents a literature review with a view to revealing the achievements and the limitations of earlier studies, which will serve as the departure point for the present study.

Chapter 3 deals with the conceptual framework of the present study. It first offers a working definition of mitigation based on a strict criterion and a delimitation that distinguishes mitigation from indirectness and politeness. It then specifies linguistic adaptation and empathy as the theories to be resorted to in the present study in accounting for mitigation.

Last, it sketches the major components of the framework, or the major aspects of mitigation to be investigated in the present study, namely, mitigating strategies, contextual constraints on mitigation, mitigating functions and the mechanism of mitigation.

Chapter 4 is concerned with the description, exploration and qualifying of mitigating strategies at the locution, the illocution and the perlocution dimensions of the speech act. Strictly following a cluster of qualifying criteria, it will offer an extensive taxonomy of mitigating strategies and substrategies.

Chapter 5 addresses the contextual constraints on mitigation. It will explore and identify the psychological and socio-cultural factors that mitigation is interadaptable with. On the basis of four criteria, it will establish the status of power, negative emotions, controversies, taboo topics and social values as the major motivators of mitigation. In addition, it will explain the use of mitigation in terms of the speaker's empathic adaptation to the constraint of the various contextual factors.

Chapter 6 offers a classification of the functions that mitigation performs in television interviews. On the basis of the criteria of linguistic evidence, local coherence and pragmatic progression, it will establish the status of image management, pacification and solidarity building as the interpersonal functions of mitigation and the status of invitations, floor manipulations and persuasions as the communicative functions of mitigation. Meanwhile, it will explain the realization of these mitigating functions in terms of the hearer's empathic adaptation to the speaker's use of mitigation.

Chapter 7 sums up the major findings, the implications, and the limitations of the present study. It closes by making some suggestions for future research.

# Chapter 2
# Literature Review

## 2.0 Introduction

Ever since the early 1970s, the linguistic phenomenon of
mitigation has captured the attention of researchers from such fields as
sociolinguistics, pragmatics and cross-cultural/interlanguage pragmatics.
An overview of its development in the three decades that have elapsed
reveals that the study of mitigation has followed the rise of these linguistic
disciplines. Mitigation first aroused the interest of sociolinguists in
the1970s, when Robin Lakoff established gender differences in language
use as a research topic in sociolinguistics and associated mitigation with
women's gender identity.

As pragmatics rose and prospered throughout the 1970s and 1980s,
mitigation became an area of research in this field. Pragmatic studies of
mitigation are represented by Fraser (1980), Holmes (1984), Haverkate
(1992), Caffi (1999), Sbisà (2001), and Huo (2004), and are characterized
by a heavy reliance on pragmatic theories such as the speech act theory
(Austin, 1962; Searle, 1969, 1976; Grice, 1975) and the politeness theory
(Brown and Levinson, 1978, 1987; Leech, 1983).

Cross-cultural/interlanguage pragmaticists began to pay systematic
attention to mitigation in the 1980s, when a team of western researchers
launched an influential research project on the realizations of speech acts
across eight cultures in eight languages, which is often referred to as

CCSARP. The project was set up to validate the universality of politeness hypothesized by Brown and Levinson (1978, 1987), and to establish culture-specific patterns of being linguistically polite. Mitigation came into the picture as a means of politeness and was put under systematic scrutiny. Another motivation for the CCSARP was to expand the scope of second language acquisition research from linguistic competence to communicative competence, a move largely inspired by Hymes (1972). Mitigation is taken as part of the language learner's communicative competence and is scrutinized with respect to its development in the learner's interlanguage. Cross-cultural/interlanguage pragmatic studies of mitigation abound, but are represented by House and Kasper (1981), Blum-Kulka et al.(1989), Kasper and Rose (2002) and further studies inspired by the CCSARP (Trosborg,1995; Barren, 2003; Skewis, 2003).

This chapter will review the different approaches that have been taken towards the study of mitigation, with special attention to their research concerns and major findings. Their achievements will be summarized so as to establish the departure point and direction for the present study.

## 2.1 Terminological Issue

Although mitigation is an understudied pragmatic phenomenon, as can be inferred from the limited literature available in academic publications, there is not a generally-adopted term to refer to it. Up to date, three terms have been employed by linguists who approach it from different perspectives with different foci of interest.

Fraser first introduced the notion of mitigation into pragmatics in the late 1970s and early 1980s and used the term *mitigation* to refer to the reduction of an unwelcome effect of the speaker's utterance on the hearer.

This is also the term taken up by Haverkate (1992), Caffi (1999, 2007), Skewis (2003) and Huo (2004). Holmes (1984) envisages a paradigm of four ways of modifying the illocutionary forces of speech acts: boosting the illocutionary force of a positively affective speech act, boosting that of a negatively affective speech act, attenuating that of a positively affective speech act, and attenuating that of a negatively affective speech act. She refers to mitigation as *the attenuation of the illocutionary force of a negatively affective speech act.*

A third term used to refer to mitigation is *downgrading,* which is widely adopted in the CCSARP studies. Aiming to reveal the cross-cultural variations in the realization of such speech acts as request, these studies make a fine segmentation of the request sequence into the head act, the head act strategy and modification. Modification is further divided into upgrading and downgrading, according as they increase or play down the impact of the request. Downgrading, in this sense, is a strategy used to reduce the impositive force of the request or to signal in-group solidarity in order to bid for the requestee's understanding, cooperation and compliance with the request. One characteristic of downgrading, according to the CCSARP coding manual, is that it modifies the illocutionary force of the request but does not bear on its illocutionary point. In other words, downgrading is optional for the realization of the request.

These three terms, different as they sound, have much in common. In fact, Holmes (1984) uses the terms of *mitigation* and *attenuation* alternately, while in the CCSARP coding manual *mitigation* is used to define and describe downgrading. Thus I regard the three terms as interchangeable but, for the sake of consistency, *mitigation* will be used throughout the present study.

## 2.2 Approaches to Mitigation

Based on their research concerns, previous studies of mitigation can be categorized as falling under three approaches: the sociolinguistic approach, the pragmatic approach and the cross-cultural/interlanguage pragmatic approach. In this section I review these approaches and summarize their findings and their implications for the present study.

### 2.2.1 The Sociolinguistic Approach

Studies under this approach are concerned with the relationship of mitigation with the social factor of gender, focusing on the question of whether women use more mitigation than men, and if so, whether it is symbolic of women's subordinate status in a male-dominated society.

The pioneering study that concerns itself with this question is Lakoff (1975), which hypothesizes that women's language is marked by the use of hedges (such as *you know*, *sort of*, *I think*) and tag questions, which shows women's tentativeness and subordinate status relative to male domination. Such tentativeness and subordinate status, according to Lakoff, are constitutive of women's gender identity, which originates from social conceptions of womanhood and gets reinforced through children's socialization. In a male-dominated society, women are brought up to think of assertion and forcefulness as masculine qualities which are undesirable in women, but to think that weakness and unassertiveness are desirable feminine qualities. These conceptions get inculcated and strengthened in young girls, as they tend to look up to their mothers as a role model.

Lakoff's hypothesis gave rise to a couple of subsequent debates. One of these debates centers on whether women, as a rule, use mitigation more frequently than men, as assumed by Lakoff's hypothesis. Studies that support the hypothesis include Austin et al.(1987), Kyratzis and Ervin-Tripp (1999), Miller et al. (1986), Leaper (1991), Sachs (1987), Sheldon (1990), Thornborrow and Morris (2004), among others. Miller et al.(1986) study same-sex arguments of children and find that girls use more mitigation strategies, including compromise and evasion, whereas boys use a more assertive style. Sachs (1987) analyzes the use of mitigated and unmitigated language forms in pre-school children's pretend play and finds that girls have 65% of their obliges mitigated while boys mitigate their obliges in only 34% of the cases. Further evidence is offered in Thornborrow and Morris (2004), who study gossip as a talk management strategy and find that women try to establish alignment with each other by mitigating their evaluations of others while men do this by aggravating their evaluations. Such findings indicate that mitigation is more associable with women than with men. However, counterevidence is equally abundant and weighty: many studies have found no significant cross-gender differences in the use of mitigation (Farris,1991, 2000; Goodwin, 1990, 1998; House,1989; Kakava, 2002; Kyratzis and Guo, 2001; Ladegaard, 2004; Sheldon:1992, 1996; Wouk, 1999). Ladegaard (2004), for example, finds that in Danish children's language in play both girls and boys predominantly leave their obliges unmitigated, indicating that girls are equally capable of being assertive when the need arises. Wouk (1999) studies the Indonesian pragmatic particles *kan* and *iya/ya* and finds that both men and women frequently use these articles for mitigating purposes. More interestingly, Dubois and Crouch (1975) find that at academic conferences men use tags far more frequently than women, diametrically opposite to what Lakoff's hypothesis predicts (cited in Cameron et al., 1988: 77).

The other debate is on whether the mitigating features in women's language invariably mark their subordination to male dominance. The female-subordination view is most eloquently expressed by Eckert's saying "femininity is a culturally defined form of mitigation or denial of power, whereas masculinity is an affirmation of power" (Eckert, 1989: 257), and is supported by Fishman (1983), Kiesling (1998), West and Zimmerman (1983), Woods (1988), and many others. However, opposing views are voiced in Ladegaard (2004), Sheldon (1996), Smith-Heffner (1988) and Sollitt-Morris (1997). Sheldon (1996), for example, finds that girls in her study frequently use what she calls a "double-voice discourse", an assertive negotiation strategy in which they can exploit mitigation to soften the blow while promoting their wishes. Similarly, Ladegaard (2004) finds that girls can use mitigation to assert power and control, e.g. to get themselves heard, to get their messages across or to get their way. Wouk's(1999) findings are also inconsistent with the female-subordination view: given that both men and women in his study use mitigation with an equally high frequency, it would be hard to explain who are subordinate to whom.

Such controversies have led some sociolinguists to reflect on Lakoff's (1975) research methodology and basic conception of mitigation. In short, Lakoff's hypothesis has been criticized as being simplistic. Firstly, it has taken a one-to-one correspondence view of the form-function relationship. For example, tag questions are held by Lakoff to signal tentativeness and/ or desire for approval except when it can be seen that they are requesting information unknown to the speaker. This view has obviously failed to take account of the many different functions that mitigating devices can perform across contexts (Holmes, 1983, 1984, 1986, 1997; Ladegaard, 2004; Wouk, 1999). Thus, simply counting and comparing the frequency of mitigating devices across genders, as is the case with Lakoff (1975) and many subsequent studies, is unilluminating. Secondly, it overemphasizes gender at the expense of other variables such as social value, participant status, conversational role and communicative intention (Cameron et al., 1988; Sheldon, 1996; Wouk, 1999). Mitigation, like any other phenomenon of language use, is situated in contexts and its occurrence and functions are co-determined by a number of interwoven factors which may take on different degrees of salience in different contexts. To give just one example, Cameron et al.(1988) finds that although tag questions are markers of tentativeness in casual conversations, they function as tools of control used by the powerful party in unequal encounters. In casual conversations it is conversational role that is determinant while in unequal encounters it is status that predominates. In neither case, they argue, does gender bear any special relevance.

Alternative to Lakoff's simplistic view of the relationship of mitigation with gender, a multifunctional view has been advocated to take account of the various functions of mitigation. It has been found that tag questions can not only express uncertainty or tentativeness, but also perform a number of other functions, ranging from softening (attenuating a criticism or directive), facilitation (inviting the hearer to participate in the interaction), to challenging (expressing aggression) (Holmes, 1983, 1997; Wouk, 1999). Similarly, hedges such as *I think* and *you know* can express tentativeness or conviction, depending on the context in which they are used (Fasulo and Zucchermaglio, 2002; Holmes, 1985, 1986, 1997; Ladegaard, 2004; Sheldon, 1996; Shiffrin,1987). Given the functional complexity of mitigating devices, it is assumed, both men and women are equally likely to exploit them to perform different functions as required by contextual factors and the speaker's communicative intention (Erman, 1992; Holmes, 1983, 1984, 1986; Nordenstam, 1992;. Smith-

Heffner, 1988; Wetzel, 1988).

To sum up, sociolinguistic studies of mitigation have centered around Lakoff's hypothesis, which deals with the relationship of mitigation and gender. The controversies of the hypothesis have inspired researchers to explore the different functions that mitigating devices can potentially perform in different contexts. However, the attention of the proponents of the multifunctional view is limited to hedges like *you know*, *I think*, and tag questions. Whether or not other mitigating strategies can also perform such multifunctions is a question that merits further investigation.

### 2.2.2   The Cross–cultural/Interlanguage Pragmatic Approach

Cross-cultural pragmatic studies of mitigation are concerned with the universality and culture-specificity related to mitigation and the reasons for possible variations in the mitigation pattern across cultures. Drawing on Brown and Levinson (1978, 1987), which treats indirectness as a superstrategy of politeness, these studies have focused their attention on the issue of directness versus indirectness in the realization of speech acts.

One of the basic hypotheses underlying these studies is that indirectness is linearly related to politeness. This hypothesis has not been validated, however. Blum-Kulka (1987), for example, finds that indirectness and politeness are not the same thing. In fact, the most favored way of performing a request and the one perceived as the most polite is not maximal indirectness but rather conventional indirectness. Conventional indirectness is polite because it involves a reasonable degree of illocutionary transparency whereas overindirectness is impolite because it imposes on the hearer the tedious task of inferring the speaker's illocutionary intention. Similarly, Skewis (2003) finds that in the Chinese context, the requestive strategy most opted-for is the mood derivable, which is the most direct way of performing a speech act. Assuming that the Chinese are polite, it can be inferred that indirectness is not linearly related to politeness.

Another basic hypothesis underlying cross-cultural pragmatic studies of mitigation is that there are great cross-cultural variations in the level of indirectness in language use. This hypothesis has largely been borne out. Blum-Kulka and House (1989), for example, compare five language groups: Hebrew, Canadian French, Argentine Spanish, Australian English and German, and find that speakers of Argentine Spanish are the most direct in their language use, followed by those of Hebrew, Canadian French, German and Australian English, in that order. Other findings include that Americans are more indirect in their speech than Greeks (Tannen, 1981), that speakers of German are more direct than speakers of British English (House and kasper, 1981), and that Hebrew speakers are more direct than speakers of American English (Blum-Kulka, 1982, 1983). Extending beyond indirectness, American judges have been found to mitigate to lesser extent their criticisms of other judges on the same bench, compared with their British counterparts (Kurzon, 2001).

Such variations in the level of indirectness have been attributed to cross-cultural divergence in the perception of social reality. House (1989), for instance, explains the difference in the use of imperatives between Germans and speakers of British English by assuming that Germans perceive the situations as standard situations where the use of the imperative is licensed by the established rights and obligations while speakers of British English perceive the same situations as nonstandard situations where the use of imperatives is inconsistent with the need to currently negotiate the rights and obligations.

The findings from the cross-cultural pragmatic studies of mitigation have important implications for cross-cultural communication in the sense that they warn against uninformed prejudiced judgments of people from another culture, help raise people's cultural awareness and avoid cross-cultural communication breakdowns. Of particular pertinence to the present study, however, is the implication that indirectness as a strategy of mitigation does not enjoy a comparable status in different cultures.

Interlanguage pragmatic studies of mitigation regard it as part of the learner's pragmatic competence and are concerned with the series of its acquisition and the pattern of its development in the language learner.

Concerning the series of acquisition, language learners have been found to overuse external mitigation but to underuse internal mitigation. In a study of the acquisition of mitigation by Australian adult learners of Indonesian, Hassall (2001) finds that the learners use far more external mitigation than the native speakers of Indonesian but never or seldom use the negator and the downtoner, both of which are used by the natives with a high frequency. Similarly, Faerch and Kasper (1989) find that Danish learners of English and German use the grounder to a greater extent than the native speakers of English or of German. In terms of internal mitigation, the learners overuse the German politeness marker *bitte* and underuse the downtoner.

Two hypotheses have been proposed to account for this pattern: the complexity hypothesis and the clarity hypothesis. According to the complexity hypothesis, external mitigation is preferred over internal mitigation because adding internal mitigators to the head act would increase the pragmalinguistic complexity and requires more processing ability than the learner possesses while external mitigators are placed outside the head act and this makes them easier to process. According to the clarity hypothesis, external mitigators are more explicit in their politeness function and so learners may feel more confident that their intended politeness message is successfully conveyed if they use them instead of internal mitigators. The preference for the politeness marker can also be explained in terms of the learner's concerns with politeness and illocutionary explicitness.

Concerning the developmental pattern of mitigation, studies have revealed a general trend of slow and marginal convergence to the target norm. Trosborg (1995), for example, discovers a regression rather than a development in the learners' mitigation with an increase in proficiency. Barren (2003) studies Irish learners of German in a study-abroad context and finds that with time spent in the target speech community, learners converge to the native norm in the frequency of the use of the politeness marker *bitte*, but diverge from the native norm with regard to the position in which the marker is used: while native speakers normally use it in an embedded position the learners use it in the sentence-final position. Kasper and Rose (2002) also find that the learners' mitigation never reaches, and often deviates from, the target norm.

The reason for this slow development has been unanimously attributed to negative transfer from the first language. As Felix-Brasdefer (2004) states, mitigation is the area where negative pragmatic transfer prevails. It can thus be concluded that mitigation is that part of pragmatic competence which is most resistant to development, in comparison with other parts: even with explicit instruction and high proficiency levels the acquisition of mitigation still lags behind. Of relevance to the present study is the implication that mitigation is closely related to the specific value orientations of the culture involved, which adds to its attractiveness as a topic of research.

### 2.2.3   The Pragmatic Approach

Studies of mitigation under the pragmatic approach are concerned with identifying and classifying mitigating devices or strategies, examining the semantic/pragmatic properties of mitigating strategies, spelling out the conditions of the use of mitigation and unveiling the psychological motivations behind the use of mitigation. According to their concerns these studies can further be classified as representing the following four trends: the pragmalinguistic trend, the semanticopragmatic trend, the sociopragmatic trend and the psychopragmatic trend.

#### 2.2.3.1   The Pragmalinguistic Trend

With regard to the pragmalinguistic trend, four taxonomies of mitigating strategies have been proposed, represented by Fraser (1980), Holmes (1984), Blum-Kulka et al.(1989), and Caffi (1999, 2007), respectively. According to Fraser's (1980) taxonomy, mitigating strategies include indirect speech acts, distancing strategy or immediacy, and the use of disclaimers, parenthetical verbs, tag questions and hedges. These strategies aim either to weaken the unwelcome effect that the utterance is likely to produce on the hearer, or to reduce the hearer's hostility towards the speaker for performing the speech act, or both.

Following and elaborating on Fraser (1980), Holmes (1984) proposes a taxonomy of mitigators which include prosodic devices, syntactic devices, lexical devices and discoursal devices. Prosodic devices refer to fall-rise intonation, weakened stress, low volume and high pitch. Syntactic devices include tag questions, passive construction, agentless constructions, nominalization, impersonal pronouns and double negatives. Lexical devices, the most elaborative subcategory and termed downtoners, include disclaimers and some of George Lakoff (1972)'s hedges. Discoursal devices are such items as *by the way*, *that reminds me* and *while I think of it*, which Brown and Levinson (1978) refer to as 'relevance hedges'. All these mitigating devices serve to reduce the illocutionary force of a negatively affective speech act.

A third categorization of mitigating devices is given by the CCSARP studies and presented in Blum-Kulka et al. (1989). According to this categorization, mitigating strategies subsume syntactic mitigators, lexical-phrasal mitigators and sentential mitigators. In addition, a fine distinction is made between internal mitigators and external mitigators, according as they occur inside or outside of the head act. Syntactic mitigators include interrogative, negation of preparatory condition, subjunctive, conditional, aspect, tense and combinations thereof; lexical-phrasal mitigators include the politeness marker *please*, understater, hedge, subjectivizer, downtoner, cajoler, appealer, and combinations thereof; sentential mitigators include preparatory, getting a precommitment, grounder, promise of reward and cost minimizer. This categorization has found wide application in studies of cross-cultural pragmatics and interlanguage pragmatics.

The fourth taxonomy of mitigating strategies is provided by Caffi (1999, 2007). On the basis of her broad definition of mitigation as the weakening of the value of one of the interactive parameters and all its possible effects, Caffi identifies three such parameters, namely the proposition, the speaker's illocutionary endorsement and the deictic origins of the utterance. Such parameters or scopes of mitigation serve as the criteria for three major strategies of mitigation: bushes, hedge and shields, respectively. Thus bushes operate on the proposition of the utterance (including referential vagueness and predicate downgrading), hedges operate on the endorsement (including illocutionary vagueness and propositional attitudinal uncertainty), and shields involve a deviation from the implicit deictic center of utterances (including the person deixis and the spatio-temporal deixis).

Further mitigating strategies include deictic categories such as time deixis and person deixis (Haverkate, 1992), negation (Giora et al., 2005; Holmes, 1984) and code-switching (Kang, 2003) and some discourse markers (Ran, 2000), but these do not constitute an independent taxonomy and need to be incorporated into other taxonomies.

### 2.2.3.2 The Semanticopragmatic Trend

Concerning the semanticopragmatic trend, a number of semantic/pragmatic properties of mitigating strategies have been identified. First, mitigation involves the speaker's reduced commitment to the validity of the proposition (Fraser, 1980; Holmes, 1984; Haverkate, 1992), so that in the use of mitigation the speaker expresses his epistemic uncertainty, or his reservation about the corresponding state of affairs holding. Second, mitigation involves a deresponsibilization mechanism that shifts from the speaker the responsibility for the negative effect of the utterance on the hearer (Fraser, 1980; Holmes, 1984; Haverkate, 1992) or for qualifying the relationship between the speaker and the hearer (Caffi,1999, 2007). Third, mitigation is achieved by the speaker through making an explicit reference to one of the felicity conditions of the current speech act (Haverkate, 1992), thereby suspending the condition and rendering the act infelicitous. Thus the speaker can mitigate a request by referring to the preparatory condition as in *Can you make coffee?* Or he does it by referring to the sincerity condition as in *I would like you to make coffee.* Fourth, as observed by Haverkate (1992), mitigation involves an iconic distance and a corresponding metaphoric distance. Thus in *I would like you to cut my hair* an iconic distance exists between the sincerity condition and the propositional content of the directive since the former is expressed in the embedding clause while the latter is expressed in the embedded clause. The metaphoric distance is created by the hypothetical reading of the conditional *would*, which denotes a state of affairs that holds at some time other than the coding time, or in a possible world rather than in the actual world. This creates the impression that the speaker's request does not bear on the hearer's immediate action or even that the request does not exist at all. It is this modification of the speaker's intention that constitutes mitigation. Fifth, mitigation functions to regulate human verbal activities in the sense of bringing harmony to the activities and facilitating its smooth running by diffusing conflicts along the social, physical and mental dimensions therein involved (Huo, 2004). Sixth, as observed by Holmes (1984), mitigation expresses the speaker's affective meaning, i.e., his attitude to the hearer in the context of utterance. Thus mitigating a negatively affective speech act such as criticism contributes to the development or maintenance of the speaker-hearer relationship, to decreasing the social distance between the speaker and the hearer, to expressing the speaker's positive feelings for the hearer and to enhancing the solidarity of the relationship. Last, mitigation is a negotiation or a reshuffling of rights and obligations between the speaker and the hearer, in terms of the speaker's entitlement and commitment and the hearer's obligations that are achieved by means of intersubjectivity (Sbisà, 2001). These semantic/pragmatic properties of mitigation are to be integrated in a comprehensive account of mitigation to be adopted in the present study.

### 2.2.3.3   The Sociopragmatic Trend

Studies of mitigation under the sociopragmatic trend are concerned with tracking down the social factors that motivate the use of mitigation and with describing  speaker's sociopragmatic competence necessary for, and indicated in, the employment of mitigating strategies.

Overstreet and Yule (2001), in a study of formulaic disclaimers in the form of *Not* X *or anything, but* Y, observe that the need to mitigate arises when the speaker intends to perform a socially problematic verbal action. The problematicity of a verbal action is judged against a stock of socially-derived knowledge of social rules and conventions, thus a verbal action is viewed as problematic if it violates one or more of the rules or conventions. Some of the rules identified in their study include 'Don't insult' and 'Don't lose control of yourself', to name just two examples.

Included in this stock of knowledge is a network of typifications of human beings based on social roles, interpersonal roles, moral character, and other criteria. When the speaker's verbal action does not seem characteristic of the type of person that he is assumed to be, it leads to a reevaluation of the speaker's social identity, or a retypification of him. Such being the case, the speaker's wish to claim identity motivates him to mitigate the possibility of being negatively evaluated.

Implied in the use of disclaimers as a mitigating strategy are two types of sociopragmatic competence: social competence and strategic competence. Social competence refers to the speaker's awareness of the social rules and conventions established by the socio-cultural community that he belongs to, of what constitutes a violation of these rules and conventions and qualifies as a problematic action, and of the fact that a problematic action might be taken as a cue for a possible negative retypification. Strategic competence includes, on the one hand, the speaker's metapragmatic competence to use formulaic disclaimers to create constraints on social interpretations of the expression of problematic actions, and the speaker's metapragmatic awareness that his attempt to forestall a negative retypification can indeed bring about the desired result, on the other hand. To sum up, in using a disclaimer, an individual (i) claims status as a competent member of society who is aware of social rules and the potential risks involved in violating these rules, (ii) asserts his intention to perform a potential problematic action, and (iii) asks his interlocutor to dissociate his identity from the problematic action he is about to perform (Overstreet and Yule, 2001:49).

Similar views are held by Heisler et al.(2003), who, in a study of evaluative metadiscursive comments, maintain that in the use of such a comment the speaker accepts responsibility for the unpleasing or unexpected nature of the content of his utterance, all the while signaling that he himself should not be prejudiced by a negative judgment that may stem from his talk. The unpleasing or unexpected nature of the utterance lies in a deviation from shared assumptions about sense making which are rooted in the social mentality of a community. Given that what the speaker says communicates as much about himself as about the external world, such deviations reflect negatively on the speaker and might prompt the hearer to formulate a negative evaluation of the speaker's utterance, and by extension, of his moral, ethnical or psychological worth. It is the unpleasantness or unexpectedness of the speaker's utterance and the need to avoid a negative evaluation that motivate the speaker to mitigate his utterance. By prefacing his utterance with a comment in anticipation of the hearer's reaction to the utterance, the speaker attempts, and more often than not manages, to eliminate the possibility of the hearer actually voicing such a negative evaluation.

As is the case with the use of formulaic disclaimers, the use of evaluative metadiscursive comments indicates the speaker's social competence, which manifests itself in an awareness of the shared assumptions about sense making, of what constitutes a deviation from these assumptions and what risks might be involved in such a deviation.

The use of evaluative meatadiscursive comments also indicates the speaker's strategic competence, which manifests itself in choosing a strategy that contributes to positive self-presentation and image management.

### 2.2.3.4　The Psychopragmatic Trend

Studies of mitigation under the psychopragmatic trend are concerned with the psychological motivations behind the use of mitigation and the psychological effects produced in the speaker and the hearer.

Caffi (1999, 2007), in a study of doctor-patient interactions in the Italian context, observes that mitigation can be motivated by the psychological state of indifference. In the diagnosis episode of doctor-patient interactions, for example, the doctor may habitually play down the seriousness of the disease, sometimes to an unwarranted degree, quite unaware of the patient's concern over his own health and indifferent to his need to know the truth. Such a psychological state is the result of long-time exposure to the sufferings of patients, which has seriously desensitized the doctor to the pain or the agony. Mitigation motivated by such a psychological state typically produces an anti-empathic effect reflective of emotional fatigue. Caffi (ibid) further finds that mitigation can be motivated by the psychological state of evasion. Thus, in the history taking episode of the interaction or in a narration of family problems, the patient uses strategic examples, topical shields and deictic shields instead of a direct and explicit reference to the problem, because he is unwilling to touch upon a sensitive area of his life, or is not ready to come to terms with the fact—in a word, because he wants to evade the topic. Such mitigation creates an impression of emotive withdrawal or emotive noninvolvement on the part of the patient, because, instead of opening up to the doctor, he appears to be deeply withdrawn into himself. In a similar vein, Huo (2004) finds that mitigation can be motivated by psychological expectations of good health on the part of the patient. In the TCM (traditional Chinese medicine) clinic interviews that he investigates, the patient may mitigate the symptoms of his illness in the hope of its nonseriousness. Mitigation on the doctor's part, on the other hand, produces a comforting effect on the patient by taking away his worries.

Caffi also attempts to account for mitigation in psychological terms, borrowing Haley's (1959) disqualification theory that was used to account for the abnormal speeches of schizophrenics. The abnormality of schizophrenics lies in refusing to do what normal people always do: defining one's own relationship with another. They refuse to define the relationship by disqualifying what they say, or by negating one or more of the 'I', 'am saying something', 'to you', 'in this situation' components of an utterance. Thus, a schizophrenic who appears to be talking to me right here at this moment may be talking to someone else about something that happened in the past somewhere else. In analogy, mitigation (especially a shield) involves a deviation from the implicit deictic sources of an utterance, which correspond to the four components mentioned above. Thus, mitigation and schizophrenic disqualification share the core of deresponsibilization.

In other words, the deresponsibilization of the deictic sources of an utterance in mitigation corresponds with a deresponsibilization for defining the interpersonal relationship in schizophrenics. It is worth pointing out here that Caffi's data include the interactions between psychoanalysts or psychotherapists and patients with mental problems, and so the applicability of her conclusions to other more ordinary types of data is to be taken with great caution.

## 2.3 Achievements

In this section, I will sketch the achievements made by the previous studies of mitigation so as to establish a foundation and departure point for the present study. Although the limitations of the previous studies are theoretically as important as their achievements, they are not practically as constructive and are to be referred to in chapters 4, 5 and 6 only when they are relevant. Thus I focus on the findings of previous studies, on which I hope to draw and elaborate in the following chapters.

First, previous studies have highlighted two definitional criteria for mitigation, namely, a reduction of the illocutionary force of the ensuing speech act and a weakening of a negative effect the speech act is likely to produce on the hearer. Based on these criteria, various definitions of mitigation can be given in further studies. Adopting either one of them leads to a broad definition whereas adopting both of them simultaneously leads to a narrow definition. In the present study, I will offer a narrow definition of mitigation on the basis of a combination of a reduction of the illocutionary force and a softening of a negative effect of the speech act on the hearer.

Second, in terms of the conceptualization of mitigation, previous studies have isolated a cluster of semantic/pragmatic properties of mitigating devices or strategies, in terms of which to speak of the reduction of the illocutionary force of the speech act. These properties include epistemic commitment, deontic commitment, imposition, deresponsibilization, among other things, which are incorporated in Sbisà's (2001) notion of rights and obligations and which will be used in the present study to testify the mitigating potential of linguistic items and to qualify them as mitigating strategies.

Third, with regard to the classification of mitigating strategies, previous studies have offered four taxonomies for the present study to draw on. Worthy of special mention is that Caffi (1999, 2007) classifies mitigation into bushes, hedges and shields on the basis of the scope of mitigation involved. Inspired by Caffi, the present study will offer a taxonomy which divides mitigation into propositional mitigation, illocutionary mitigation and perlocutionary mitigation and subsumes under them the substrategies derived from other taxonomies.

Fourth, in the area of contextual constraints on mitigation, previous studies have brought to light a number of factors that motivate the use of mitigation, including social norms and violations thereof (Overstreet and Yule, 2001; Heisler et.al, 2003) and conflicts of various kinds (Huo, 2004). These constitute the basis on which the present study embarks on an exploration of the socio-cultural and psychological motivators of mitigation.

Fifth, in the area of explanation, previous studies have given various accounts of mitigation, including Huo's (2004) regulation account in terms of regulating verbal activities by diffusing conflicts along the physical, the mental and the social dimensions, and the account given by Overstreet and Yule (2001) and Heisler et al. (2003) in terms of forestalling negative evaluation or retypification of the speaker. In the present study I will draw on both of them in examining the interpersonal and the communicative functions of mitigation.

## 2.4  Summary

In this chapter, I have briefly reviewed previous studies of mitigation under three approaches, the sociolinguistic approach, the cross-cultural / interlanguage pragmatic approach and the general pragmatic approach.

Studies under the sociolinguistic approach have revolved around Lakoff's (1975) hypothesis that mitigation is correlated with women's subordinate status in a male-dominant world. However, they have yielded more controversies than agreement. Recent sociolinguistic studies of mitigation have highlighted the multifunctionality of mitigation, which is taken up and elaborated on by the present study.

Studies under the pragmatic approach are most fruitful in terms of hypothesis generation. Taxonomies of mitigating strategies have been offered, contextual constraints on mitigation have been examined and accounts have been given of its working mechanism. These research findings, with necessary adaptation and alterations, are integrated into the present study.

Studies under the cross-cultural/interlanguage pragmatic approach are mostly applications of pragmatic theories. They have disconfirmed the assumed linear correlation of indirectness to politeness, but validated the hypothesis of cross-cultural variations in mitigating patterns. They have also revealed an overacquisition of external mitigation accompanied by an underacquisition of internal mitigation. Furthermore, they have revealed a trend of slow and marginal development of mitigation in the language learner. Interesting as these findings are, they bear little transparent relevance to the present study except for stressing, from a cross-cultural communicative and pedagogical point of view, the importance of making a systematic study of mitigation.

# Chapter 3
# The Conceptual Framework

## 3.0 Introduction

In this chapter, I am concerned with describing the framework in terms of which to conceptualize and account for mitigation. I will first review the definitions of mitigation that have been given in earlier studies and, on the basis of that, offer the working definition to be adopted in the present study. I will then draw some distinctions between mitigation and overlapping notions such as indirectness and politeness. Following this, I will supply the theoretical background of the present study by outlining the theories which will be resorted to in subsequent reasoning and exposition, which are Verschueren's (1999) adaptation theory and Davis' (1996) empathy theory. Last, I will outline the components of the conceptual framework as the aspects of mitigation that will be taken up as research questions by the present study. These are mitigating strategies, contextual constraints on mitigation, mitigating functions and the working mechanism of mitigation.

## 3.1 Definitions of Mitigation

In this section, I will first review the definitions of mitigation that have been proposed in the literature with view to revealing their strengths and weaknesses and then provide a working definition for the present study by improving on these earlier definitions.

### 3.1.1  Previous Definitions Revisited

Although mitigation has been taken up as a topic of research in various fields, its definition is an issue on which no agreement has been reached. As will be indicated by the review below, some of the studies have operated without an explicit definition, while others seriously diverge from each other in their definitions.

Labov (1976), one of the earliest studies of mitigation, does not offer a definition. One can only infer from his discussion that he means the following points by the term. Firstly, mitigation is related to indirect use of language, so that asking questions as a way of refusing constitutes mitigation while making an outright refusal counts as nonmitigation. Secondly, mitigation is a form of politeness, which makes it possible to refuse or reject without causing major confrontations. The black schoolchildren in his study, on account of directly refusing to obey their teacher's orders, were perceived as impolite and were reprimanded or even demoted.

Pragmatic studies of mitigation have offered various definitions for the term. Fraser (1980:341) defines mitigation as 'the reduction of certain unwelcome effects which a speech act has on the hearer'. In order to clarify the notion, he adds a few restrictions to his definition: the effects must be perceivably negative (unwelcome); the negative effects must be those which might arise out of the ensuing speech act, not those having already originated elsewhere; mitigation is not an independent speech act, but is related to both the illocution and the perlocution of a speech act; mitigation is not the same as politeness. Fraser's is the first definition with any explicitness and clarity, but it suffers from a weakness. Concerning what he refers to by unwelcome effects, Fraser seems to sway between the illocutionary force and the perlocutionary effect: in the case of face threatening acts, he means by mitigation the reduction of face threat, while in the case of face-neutral speech acts he refers to the reduction of the illocutionary force (e.g. assertive force).

Following and elaborating on Fraser, Holmes (1984:346) defines mitigation as the attenuation of the illocutionary force of a negatively affective speech act. Speech acts fall into positively affective and negatively affective categories, according to the speaker's attitude toward the hearer in the context of utterance. Negatively affective speech acts are those that potentially increase the social distance between the interlocutors while positively affective speech acts work in the opposite direction. The illocutionary forces of both categories of speech acts can be boosted or attenuated depending on what kind of affective meaning the speaker wants to express toward the hearer. However, mitigation exclusively operates on negatively affective speech acts and serves to strengthen the solidarity between the interlocutors and thereby enhance their social relationship. By illocutionary force, Holmes refers to the strength with which the illocutionary point of a particular speech act is presented, which is further defined in terms of epistemic modality, i.e., the speaker's attitude to the proposition embedded in the utterance. It is clear that Holmes shares Fraser's negative orientation in the definition of mitigation, but is more explicit about what mitigation consists of. However, her conception of illocutionary force as speaker's epistemic modality seems to be limited, which is a problem taken up by Sbisà(2001).

Sbisà (2001) also defines mitigation as the weakening of the illocutionary force of a speech act, but unlike Holmes, she views illocutionary force as determined by the interlocutors' rights and obligations presupposed by the performing of a speech act, which she calls its 'core illocutionary effects'. These rights and obligations come in the forms of the speaker's entitlement (referring to the speaker's power, status or authority that entitles him to perform the speech act), the hearer's obligation (the need, created by the speech act, for the hearer to perform a subsequent verbal or nonverbal action), and the speaker commitment (a commitment to the truth of a proposition or to the undertaking of a future action). Mitigating the illocutionary force of a speech act, perceived in such a light, consists in restricting the speaker's entitlement, removing the hearer's obligation and lowering the speaker's commitment. Two points about Sbisà's definition of mitigation are noteworthy. Firstly, she expands the notion of illocutionary force from epistemic modality to deontic modality, which represents a broader view than Holmes (1984). Secondly, the illocutionary effects in terms of which illocutionary force is conceived are conventional, in the sense that they are founded on intersubjective agreement. Thus mitigation serves the function of adjusting or fine-tuning the interpersonal relationship between the interlocutors. Sbisà's study is oriented to speech act theory in the sense that she attempts to provide a unified account of mitigation (together with reinforcement) and illocutionary force in her reformulated model of speech acts. In other words, she regards mitigation as an inherent property of language use in general and speech act performance in particular. Of special interest to the present study is her notion of deontic modality, which I will adopt as the basis of my working definition of mitigation.

Caffi (1999, 2007) defines mitigation as the result of the weakening of one of the parameters involved in a certain interaction. The basic assumption behind this definition is that human communication, viewed under the systemic theoretical framework, involves a set of parameters whose values vary with the circumstances of their application and whose importance overrides that of the system's initial conditions. Mitigation, in this sense, plays an indispensable role in human communication. Caffi then identifies three such parameters, namely, propositional precision, illocutionary endorsement and deictic source of the utterance, which mitigation operates on and which form the basis of three major mitigating strategies (bushes, hedges and shields). The result arising from mitigation comes in the form of the increasing or decreasing of social distance, psychological distance and emotive distance. Embodied in this definition is an important divergence from Fraser's conception of mitigation: while Fraser views mitigation as associated with such negative aspects of a speech act as face threat, Caffi goes far beyond this. For Caffi, face threat is only one of the parameters that may be involved in human communication, and it bears no relevance to institutional interactions such as doctor-patient conversations, where other parameters predominate. Caffi's conception of mitigation also differs from Holmes' and Sbisà's in that it is not restricted to the social dimension of communication, but rather extends to the psychological and emotive dimensions. It can be seen that Caffi's notion of mitigation is more comprehensive than the others. However, it suffers from a few weaknesses. Firstly, her list of interactional parameters is not exhaustive: exactly how many parameters are involved in communication and what are the other parameters than the three she has isolated? Secondly, parameter is too general a term to be operational in further studies of mitigation, especially in the characterization of other cases of mitigation than those she has identified. Most importantly, perhaps, her study is based on doctor-patient interactions in psychoanalytic interviews, therefore the extent to which her explanations can be generalized to other genres of speech should be taken with caution.

The definition of mitigation adopted in cross-cultural/interlanguage pragmatics is given in the coding manual of the CCSARP study of the speech act of request, which is presented in Blum-Kulka et al.(1989, 281-288). Mitigation is defined as a politeness strategy that functions by reducing the threat to the hearer's positive or negative face. More specifically, mitigation consists in the reduction of the impositive force of the request, or in the signaling of the requester's solidarity with the requestee, both of which contribute to a reduction of the weightiness of the FTA and constitute polite requesting. One characteristic of this definition is that it is largely dependent on Brown and Levinson's (1978, 1987) politeness theory. Another is that it is given with reference to the speech act of request and meant to be extended to other speech acts such as apology, complaint, offer and refusal of offer.

More recently, Huo (2004: 108) defines mitigation as 'a pragmatic strategy which functions to defuse or weaken a social, physical or psychological conflict by choosing a linguistic device to reduce a pragmatic parameter so as to regulate, maintain and manage an activity interaction, thereby restoring and improving harmony of different kinds'. Implied in this definition is the assumption that human social activities, including language use, are conflictive in nature, and conflicts of various kinds may threaten the smooth progression of the current activity interaction, which may be set right again by reintroducing harmony into the interaction. This motivates the rational language user, who is bestowed with metapragmatic awareness, to weaken the conflict and thus facilitate the progression of the interaction. Conflicts can occur along the physical, the psychological and the social dimensions, along which mitigation operates. Specifically, physical conflicts assume the form of a disagreement or mismatch between a linguistic fact (i.e. the proposition in an assertion) and the real world fact, psychological conflicts take the form of an opposition between the different psychological states or intentions of the interaction participants, and social conflicts are reflected in a range of real or potential interpersonal oppositions or frictions of different sizes. Such conflicts can be weakened or defused by weakening pragmatic parameters such as propositional precision, impositive illocutionary force or face threat.

It can be seen that, drawing on the familiar concepts of proposition, illocutionary force and face threat, Huo tries to characterize mitigation in its full complexity. One of the merits is that his definition has gone beyond previous ones by foregrounding the role that mitigation plays in facilitating the progression of the interaction in which mitigation occurs, which I take to be one of the major roles of mitigation and which has long been neglected in the literature. In defining mitigation, Huo follows Caffi (1999) in adopting the notion of parameter and further claims that pragmatic parameters constitute an open set. This means that he may inherit Caffi's weakness of questionable operationality. Moreover, he has only partly answered the question of exactly how mitigation can achieve its facilitative goal by stating that mitigation is cognitively made possible by the language user's metapragmatic awareness.

To sum up, previous definitions are related to, but different from, one another. Such diversity has brought to light various aspects of the notion of mitigation. As Caffi(1999, 885) rightly points out, mitigation is a three argument predicate: someone mitigates something through something else. This can be interpreted as meaning that there are at least three aspects involved in mitigation: the agent, the means and the end. The means refers to the cluster of semanticopragmatic features of an utterance, or to use Caffi's term again, the parameters whose values may be weakened. The end refers to the negative effect that mitigation serves to soften in the performing of a certain speech act. Seen in this light, some of the aforementioned definitions are means-oriented while others are end-oriented. The merits and demerits of such definitions will be sketched in the next section, where I present my working definition of mitigation.

### 3.1.2   A Working Definition of Mitigation

As pointed out above, some of the earlier definitions of mitigation are means-oriented. Holmes (1984), Caffi (1999, 2007) and Sbisà (2001) have all defined mitigation in terms of a reduction of the illocutionary force of a speech act. The adoption of this criterion is important because the illocutionary force of a speech act is located at the interface of semantics and pragmatics, and its adoption makes the treatment of mitigation both semantically informed and pragmatically oriented.

Some other definitions of mitigation are end-oriented. The most typical example is that of Fraser (1980), which is given in terms of the reduction of certain unwelcome effects which a speech act has on the hearer. In a similar fashion, Huo (2004) stresses the end result of mitigation, which comes in the form of the cushioning of a physical, social or psychological conflict. The adoption of this criterion is reminiscent of the use of the notion in natural sciences, where it concerns the reduction of bad consequences such as damage to the environments.

It is evident that these two aspects, the reduction of the illocutionary force of a speech act and the avoidance of an unwelcome effect, are both highly relevant to an examination of the nature of mitigation. Therefore it makes sense to integrate them into my working definition of mitigation.

*A working definition of mitigation:*

Mitigation is a pragmatic strategy whereby the speaker reduces the illocutionary force of his speech act in order to soften an unpleasant effect that is detrimental to his communicative goal.

A few clarifications and justifications are given as follows.

First, by illocutionary force I mean the strength with which the speaker performs a speech act. This is operationalized as the determination, endorsement or unreservedness with which the speaker gets on record performing the speech act. My notion of illocutionary force incorporates Holmes' (1984) and Caffi's (1999, 2007). It also goes beyond Sbisà's (2001) by including not only deontic modality related to possibility and necessity, but also deontic modality related to social and/ or moral appropriateness. Thus the reduction of the illocutionary force of the speech act may take the form of propositional vagueness, illocutionary nonendorsement and perlocutionary concern. If the proposition embedded in a speech act is made imprecise, or if the speaker's propositional attitude is made uncertain, the illocutionary force is viewed as having been reduced. Likewise, if the speaker dissociates himself from the illocutionary point of a speech act, the illocutionary force is rendered weaker. If, while attempting to perform an illocutionary act, the speaker singles out one perlocutionary effect and shows concern over it, the illocutionary force is downgraded in a similar fashion.

Second, the effect of a speech act that is to be softened by mitigation is necessarily negative. When Caffi (1999, 2007) speaks of extending the notion of mitigation beyond negativity, she is actually confusing the perlocutionary effect that gets mitigated and the mitigating functions that are produced at the interpersonal and the communicative levels. In my view, the mitigated perlocutionary effect is always negative and the functions of mitigation are always positive. Besides, from the perspective of human rationality, there is no motivation to mitigate something positive, which is why it is reasonable to stick to negativity at the definitional stage.

Third, by unpleasant effect I mean some perlocutionary sequels or side effects of the speech act that are different from, and detrimental to, its main perlocutionary effect and/or the communicative goal of the speaker. Fraser (1980) has this distinction in mind although he does not make it explicit. The distinction is made apparent in Huo (2004) when he states that mitigation functions to diffuse conflicts along various dimensions so as to regulate interactions and restore or improve harmony of various kinds. Mitigation must be defined with reference to perlocutionary sequels, which are perceivably detrimental to the release of the main perlocutionary effect of the speech act or the achievement of the speaker's communicative goal. It cannot be defined with reference to the speaker's communicative goal because from the perspective of human rationality there is only justification in boosting one's own communicative goal. It cannot be defined with reference to the main perlocutionary effect because it would presuppose that the speaker is engaged in a malicious speech act whose main perlocutionary effect is inherently negative, given the condition that mitigation is negativity-oriented. It can not even be defined in terms of a reduction of the risk of communicative failure because, given that mitigation serves exactly that function, such a definition would end up being circular. This distinction has practical importance because it disqualifies the politeness marker *please* and deferential terms of address as falling into the domain of mitigation. The picture is that mitigation operates by counteracting something bad (negative effects that are detrimental to smooth running of communication) to achieve something good (communicative success).

Fourth, the present working definition is a strict one in the sense that it postulates two conditions, separately upheld by earlier definitions, which must be simultaneously satisfied. That is, for something to qualify as mitigation, it must first involve a reduction of the illocutionary force of a speech act and then a corresponding softening of an unpleasant effect that the speech act has on the hearer. Hopefully, the adoption of the strict definition has the advantage of capturing the nuclear cases of mitigation and excluding the borderline or marginal cases.

## 3.2   Delimitation of Mitigation

Having given a working definition of mitigation, it is necessary to examine its relationship with such overlapping notions as indirectness and politeness.

### 3.2.1   Mitigation and Indirectness

In its research history, mitigation has been associated with indirectness of language use, defined as the extent of illocutionary opaqueness. Labov (1976) notes that asking questions as an indirect way of refusing mitigates the challenge to the school teacher's authority, while a direct refusal definitely constitutes such a challenge. Fraser (1980) lists indirect speech acts as the first mitigating strategy, arguing that the use of an indirect speech act on the part of the speaker assigns to the hearer more responsibility of inferring the illocutionary point of the speaker and thus reduces the possibility of antagonism being directed toward the speaker, thereby achieving a kind of self-serving mitigation. Brown and Levinson (1978, 1987) envisage five strategies of performing face threatening acts, which range from *go boldly on record* , *negative face redress*, *positive face redress*, *go off record* to *withhold FTA*, on the basis of their levels of indirectness. The level of indirectness is assumed to be causally related to the weightiness of the FTA, with the most indirect strategy (*withhold FTA*) being chosen for the most serious FTA. Thus indirectness is perceived as functioning to counteract the weightiness of FTAs. Following and elaborating on Brown and Levinson, the CCSAR researchers (cf. Blum-Kulka et al., 1989:278-281) isolated nine levels of indirectness, on the basis of which nine requestive strategies are postulated, which range from mood derivable to mild hint. Given that a request is an FTA impeding the requestee's freedom of action, indirectness in the requestive strategies is seen as functioning to mitigate threat to the requestee's negative face. One implication that is derivable from Brown and Levinson's conceptualization and from the CCSAR coding manual is that not only is indirectness associated with mitigation, but its level is positively correlated with its mitigating potential.

However, contrary to what Brown and Levinson implicitly hold, indirectness is not in a linear relationship with mitigation. Blum-Kulka (1987) finds that the most acceptable way of performing speech acts is not the most indirect one but the conventionally indirect one, which encodes an acceptable level of indirectness and desirable illocutionary transparency. Blum-Kulka argues that overindirectness imposes on the hearer the burden of inferring the illocutionary intention of the speaker. More radically, Skewis (2003) finds, in a study of the directive speech acts between the male characters in the Chinese novel *Hongloumeng*, that the most favored strategy is mood derivable, the most direct on the CCSARP coding manual. This may imply that indirectness as a mitigating strategy is not resorted to as much as predicted by Brown and Levinson (1978:198), at least not in the context of the Chinese culture.

The conclusion to be drawn is that there is a limit to the mitigating potential of indirectness and to the domain to which it is applicable.

Indeed, the establishment of indirectness as a mitigating strategy and the systematic attention it has enjoyed in the literature is a reflection of the negative-face orientation of western cultures. In the case of the solidarity-oriented Chinese culture, other mitigating strategies than indirectness may be more interesting, both theoretically and practically. It is for this and a few other reasons to be specified below that I exclude indirectness from the present study.

One of these additional reasons is that indirectness, unlike the other mitigating strategies in my data, does not contain an explicit mitigator, i.e., a linguistic item that is a necessary and sufficient condition for its mitigating status. Another reason is that it is resistant to further classification and thus makes systematic study difficult, if not impossible.

Other kinds of indirectness include the preparatory work the speaker does before introducing the illocutionary point (as illustrated in small talk) and implicit and vague reference to a taboo topic (as illustrated in euphemism), which occur more frequently in language use. However, these do not occur frequently in my data, so they are excluded from the present study.

### 3.2.2   Mitigation and Politeness/Facework

Throughout the research history of mitigation, its relationship with politeness has exerted much fascination on researchers. Two different views have been proposed as regards the nature of this relationship.

One of these views is that mitigation is somewhat inherently related to politeness. Fraser (1980:344), for instance, explicitly states that mitigation entails politeness, although not the other way round. He concludes that mitigation occurs only if the speaker is also being polite and that it is hard to construct a case where the speaker is viewed as impolite but as having mitigated the force of his utterance. Similarly, Haverkate (1992:505) holds that mitigation is a special form of politeness.

More explicit about the relationship of mitigation with politeness are Brown and Levinson (1978, 1987) and Leech (1983). For Brown and Levinson, linguistic politeness consists in the hearer's positive and negative face wants being satisfied, and mitigation contributes to politeness by minimizing the weightiness of the face threatening act, or more specifically by softening the threat posed by the FTA to either the positive face or the negative face of the hearer. Thus mitigation is causally linked to politeness, which is taken as a language universal. Similarly, Leech (1983) incorporates mitigation under politeness on the assumption that mitigation constitutes a sufficient condition for politeness, as is demonstrated in his politeness maxims in which the minimizations of cost to other, benefit to self, dispraise of other, praise of self, disagreement between self and other, and antipathy between self and other are each thought to lead to politeness.

This view of the relationship of mitigation to politeness is carried to an extreme by the studies in the CCSARP project, whose coding manual of mitigation is widely adopted in subsequent cross-cultural/ interlanguage pragmatic studies of mitigation. According to this coding manual, mitigation and politeness are one and the same, in the sense that the functions of mitigation are conceived largely in terms of its contribution to politeness and politeness potential is one of the criteria used for qualifying a linguistic item as a mitigator. In fact, there has been an attempt to relate kinds of mitigation with kinds of politeness. Blum-Kulka (1992), for example, states that internal mitigation redresses face by stressing in-group membership and is oriented to positive politeness whereas external mitigation appeals to the hearer as a rational agent in need of persuasion and is interrelated with negative politeness. Skewis (2003) advertently follows this and concludes that mitigation compensates for the lack of politeness incurred by the choice of mood derivable, the most direct and thus impolite request strategy.

The other view regarding the relationship between mitigation and politeness is that these concepts differ from each other on various grounds. Fraser (1980), for example, points out that although mitigation entails politeness, they are different by their nature: whereas mitigation is an attempt on the part of the speaker to soften some unwelcome effect that the ensuing speech act is likely to have on the hearer, politeness depends on the extent to which the speaker's linguistic behaviors conform to what he calls the conversational contract, i.e., the implicit understanding that both interlocutors bring to the interaction of the rights and obligations assigned to them respectively. Mitigation also differs from politeness in terms of their status: politeness is regarded by some researchers (e.g. Gu, 1990) as a social norm, which mitigation can never be. Thus, while politeness is a compulsory requirement and an explicitly expected pattern of behavior, mitigation is often an idiosyncratically flavored pragmatic strategy. In addition, as suggested by Thomas (1995), politeness is determined by the semantic content of an utterance or the illocutionary point of a speech act in accordance with the extent to which they have conformed to the social norms of appropriateness, mitigation does not have an illocutionary point of its own as it is not an independent speech act. Thus mitigating the illocutionary force of an impolite speech act does not make the act qualitatively polite. In other words, although mitigation can reduce the severity of the impoliteness involved, it does not alter the impolite nature of the speech act to which it is affiliated. Further, Caffi (1999, 2007) observes that mitigation and face are two extensionally divergent notions. She holds that mitigation is the weakening of one of the interactive parameters involved in a communicative event and face is only one of those parameters, so mitigation extensionally incorporates facework. More recently, some researchers have even voiced doubt on the necessary relation of mitigation to politeness. Martinovski (2006), for example, shows that mitigation in courtroom examinations functions not to express politeness, but rather to modify discourse plans and social contexts, and most importantly to protect life.

It can be seen that mitigation and politeness/facework only coincidentally overlap. In the present study, I maintain that they are separate concepts on the following grounds. First, treating mitigation and politeness as interchangeable or equivalent can lead to absurdities. For instance, in interlanguage pragmatic studies of mitigation, mitigating strategies are thought to perform the sole function of politeness while some politeness strategies like the use of the politeness marker *please* is listed as the first lexical mitigator. This invites the question: which precedes which? Does mitigation lead to politeness or does politeness lead to mitigation? This chicken-egg question obviously suggests the circularity in the conceptualization of mitigation by these studies. In fact, *please* is not only a politeness marker, but also an IFID (House, 1989) that marks the illocutionary point of the speech act as requestive and makes it more explicit. Taking this into consideration, it is easy to see that *please* does not reduce the illocutionary force of the speech act but rather boosts it. It does not fit the strict definition offered in the present study. This view is consistent with Fraser (1980: 344) when he says 'if I say "Please sit down", I have requested in relatively polite but relatively unmitigated way'. To push the argument a little further, if I say 'Please help yourself to the fish', what have I mitigated, your refusal or my hospitality?

Neither, there is actually nothing to mitigate in this case. The conclusion to draw is that politeness is not an inherent property of mitigation. The treatment of deferential terms of address as mitigators is also absurd. Deferential terms of address mark a social distance so that, other things being equal, they increase the weightiness of the FTA as calculated by the equation $W_x = P(S,H) + D(S,H) + R_x$ Therefore the use of deferential terms of address is polite but does not mitigate. Second, in much of pragmatic research since Leech (1983), whose Politeness Principle is said to 'rescue' Grice's (1975) Cooperative Principle, politeness has been considered as the ultimate goal of communication, so that if mitigation is an effective communicative strategy it must serve the function of politeness. But this is a wrong assumption. If the speaker's goal in using mitigation was to be polite, he might as well have withheld the speech act or have gone off record, because those are more polite ways to behave. If the speaker goes on record in a mitigated manner, he must have been otherwise motivated, e.g., to enhance the effectiveness of the communication. In fact, what has often led to the confusion between politeness and mitigation is that they are both effective communicative strategies. Third, even though mitigation occasionally produces a politeness effect, this effect is context-dependent. For example, while it is polite to mitigate one's utterance in casual relationships, this is not true in close or intimate relationships. In intimate relationships, mitigation can be viewed as impolite, ironic or even hypocritical, whereas boasting, directness, exaggerating and playful insulting can be taken as extremely polite. What's more, Brown and Levinson's (1978, 1987) notion of face is fraught with problems due to its Anglocentricity. Although there are two face types, far more attention has been given in the literature to negative face, the wish not to have one's own freedom of action impeded. This reflects the individualistic orientation of western cultures. In eastern collectivism-oriented cultures, in-group solidarity and interdependence are far more highly valued. Apart from this orientational divergence, there is an intensional difference between the Chinese notions of *miànzi* (面子), *liǎn* (脸) and Brown and Levinson's notion of face. Though *miànzi* and *liǎn* are occasionally interchangeable, *miànzi* is mainly a social concept referring to social prestige or reputation and *liǎn* is mainly a moral concept referring to moral worth or sense of shame. (cf. Mao, 1994: 457) Neither of these is consistent with Brown and Levinson's positive face or negative face. Such cross-cultural differences in the conceptualization of face should be borne in mind when deciding to use it as a technical term.

For the aforementioned reasons, I take mitigation as theoretically unrelated to politeness and give up the notion of politeness in conceptualizing, characterizing and accounting for mitigation. I also distinguish between mitigation and facework: although I am fully aware that mitigation can occur within FTAs and serves to reduce face threat, I maintain that what is involved and achieved goes far beyond that. Thus, in the exposition to be given in chapters 4, 5 and 6, the notion of face in sense of Brown and Levinson (1978, 1987) will be mentioned only in passing. The thrust of the argumentation lies elsewhere.

## 3.3 Theoretical Background

The theoretical background of the present study consists of Verschueren's (1999) adaptation theory and Davis' (1996) empathy theory.

### 3.3.1 Linguistic Adaptation

Verschueren's (1999) adaptation theory is an evolutionarily

inspired general theory of pragmatics. According to this theory, just as species adapt themselves to environmental changes to flourish in their evolutionary process, so the language user adapts himself to the context to survive linguistically and socially. Language use is viewed in this theory as a means of human life and survival that centers on linguistic adaptation.

Linguistic adaptation consists in the constant making of linguistic choices, which operates at all levels of linguistic structuring ranging from phonemes, morphemes, words, utterances, discourses and beyond. The choices made include not only linguistic items but also communicative strategies such as mitigation. Linguistic choice making occurs not only in the process of language production but also in that of language comprehension. Seen in this light, linguistic choice making pervades the use of language.

The continuous making of linguistic choices is possible because language has three properties: variability, adaptability, negotiability. Variability is the property of language which defines the range of possibilities from which choices can be made. It refers to the wide array of linguistic resources that the language user avails himself of in making linguistic adaptations to satisfy his specific communicative needs. It is claimed that languages have developed to the point of providing their users with all the linguistic means necessary to express what they want to convey. Negotiability is the property of language responsible for the fact that choices are not made automatically or according to strict rules or fixed form-function relationships, but rather on the basis of highly flexible principles or strategies. Since linguistic adaptation also occurs in the process of language comprehension, negotiability also pertains to meaning generation. Adaptability is the property of language that enables language users to make negotiable choices in such a way as to approach points of satisfaction for their communicative needs. It also involves the contextual factors that linguistic choice making is interadaptable with.

Verschueren (1999) proceeds to highlight four angles or perspectives of investigation for any specific pragmatic phenomenon. These are structural objects of adaptation, contextual correlates of adaptation, dynamics of adaptation and salience of adaptation. The structural objects of adaptation are the linguistic resources within which linguistic adaptation operates and manifests itself. Contextual correlates of adaptation refer to the contextual constraints that motivate the making of linguistic choices, and include factors in the physical world, the social world and the mental worlds of language users. Dynamics of adaptation refers to the ever-going process of language production, context construction and meaning generation. It is also concerned with the ways that communication principles and strategies are used in the making and negotiation of choices of production and interpretation. Salience refers to the fact that not all choices are made with the same degree of consciousness: some are quite automatic while others are highly motivated. It implies that language use is subject to the constant monitoring of the 'mind in society'.

With the main points of the adaptation theory in mind, we are ready to examine its advantages over other pragmatic theories. The first advantage is that adaptation theory incorporates a social, a psychological and a cognitive dimension into its framework so that it provides a multidimensional approach to the study of language use and has the promise of bringing the many facets of language use in general, and mitigation in particular, to light. The second advantage is that it addresses both language production and language comprehension so that it is more integrative than most other pragmatic theories and has more explanatory power. One more advantage is that it attempts to reveal the physical, social and mental factors that motivate the making of linguistic choices and thus establish a relationship between language and the world. The last and most important advantage is that it pays special attention to the dynamic process of adaptation and negotiation. This makes it possible not only to examine the end result of adaptation from a static perspective but also to track down the development over time of the adaptation so as to get a glimpse of the mechanism behind the adaptation. The dynamic negotiation process of meaning generation is especially relevant to the study of mitigation because mitigation often involves a second processing of the utterance, which is rendered necessary by an inconsistency or even contradiction between the literal meaning of the mitigator and what the speaker intends to be doing with mitigation.

Because of these advantages the adaptation theory is taken as one of the theories that can best account for mitigation.

### 3.3.2   Empathy

A pragmatic theory is incomplete without giving an account of emotive communication. Similarly, an account of mitigation does not tell the whole story without introducing an affective element into the account. The need for a pragmatics of emotive communication is convincingly spelled out in Caffi and Janney (1994). As far as the study of mitigation is concerned, the promising notion to address this need is empathy, to be borrowed from psychology into pragmatics.

A short history taking reveals that the notion of empathy has been given different definitions and treatments in its history of research, with different aspects highlighted and divergent views proposed. The situation was like that of the blind men with the elephant until Mark H.

Davis (1996) proposed a comprehensive perspective on the issue in his *Empathy: A Social Psychological Approach.*

Integrating various definitions of empathy, which focus on either the sharing of affect, the understanding of emotion, cognitive abilities or prosocial behaviors, Davis (1996) defines empathy as embracing a number of constructs related to experiencing emotion through exposure to the target's affect. He then enumerates the constructs that represent the components of empathy: antecedents, processes, intrapersonal outcomes and interpersonal outcomes.

Antecedents of empathy include the capacity for empathy, dispositional differences in empathic tendencies, situational strength and the degree of similarity between the observer and the target, which all influence the likelihood of engaging in empathy-related processes or experiencing empathy-related outcome during any given particular empathy episode. Of the antecedents, capacity for empathy merits special attention. Empathy is regarded as an innate human capacity with a biological basis and evolutionary advantages. It is also viewed as a variety of social intelligence that involves a capacity to understand the perspective of others and that brings status or popularity to the empathizer.

Empathy is generated through specific processes. On the basis of the cognitive effort involved and the degree of sophistication, empathic processes are classified into noncognitive processes, simple cognitive processes and advanced cognitive processes. Noncognitive processes include primary circular reaction and motor mimicry. Simple cognitive processes include classical conditioning, direct association and labelling. Advanced cognitive processes include language-mediated association, elaborated cognitive networks and role taking. Of these processes, the most primitive is the circular reaction, in which a neonate cries in response to hearing other infants cry, and which is taken as evidence for the innateness of empathy. The most advanced is role taking, which involves an effortful and conscious suppression of one's own egocentric perspective on events to entertain that of someone else.

Intrapersonal outcomes refer to the cognitive or affective responses resulting from exposure to the target's (usually negative) affect that are not manifested in the observer's overt behavior toward the target. Cognitive responses include interpersonal accuracy (the successful estimation of other people's thoughts, feelings and characteristics), causal attributions offered by observers for the target's behavior and evaluative judgments of others. Affective outcomes include parallel outcomes, which are actual reproductions in the observer of the observed affect, and reactive outcomes, which are reactions to the experience of others that differ from and go beyond the observed affect. One typical reactive outcome is empathic concern, which involves feelings of compassion or sympathy for the target.

Interpersonal outcomes refer to the observer's behaviors directed toward the target which result from prior exposure to that target. Such outcomes include prosocial behaviors like helping, antisocial behaviors like aggression and behaviors in close social relationships. The components of empathy are summarized in Figure 3.1.

It is clear that all the aspects of empathy that were the foci of previous studies are grouped together and assigned a proper place in the organizational model. This helps put an end to the unsatisfactory situation where studies of empathy were basically unrelated to each other.

Having subsumed such components under the general heading of empathy, Davis (1996) proposes that they are located at an antecedent-process-intrapersonal outcome-interpersonal outcome chain. Thus genetically, antecedents precede processes in the sense that they influence the likelihood of the observer engaging in an empathic process. The processes precede the intrapersonal outcomes in the sense that the latter prototypically result from the former. Finally, the intrapersonal outcomes motivate the interpersonal outcomes that are manifested in overt behaviors toward the target. Davis further claims that, theoretically, each of the components stands in causal relationships with the subsequent ones on the chain. Starting with antecedents, the arrows indicate that they can directly lead to processes, intrapersonal outcomes and interpersonal outcomes. Or they can cause intrapersonal outcomes via processes. Or they can cause interpersonal outcomes via processes or via the process-intrapersonal outcome route. Similarly, processes can directly cause intrapersonal outcomes and interpersonal outcomes, and they also cause interpersonal outcomes via the intrapersonal outcomes. The casual link between intrapersonal outcomes and interpersonal outcomes is obviously direct. Thus, each component of the model is linked with each and every other component. Practically, however, there is a big difference in the strength of the causal links. The strongest links exist between the immediately adjacent components, such as between antecedents and processes, between processes and intrapersonal outcomes and between intrapersonal outcomes and interpersonal outcomes. The weakest link exists between antecedents and interpersonal outcomes, which are removed from each other the furthest on the chain. Ironically, Davis points out, earlier research efforts have been wrongly put in examining the weakest link, i.e., that between antecedents and interpersonal outcomes, understandably giving rise to limited findings and unlimited confusion.

**Fig. 3.1　The Organizational Model of Empathy (reproduced from Davis, 1996:14)**

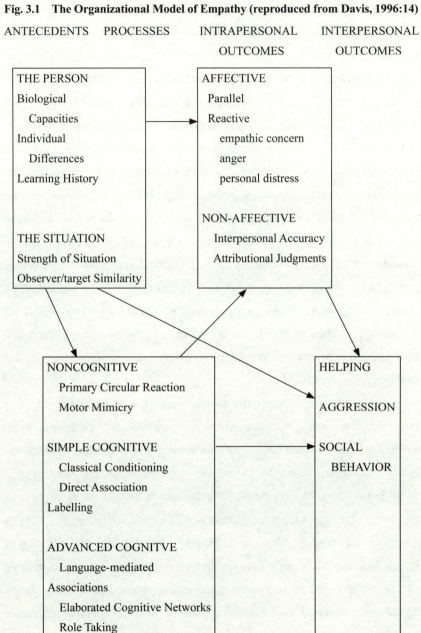

According to Davis, attention should be directed toward the links between immediately adjacent components or between the components that are only one step removed. Empirical researches have brought several patterns to light. Firstly, the subcomponents that have received systematic attention are role taking, empathic concern, actor-like causal attribution and altruistic helping. Actor-like causal attribution refers to the fact that the observer follows the actor in stressing situational forces and deemphasizing dispositional factors as responsible for his behaviors. Secondly, role taking typically leads to empathic concern and actor-like causal attributions; empathic concern is strongly associated with altruistic helping and actor-like causal attributions are strongly associated with the management of interpersonal conflicts. Thus thirdly, the two causal chains most strongly supported by empirical evidence are role taking-empathic concern-helping and role taking-actor-like causal attribution-conflict management. These propositions have general validity and consequently bear special relevance to the adoption of the notion of empathy in the study of mitigation.

The relevance of empathy to communication derives from their interrelations. Firstly, empathy cannot be separated from communication. Empathy loses much of its significance unless it is communicated and used in communication. Motor mimicry, for example, has been argued to be largely a communicative means by which the observers express to the target that they are aware of and in fact are experiencing the target's affective state (Davis, 1996: 113). Empathy has evolutionary advantages in the biological and social senses and there is no reason not to believe that it has a communicative advantage, too. More importantly, since communication involves the understanding of others' perceptual, affective, cognitive, social and judgmental perspectives, it can be enhanced by empathy. Indeed, there is ample empirical evidence that empathic concern prompts good communication in terms of more cooperation, better effectiveness of communication and larger extents to which members of a close relationship disclose to each other. The conclusion to draw is that empathy as a psychological phenomenon occurs in ordinary life and as a subject of study it overflows into pragmatics from such psychology-related fields as psychoanalysis, psychotherapy and nursing.

Empathy is relevant to mitigation on two grounds. One of the reasons is that both empathy and mitigation are related to altruism, a motivational state with the ultimate goal of increasing another's welfare (Batson, 1991:6). That mitigation can be altruistic is evident in Fraser's (1980) most important distinction between self-serving mitigation and altruistic mitigation. Although the distinction does not seem valid sometimes because egoism and altruism are often co-present in a single instance of mitigation, this does not alter the fact that altruism is one of the inherent features of mitigation. Empathy, on the other hand, is thought to be the mechanism of altruism by Batson's (1991) famous empathy-altruism hypothesis, which states that altruistic motivation is produced by feelings of empathy for a person in need and specifies that, as empathic concern for a person in need increases, the altruistic motivation to have that need relieved increases. It is clear that empathy and mitigation can be related via altruism. In fact, it would be interesting to know whether empathy provides a mechanism for mitigation, too. Caffi (1999: 904) also holds that mitigation is related to empathy, although it sometimes has an anti-empathic potential. Topical shields and strategic digressions, for example, are anti-empathic in the sense that they are noncooperation in the disguise of cooperation. Given that her data were obtained from psychotherapeutic interactions where the patients are often schizophrenics and the doctors (therapist, psychoanalyst) can experience what is technically referred to as *burnout*, an emotional fatigue caused by long-term exposure to sufferings, this anti-empathy potential of mitigation is readily understandable. But the use of more ordinary data would suggest that mitigation is pro-empathic rather than anti-empathic. Another reason why empathy is relevant to mitigation is that there is a great convergence in the functions that empathy and mitigation perform. For example, both actor-like causal attributions and mitigation are oriented to solving interpersonal conflicts. Role taking and situational attribution are strongly associated with positive evaluations being made by the observer on the target, which is completely captured by Overstreet and Yule (2001) and Heisler et al.(2003) in their respective discussions of formulaic disclaimer and evaluative metadiscursive comments. Moreover, role taking and empathic concern present the empathizer as being considerate and build up his good image, which is also a function of mitigation. In fact, there is so much in common between empathy and mitigation that it would be unfortunate not to examine mitigation in an empathic light.

In light of the interrelations of empathy to mitigation, it is desirable to integrate it into a pragmatic account of mitigation. Pioneering work has been done by He (1991), He and Ran (2002), and Ran (2007) to introduce the notion of empathy into pragmatics. He (1991), for example, defines pragmatic empathy as the communicators' taking of each other's stance for the purpose of imagining and understanding each other's intention. He further distinguishes between pragmalinguistic empathy and sociopragmatic empathy. Pragmalinguistic empathy refers to the unusual use of indexicals or other deictic expressions that are reflective of the speaker's considerateness for the hearer or his affection towards the hearer. Sociopragmatic empathy refers to the respect shown by the communicators to each other's thoughts and opinions, and is of special relevance to cross-cultural communication where the native speaker shows tolerance for the nonnative speaker's deviate use of the language by accepting his sociocultural customs. Similarly, Ran (2007) refers to pragmatic empathy as the speaker's taking of hearer's pragmatic stance and the satisfaction of the hearer's various needs. He further contrasts empathy and de-empathy, as reflected in the choice of person deixis, along the dimension of emotional and psychological convergence versus divergence. Drawing on these pioneering studies and in light of the components summarized by Davis (1996), the present study operationalizes pragmatic empathy in ordinary language use as containing *perspective taking, affective convergence, respect and analogical reasoning,* individually or collectively. Perspective taking is the process of empathy manifested by the speaker and the hearer adopting each other's perspective, imagining being in each other's place or viewing things from each other's angle. Affective convergence is the affective outcome of empathy and manifests itself in the speaker and the hearer understanding, sharing, caring for or identifying with each other's emotions. Respect is the nonaffective outcome of empathy and is embodied in the speaker and the hearer's showing respect for each other's affect-neutral qualities such as knowledge, status, rights, beliefs, views and thoughts. Analogical reasoning is the inferential mechanism of empathy triggered off by mitigation in the hearer and is characterized by the hearer attributing his rationality-based responses to the speaker on the strength of analogy. The reasoning runs as follows:

    a) The use of mitigation indicates that the speaker is aware of the problematic nature of what he is saying.

    b) Judging from this awareness, the speaker is rational, in fact, as rational as I am.

c) I would not usually say such a thing as the speaker is saying because it violates a social norm.

d) Analogically, the speaker would be saying such a thing as violates a social norm unless there is a special reason for doing it.

e) The best candidate for that special reason is that he is telling the truth, so I might as well believe what he says.

This inferential process of analogical reasoning is the generator of empathic altruism and is responsible for the outcomes of empathy. It is always at play, but is most salient when an interpretation is doubted or challenged.

## 3.4  Characterization of the Conceptual Framework

I have been attempting to build a coherent conceptual framework in order to account for mitigation. Having clarified the theoretical background of the framework, I am ready to outline the major components of the framework.

### 3.4.1  Mitigating Strategies

The basic assumption of the adaptation theory is that language use consists in the continuous making of linguistic choices, which is rendered possible by the variability of the language. Language variability refers to the infinite range of linguistic resources for the language user to choose from in order to approach points of satisfaction for his communicative needs. Choices are made not only of linguistic structure, but also (and perhaps more importantly), of pragmatic strategies. Thus pragmatic strategies, like linguistic structures, constitute part of the language user's linguistic repertoire and pragmatic competence, to which he has recourse in the dynamic use of language.

In the same way that linguistic items ready to be chosen are located at all levels of structuring, the strategies to be employed are related to different levels of the speech act. According to Austin (1962), a speech act has three constituents, the locution, the illocution, and the perlocution, which stand in a complementary relation toward one another. One assumption about the tripartite of the speech act is that these constituents are each necessary and together sufficient conditions for the exhaustion of linguistic meaning. In the absence of any of these constituents the meaning of the speech act cannot be not exhausted.

Mitigation, as a superstrategy of language use, subsumes under it a number of strategies from which to choose when the need of mitigation arises. These can occur either at the locutionary, the illocutionary or the perlocutionary dimensions, leading to the classification of mitigation into propositional mitigation, illocutionary mitigation and perlocutionary mitigation. Propositional mitigation operates on the precision of the propositional content or on the degree of certainty of the speaker's propositional attitude, i.e., illocutionary vagueness. This strategy is chosen most typically when the speaker enjoys less power than his interlocutor with regard to the state of affairs depicted in the proposition or when the speaker wants to psychologically dissociate from it. Illocutionary mitigation operates on the illocutionary nonendorsement, the noninsistence or nondetermination with which the speaker gets on record performing the ensuing speech act. This strategy is chosen when the speaker is reserved about the social and moral appropriateness of the ensuing speech act. Perlocutionary mitigation operates on the speaker's concern, direct or indirect, over the possible negative effect that the current speech act is likely to produce on the hearer. This strategy is chosen when there is a particularly imaginable negative effect which the speaker especially wants to avoid. These strategies, each of which further includes substrategies, are motivated by different contextual factors and are chosen when the factors take on special salience.

The taxonomy of propositional mitigation, illocutionary mitigation and perlocutionary mitigation is an attempt at an exhaustive overview of the strategies and substrategies of mitigation that are available to the language user to choose from in adaptation of his communicative needs and the relevant contextual factors.

To sum up, for linguistic choice making to be possible at all, there must be something to be chosen and a range of items to choose from. So the mitigating strategies take on special relevance in a comprehensive account of mitigation and constitute a necessary component of my framework. The mitigating strategies and substrategies are represented in Figure 3.2.

## Fig. 3.2   Mitigating Strategies

Propositional Mitigation
- Understaters
- Evidential
- Tag Questions
- Epistemic Modals
- Subjectivizers

Mitigation——Illocutionary Mitigation
- Disclaimers
- Deprecators
- Truth Claimers
- Hesitators

Perlocutionary Mitigation
- Simple Anticipation
- Concern Showing
- Penalty Taking
- Direct Dissuasion

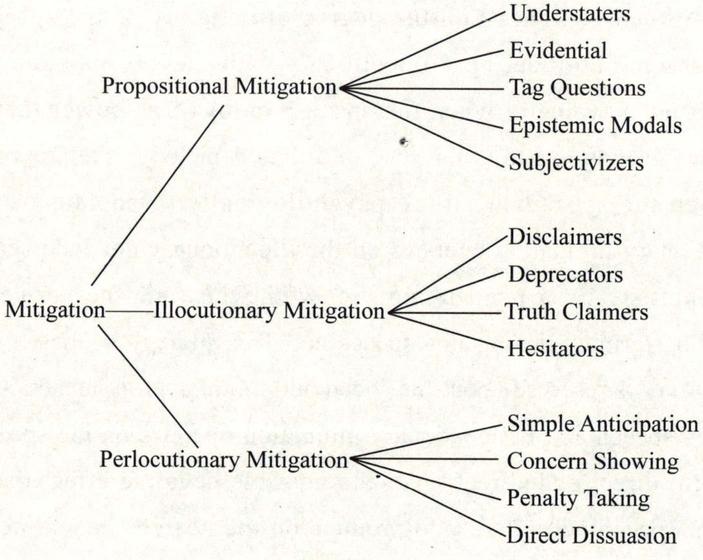

### 3.4.2   Contextual Constraints on Mitigation

In an adaptational account of mitigation, one of the most essential questions to ask is to what mitigation as a phenomenon of language use adapts itself? In other words, what factors motivate the employment of mitigating strategies and substrategies in the process of language production. As language use is anchored in contexts, it can be assumed that mitigation is interadaptable with the factors of the context in which it occurs. The contextual constraints on mitigation are depicted in Figure 3.3, adapted from Verschueren (1999: 76).

**Fig. 3.3   Contextual Constraints on Mitigation (adapted from Verschueren, 1999: 76)**

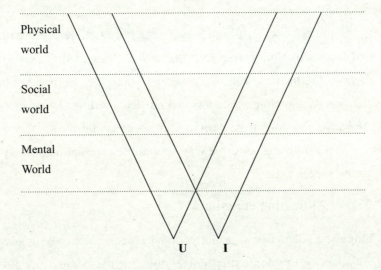

As can be seen from the figure, the context consists of the mental world, the social world and the physical world. In theory, all the factors in these worlds are part of the context with which mitigation interadapts, but in practice only those factors that appear in the area of the lines of vision are activated as contextual objects of adaptation. Specifically, a certain cluster of factors in the social and the mental worlds are of special relevance to the use of mitigation.

In the social world, power, taboo topics and social values are the constraints that prominently motivate the employment of mitigation. As a general rule, the powerless individual must speak to his powerful interlocutor in a weak, nonassertive and tentative manner. Taboo topics such as sex, privacy and unlucky words require the speaker to exercise caution in his manner of speaking so that no violation is committed of the taboos, or enough remedial work is done in the event of an inevitable violation. Values such as modesty, sincerity and restraint constrain the speaker into modifying his utterance in such a way as to present himself as upholding these values.

In the mental world, disbeliefs and negative emotions are the most essential factors that mitigation interadapts with. Assumed or perceived disbeliefs in the hearers lead the speaker to take the controversy into consideration by signaling awareness, acknowledgement and appreciation of it. Negative emotions from various sources constrain the speaker into speaking in a gentle and sensitive way so that they are not intensified by the ensuing speech act.

### 3.4.3   Mitigating Functions

Linguistic adaptation is a bidirectional process. Not only linguistic choices adapt to the contextual correlates, but the context adapts to the linguistic choices that have been made. In other words, linguistic choices have a great impact on the context as well. If mitigation results from linguistic adaptation to the speaker's communicative needs and the contextual factors in the social and the mental worlds, the question arises as to what effects mitigation produces on such dimensions. These effects are captured by the functions that mitigating performs in specific communication events.

Mitigating functions include interpersonal functions and communicative functions. Interpersonal functions have to do with the change (or lack thereof) in the opinion that the interlocutors hold of each other, or in their attitude toward each other, that is brought about by the use of mitigation. As a rule, the use of·mitigation is beneficial to maintaining the speaker's image, to soothing the hearer's negative emotions and to the establishment of solidarity between the speaker and the hearer.

Communicative functions have to do with the contribution that mitigation makes to the smooth running of the interaction and/or to the effectiveness with which the interaction is carried out. Communicative functions come in three modalities: invitations, floor manipulations and persuasions. Invitations refer to the elicitation of a narration, an elaboration or a comment from the hearer. Mitigation performs such functions by creating an informational gap, an obligation to fill up the gap and an assignment of the obligation to the hearer, who stands in a powerful position in relation to the speaker. Floor manipulations refer to the taking, keeping and yielding of the speaking floor in the negotiation of turns. Mitigation realizes these functions by means of its performative, attention-seizing and judgment-suspending character. Persuasions refer to the achievement of the speaker's chief communicative goal or the enhancement of the main perlocutionary effect of the speech act. Mitigation performs these functions by making what is said easier to accept or more difficult to refute. The mitigating functions are summarized in Figure 3.4.

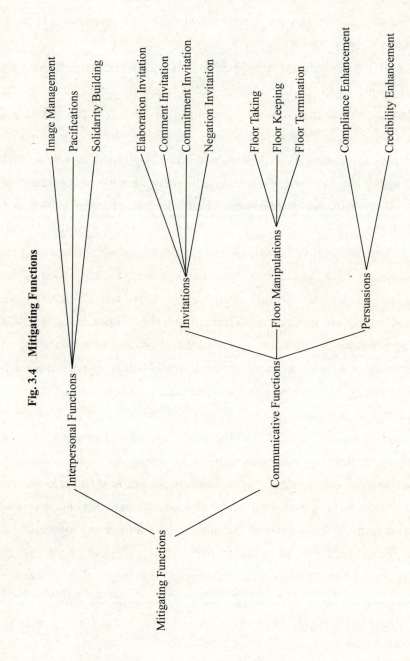

**Fig. 3.4   Mitigating Functions**

### 3.4.4   Adaptation, Empathy and Mitigation

Having chosen the theory of linguistic adaptation proposed by Verschueren (1999) and the theory of empathy advocated by Davis (1996), it is necessary to examine their compatibility and the potential of integrating them into a unified account of mitigation.

The similarities and differences among the notions of adaptation, empathy and mitigation can be explored in the following aspects: object, emotion, attitude, and benefit. Empathy, the experiencing of a vicarious affect through the process of perspective taking, involves an affect (predominantly but not exclusively negative) as its object. Mitigation, on the other hand, is related to a negative effect of the speech act, but the effect is not necessarily affective. Such a requirement is irrelevant to adaptation as one can adapt to something affective or nonaffective, or to a positive affect or a negative affect. It is clear that mitigation is more closely related to empathy than to adaptation. In terms of emotion and attitude, the empathizer is emotionally involved in the empathizee's affect and is attitudinally positive toward the empathizee. Mitigation also denotes an emotional involvement and a positive attitude. Adaptation, however, indicates an emotional detachment and a neutral attitude. In other words, while one has to be emotionally aroused and attitudinally well-disposed to count as engaging in empathy or mitigation, one can adapt to something (a change in the environment, for example) whether one likes it or not. More importantly, in terms of benefit, empathy is other-oriented in that it involves the adoption of someone else's perspective and a convergence to someone else's affect, and leads to prosocial behaviors. Adaptation, either in its biological sense or pragmatic sense, is oriented to enhancing the chance of the individual's own survival. Although no explicit definition is given of adaptation in Verschueren (1999) and no specifications are made as regards its benefit orientation, from his definition of adaptability as "the property of language which enables the human beings to make negotiable linguistic choices from a variable range of possibilities in such a way as to approach points of satisfaction for communicative needs" (Verschueren, 1999: 61), one can infer that linguistic adaptation as envisaged by him is egoistically-oriented. Besides, in the biological sense of the word, adaptation denotes the change of the organism in response to a change in the environment to enhance the chance of survival or gain other evolutionary advantages for the organism. This also points to the egoistic orientation of adaptation. Empathy has been established by Batson's (1991) famous empathy-altruism hypothesis not only as altruistically oriented but also as the mechanism of altruism in human nature. Mitigation is beneficial to both the self and the other, is both egoistic and altruistic, and is egoistic by means of being altruistic. Thus it displays a combination of adaptation and empathy.

The relationship of adaptation, empathy and mitigation is depicted in Figure 3.5 below.

Intensionally, mitigation entails empathy, which in turn entails adaptation. Extensionally, adaptation incorporates empathy, which in turn incorporates mitigation. Therefore, mitigation is necessarily empathic while empathy does not have to be expressed through mitigation, for there are other kinds of empathy, such as nonverbal empathy or reinforcing empathy, in addition to mitigating empathy. Likewise, while empathy is definitely a special type and mode of adaptation, adaptation does not have to take the form of empathy, the other alternative being antipathy (as exemplified in confrontational encounters where the interlocutors want to hurt each other as much as possible). The same entailing relationship holds between mitigation and adaptation.

**Fig. 3.5    The Relationship of Mitigation, Empathy and Adaptation**

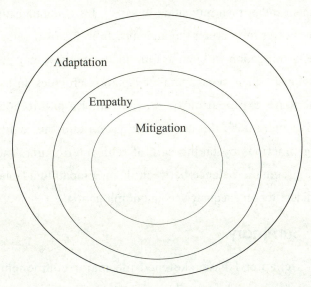

In light of the relationship of mitigation with adaptation, empathy and the compatibility of adaptation with empathy, it makes sense to conceive of mitigation in terms of empathic adaptation, i.e., empathizing with one's interlocutor while adapting to a contextual constraint or to a mitigating strategy. Given the egoistic orientation of adaptation and the altruistic orientation of empathy, empathic adaptation denotes an altruistic egoism, that is, the achievement of egoistic ends by altruistic means. This is consistent with the copresence of egoism and altruism in mitigation and, in fact, describes the very nature of mitigation. Thus, the notion of empathic adaptation is meant to combine the complementary roles of adaptation and empathy in accounting for mitigation. Adaptation is necessary for the explanation of the use of mitigation and the realization of mitigating functions, in the basic sense that without adaptation no communication would be possible at all. However, mere adaptation or nonempathic adaptation would probably lead the speaker to use reinforcement rather than mitigation to satisfy his communicative needs, or lead the hearer to interpret the utterance from his own perspective. If this happens, mitigation will not perform its functions or may not be used at all. Obviously, then, nonempathic adaptation provides an incomplete and inadequate explanation of mitigation. Empathic adaptation, conversely, guarantees the use of mitigation and the realization of mitigating functions by taking care of both interlocutors' needs and securing a pragmatic balance between them. Empathic adaptation is a good candidate for an adequate account of mitigation.

## 3.5　Summary

In this chapter I have sketched the major components of the conceptual framework, namely, mitigating strategies, contextual constraints on mitigation, mitigating functions and empathic adaptation. These components, together with their interrelations, are visually represented in Figure 3.6.

**Fig. 3.6　The Flowchart of Mitigation**

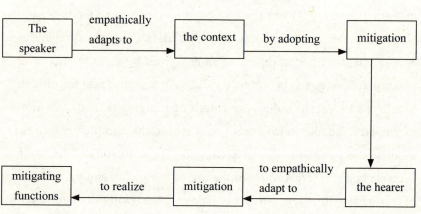

As indicated in the figure, communication invariably takes place in contexts and is thus subject to the constraint of various contextual factors. These exist along the social, the mental, and the physical dimensions and include power, negative emotions, controversies, taboo topics and social values. Thus the speaker, when engaging in communication, must take into consideration the impact of these factors in order to get the communication started and move it forward. Given his wish to satisfy his communicative needs and confronted with such factors, the speaker can opt either to boost or to mitigate his illocutionary force. However, since the speaker must not only adapt to the constraint of the contextual factors but also empathize with the hearer, he is left with only one choice, namely, to use mitigation. Therefore, the speaker's empathic adaptation to contextual constraints is a necessary and sufficient condition for his employment of mitigation. In other words, mitigation serves as the means by which empathic adaptation is achieved. Mitigation comes in different strategies, including propositional mitigation, illocutionary mitigation or perlocutionary mitigation, together with their substrategies. Which strategy is chosen is a function of the contextual factor to adapt to, the social norm related to the factor and the speaker's linguistic idiosyncrasy. The mitigating strategy does not lead an independent life once it is chosen, however. The speaker communicates the metapragmatic message that he expects the hearer to empathically adapt to his mitigating strategy while interpreting the utterance. This reflects the speaker's empathic intention which is explicitly marked by the juxtaposition of the strategy and the performing of the inappropriate illocution. The speaker's expectation is justified on the ground of reciprocity, i.e., the exchange of empathy for empathy, and is motivated by his desire to realize mitigating functions at the interpersonal and the communicative dimensions. In the interpretation process, the hearer has two options, theoretically. He may either take his own perspective and make a conventional interpretation of the mitigated utterance or take the speaker's perspective and thereby make an interpretation that is advantageous to the speaker. Practically, however, the hearer has to empathically adapt to the speaker's mitigating strategy, which means that he can only opt for an altruistic interpretation. Thus, the hearer's empathic adaptation constitutes a necessary and sufficient condition for the realization of the mitigating functions. If and only if the hearer empathizes with the speaker while adapting to the mitigating strategy can he be expected to comply with a request, accept an invitation or believe an utterance, for example. Seen in this light, mitigated communication is an exchange of empathy between the speaker and the hearer.

# Chapter 4
# Mitigating Strategies

## 4.0 Introduction

This chapter will be devoted to a description of the mitigating strategies that can be isolated on the basis of my data. The describing will be done in terms of the semantic features and pragmatic properties of the linguistic items contained in the strategies, and the pragmatic implicatures derivable from them.

This chapter will also explain in what sense such items function as mitigators, i.e., in what sense their semantic features and pragmatic properties constitute a reduction of the speaker's illocutionary force and why their implicatures warrant the inference of the softening of a negative effect. To this end, Sbisà's (2001) notion of rights and obligations, covering the speaker's entitlement and commitment and the hearer's obligations, will be resorted to. Meanwhile, other notions such as imposition, face threat and discursive responsibility, in terms of which mitigation has been accounted for in earlier studies, will be adopted to examine the compatibility of the present account with previous ones.

## 4.1 Propositional Mitigation

Propositional mitigation operates on the proposition of the utterance in which the mitigator occurs, especially the speaker's propositional attitude. In using mitigation of this kind, the speaker reduces his commitment to the truth or validity of the proposition. Used in different speech acts or contexts, it softens unpleasant effects of various kinds. This strategy of mitigation subsumes the substrategies of understaters, evidentials, tag questions, epistemic modals and subjectivizers.

### 4.1.1  Understaters

Understaters are linguistic expressions which underrepresent the state of affairs denoted in the proposition of the utterance in which they occur. The most commonly used undestaters in my data are "一点儿", "有点" and their variants, which are approximately equivalent to *a little*, *a bit*, or *somewhat* in English. When used to modify a state or an action, for example, they make it peripheral to a category that it would otherwise be typical of. As mitigators they render the proposition imprecise and thereby soften the illocutionary force of the speech act in which they are imbedded (Caffi, 1999, 2007). In terms of rights and obligations, understaters reduce the speaker's entitlement (authority that the speaker appeals to in making a statement or a judgment), as well as the hearer's obligation to accept the proposition (Sbisà, 2001). In specific contexts, the understaters weaken various negative effects which a speech act may produce on the hearer.

In my data, they co-occur with such speech acts as disagreeing, accusing and judging. Consider example (1) below:

（1）嘉　宾：我对你这个观点还是*有点*不同的看法。我认为，孩子你
　　　　　别说有百分之二十五的希望，哪怕是百分之一的希望，
　　　　　也要去争取。(《想说爱你不容易》)

In this example, the honored guest is expressing disagreement with her interlocutor, another honored guest invited to the interview. The understater "有点" semantically denotes nontypicality and pragmatically implies partial disagreement and lack of importance or severity of the disagreement. Thus a reduction of the speaker's illocutionary force is created. In terms of rights and obligations, the speaker appeals to little power in making the assertion and the hearer has little obligation to accept what the speaker is going to say or to take it seriously. Thus imposition is also reduced. Concerning the negative effect to be softened by mitigation, the use of the understater reduces the threat to the hearer's positive face posed by the act of disagreeing. Alongside this, there is a mitigation of the threat to the harmonious atmosphere of the conversation and of the likelihood of objections or negative emotions arising in the hearer.

Example (2) below can be analyzed along similar lines.

（2）嘉　宾：我跟斗哥有点不同的看法，因为我自己是感觉到这两年的相声，不止这两年了，五六年了，还是不景气。(《说相声》)

In this example, the honored guest prefaces the expression of his divergent view with the understater "有点", which indicates, by inference, that he is not in total disagreement with his interlocutor and that the disagreement is not important. This not only saves his interlocutor's positive face, as analyzed above, but also mitigates the tension that might be introduced into the interaction. In terms of rights and obligations, the speaker appeals to little authority and commits himself to less responsibility for his utterance's possible negative effects. The hearer, on the other hand, has less obligation to take the disagreement to heart and little right to brew hostility towards the speaker, on account of the use of the understater.

Understaters are also used by the speaker to make accusations less fierce. In example (3) below the audience member is accusing a guest of entertaining commercial motivations such as bidding for publicity in the name of training government employees.

（3）主持人：你觉得有炒作的意思，是吗?

观　众：有一点嫌疑。(《我在南边听好的》)

At the semantic level, the understater makes the proposition imprecise, leading to a vague characterization of the target behavior. This constitutes a reduction of the speaker's illocutionary force. In terms of rights and obligations along the lines of Sbisà (2001), the speaker is appealing to less authority in making the accusation and the hearer has little obligation to accept the speaker's view. Different from the previous cases, this example instantiates a reduction of imposition on the guest, who, as a result of the speaker's mitigation, may feel less guilty than he would otherwise do. The antagonism that might arise in the guest from the accusation is also mitigated. From the speaker's perspective, his discursive responsibility is greatly reduced so that there is less chance that the hearer will show hostility towards him due to the accusation.

（4）主持人：你觉得王先生愧对这个 "男" 字，是吗?

观　众：我认为有这点意思。(《住家男人》)

Again, the audience member is accusing a guest of not assuming a man's social responsibilities. The understater indicates that the guest is not guilty of what he is accused of in an entire sense. This categorical nontypicality and the limited authority indicated by the use of the understater help to create the impression that what is at issue is still an open question. All of this softens the effect of the speech act on the interlocutor, such as the feeling of guilt or displeasure. It also reduces the speaker's discursive responsibility and the hearer's right of entertaining hard feelings against the speaker.

Another possibility is that the understater is used to make a judgment of a general state of affairs. In the following example, the honored guest is offering such a judgment in response to the host's question.

（5）主持人：有外向的吗，射击队，像我这样的天天想到处乱跑的这
　　　　　种？
　　嘉　宾：好像少点。(《勇敢的心》)

What is interesting about example (5) is that the honored guest is appealing to far less authority than she is entitled to. Although she knows for sure that the answer to the host's question is absolutely negative, she downgrades it to a partial negation. In general terms, this leaves her answer inconclusive and open to further negotiation. One special effect of the understater in this particular context is that it makes the host's question sound less unreasonable, which would be the case if the guest's answer were a straightforward *no*. More importantly, the honored guest's mitigation is more congruent with the host's playfulness than nonmitigation, which means that it reduces the potential of disharmony in the interaction.

### 4.1.2   Evidentials

Evidentials are linguistic expressions which provide evidence or source of information for what the speaker says. Instead of bearing on the proposition proper, as is the case with understaters, they bear on the speaker's attitude to the proposition. Therefore, while the proposition may be transparent, the speaker's attitude to its truth is marked by various degrees of uncertainty. In the use of evidentials, the speaker appeals to less than absolute authority in making assertions or other speech acts. On the other hand, the hearer's obligations undergo a change from having to accept the truth of the proposition to having to verify it. As far as the speaker's commitment is concerned, he is not responsible for the truth of the proposition and, by extension, for any possible negative effects that may result.

The first type of evidentials in my data are hearsays such as "听说", "据说", "他们说", which are used in various contexts to produce various mitigating effects. Hearsays are first used to inquire of the interlocutor's life experience, as in example (6):

（6）主持人：我*听说*您最痛苦的时候有过自杀的念头。

客　人：是。(《有话慢慢说》)

The mitigator "听说" attributes the source of the information to some party other than the speaker and the hearer. It indicates that the speaker is not committed to the validity of the proposition, and therefore it is the hearer's obligation to check out on it. In the present case, it is the guest's obligation to confirm or disconfirm what the host has heard, which she does in her response to the host's inquiry. Moreover, in having her secret exposed, the guest may experience feelings of shame or humiliation. However, the mitigating strategy either soothes out such feelings or shifts the responsibility for having stirred up such feelings to some unknown party.

In example (7) the speaker claims to have heard about an impersonal matter:

（7）主持人：我*听说*模仿也有高境界，*据说*在美国办过模仿卓别林的大赛，卓别林自己也去参加了，结果得了个第三。(《"看上去很像"》)

Again, the source of information is attributed to some unknown third party, and correspondingly, the responsibility for the truth of the proposition is explicitly assigned to this unknown party. Put in other words, the speaker is not sure of the truth of what he has heard. In the use of "听说" and "据说", the speaker appeals to less authority than if he made a direct or bare assertion, whereby the illocutionary force of the speech act is greatly weakened. It is the hearer's obligation to ascertain the validity of the information if he wants to put it to further uses, e.g., committing it to long-term memory. On the other hand, should the information turn out to be untrue the speaker would more easily avoid being blamed or other unpleasant effects. This is what Fraser (1980) terms self-serving mitigation.

The second type of evidentials include modals like "应该"and "应该说", which, like hearsays, occur with a high frequency in my data. These constitute mitigation, i.e., a reduction of the illocutionary force of a speech act, in the following senses. At the primary level, they reduce an assertion, a prediction or a judgment to a simple report of obligation. The result of this is a decrease in the assertive force, for the reason that reports are totally objective and there is no room for subjective assertiveness in a report. Moreover, the report of obligation goes hand in hand with the providing of evidence, but such evidence is very often left implicit so that the speaker, in using such evidentials, indicates that he is basing his judgment on incomplete evidence or on general course of events and therefore he is not absolutely certain of the soundness of his judgment. In addition, the fact that the speaker bothers to provide evidence indicates that he does not take it for granted that the state of affairs denoted in the proposition holds. This is a sign of tentativeness. Another way of viewing this is that the speaker is not talking from the perspective of an authority, but as an ordinary conversational partner who needs to provide evidence for whatever he says. The general impression thereby created is one of maximal flexibility, negotiability, tentativeness and inconclusiveness.

Evidentials of this type are used to make judgments, attributions, recollections and corrections or objections. Consider example (8):

（8）主持人：您出去的时候有没有人对相声有误解，认为它不是一门
　　　　　 语言艺术？
　　嘉　宾：*应该是有的*。比如说我们上厕所进门，是客满。那么我
　　　　　 们想去，又出来，一趟一趟的。他就说了："金斗，好
　　　　　 好说一段我就让给你。"（《说相声》）

In this example, the honored guest is making a general judgment in response to the host's question. Theoretically he could have given a simple answer, either negative or affirmative, to the host's question, but that would sound conclusive and arbitrary. As it is, he asserts himself much less arbitrarily, for his use of the evidential suggests the existence of implicit evidence or evidence that is to be spelled out. His account of the insult inflicted on him serves as an explicit piece of evidence to support his judgment. What is interesting from an interactive perspective is that the hearer, as well as the speaker, has a role to play in meaning generation, because the use of the evidential and the providing of explicit evidence indicate that the guest's judgment is open to negotiation and subject to confirmation. Indeed, the hearer is encouraged to engage in an inference of his own and see for himself whether the speaker's judgment is sound or not. As the hearer does not have to accept the speaker's view, imposition is greatly reduced. This is one more sense in which the use of the evidential constitutes a mitigation of the illocutionary force of the speech act.

Evidentials can also be used to make an attribution, as is the case with the following example.

（9）主持人：我觉得你当时还*应该*有些犹豫，就是说，可能一些人是假的，但是有可能有一些人是真的。（《擦亮你的眼睛》）

In example (9) the speaker is attributing a psychological state of hesitation and a thought process to the hearer. As one has no direct access to another's mental activities, one has to rely on inferences from whatever evidence is available. This is implicitly conveyed in the use of the evidential "应该". The evidential indicates that the evidence the speaker has for making the attributions is implicit and probably not solid, and that the speaker is resorting to what he perceives as a general course of events or common sense, which does not necessarily apply to particular situations. Thus a reduction of the speaker's illocutionary force is achieved. The evidential also indicates that, since what is at issue is a hearer-event (i.e., the hearer has more authorities than anyone else on his own mental states), the speaker is not claiming to be right in his guess. Rather, the speaker is subjecting his guess to the hearer's confirmation or disconfirmation. The negative effect softened by the evidential is the speaker's arbitrariness.

Evidentials are often used in making recollections of past events, as illustrated in the following example.

（10）主持人：上学的时候在忙于干什么？
　　　客　人：当时*应该*是忙于睡觉、看小说、打游戏。（《聪明的烦恼》）

In answer to the host's question, the guest makes a count of the things he did as an under-aged student in college, but he prefaces his count with an evidential which refers to the existence of implicit evidence. The evidence, which is related to the guest's vague memories of his long-past college days, is less than solid. In addition, the fact that evidence is provided and the nature of the evidence combine to make the guest less certain of his recollection. This is the first sense of mitigation of this example. Another sense of mitigation derives from the fact that the memory made vague by the evidential corresponds with a reservation about revealing what might be perceived as irresponsible behaviors, i.e., deviations from what was expected of a genius youth who entered university at the age of 14. The speaker entertains an evasive attitude which represents an attempt to shield himself from feeling ashamed of, or being blamed for, what he did. This is self-serving mitigation in Fraser's (1980) sense.

Evidentials used in making corrections or raising objections help to soften the impact of the speech act on the hearer. Consider example (11):

（11）观　众：科学家叔叔，电脑里面的照片，他们在进冰缝的时候，我看见那个冰缝是圆的，而且有的地方是横着的，我觉得*应该*叫冰洞。
主持人：纠正科学家一个说法，那不叫冰缝叫冰洞。人在里面呆长了叫冰棍。(《人在南极》)

The reduction of the illocutionary force in this example can be analyzed in a similar fashion to the previous cases: the speaker is less certain of his view as he is appealing to evidence instead of authority, which he totally lacks anyway. The negative effects to be avoided or diffused include a feeling of antagonism against the audience member. Correcting is an FTA that threatens the hearer's positive face but the evidential, by weakening the force of the correction, minimizes its face-threatening potential. On the other hand, the evidence that the speaker mounts up seems to override the need to have one's face protected and thus disarm the hearer's antagonism or other negative emotions against the speaker. This is a case of self-serving and altruistic mitigations combined in one. Such mitigating effects, by the way, are further enhanced by the host's humorous metapragmatic comment. "人在里面呆长了叫冰棍", which plays down the seriousness, and perhaps the relevance, of the correction.

### 4.1.3  Tag Questions

Tag questions as mitigators have enjoyed wide attention. Lakoff (1975) points out that tag questions, which women use to a greater extent than men, characteristically express unassertiveness and the lack of power. Fraser (1980: 349) also stresses that tags are a softer way of making assertions. Holmes (1984) elaborates on Fraser by adding that same-polarity tags, apart from the contrastive tags dealt with by Fraser, serve as mitigators. She also observes that tags with either a rising intonation or a falling contour can perform a mitigating function. Similarly, Huo (2004: 180) notes that tags semantically imply a tentative judgment on the part of the speaker, whereby he requests a confirmation of his statement by the hearer. It seems that the mitigating potential of tags has been widely recognized, but the senses in which tags reduce the speaker's illocutionary force are yet to be spelled out.

In using a tag, the speaker is subjecting his judgment to the hearer's confirmation or disconfirmation, although he is also requesting confirmation by the hearer, as suggested by Huo (2004). In general terms, this can mean that the speaker is not wholly committed to the validity of the proposition, is not certain of the truth of what he asserts, and by extension, he is not responsible for any possible negative effect derivable from his statement. This is one sense of mitigation. From another perspective, tags introduce negotiability into the talk. The negotiability originates from the juxtaposition of contrastive polarities, which represent different points of view entertained by the speaker and the hearer. Same-polarity tags like "是吧" can be taken as meaning "是不啊"(cf. Ran, 2004) and can be analyzed along similar lines. This is another sense of mitigation. One more sense of mitigation lies in the options given to the hearer either to confirm or disconfirm the speaker's statement, which reduces imposition on him.

Tag questions in my data include same-polarity tags such as "是吗" and "是吧" and contrastive-polarity tags such as "对不对", "好不好" and "是不是". In distributional terms, same-polarity tags occur mostly in inquiries while contrastive-polarity tags occur in representatives like assertions, expositions, and directives like persuasions and requests. Consider example (12):

（12）主持人：那你是有具体的经济压力的时候才开始想到了挣钱，
　　　　　　 是吗?
　　　客　人：会，尤其在大学的时候。(《又见罗大佑》)

In this example, the tag is attached to a representative which attributes a reason to the hearer's engaging in commercial activities at the expense of his artistic pursuits. The truth value of the proposition can not be determined before it is confirmed or disconfirmed by the hearer himself. Thus the speaker's propositional attitude is one of uncertainty. Besides, he is assigning the discursive responsibility to the hearer, who has to confirm or disconfirm the statement. The illocutionary force is reduced as the representative is downgraded to a guess. From the hearer's perspective, he does not have to accept the host's attribution, so the imposition on him has diminished. In terms of the softening of negative effects, the tag prevents the hearer from viewing the speaker as being arbitrary.

（13）主持人: 您刚才说那个付出代价就是他们重归于好, *是吗?*

嘉　宾: 那是。(《想说爱你不容易》)

In example (13) the host is offering a reformulation, or making an interpretation, of what the honored guest has previously said, as marked by "就是" in "就是他们重归于好". Since it is someone else's viewpoint that is being clarified, the host cannot but appeal to little assertive force, which means that he cannot be certain of the soundness of the interpretation until it is confirmed or disconfirmed. On the other hand, since it is up to the hearer to confirm or disconfirm the speaker's interpretation and the hearer can actually reject it, the imposition of the speaker's utterance is greatly reduced. The mitigation in this example consists mainly in the reduction of the force with which the speaker makes his attribution and the softening of imposition thereby implied.

In the following example, the tag is used in a context where the speaker is drawing a conclusion, or making an inference, from what has been said by his interlocutor, as indicated by the marker "那就是说".

（14）主持人: 那就是说随他便, *爱盗就盗, 是吗?* (《盗版怎么反》)

At a general level, the tag constitutes mitigation in the senses described above, namely, the speaker's undercommitment to the truth of the proposition, his lack of absolute authority, the reduction of the imposition of the conclusion on the hearer, and the shifting of his responsibility for the utterance and its possible negative effects. In addition to these, there is a more specific sense of mitigation associated with this example. Note that the conclusion or inference instantiates a case of *reductio ad absurdum*, which implicitly accuses the hearer of neglecting his duties in fighting plagiarism. Accusing is an FTA that threatens the positive face of the accused, as a result of which feelings of guilt or embarrassment might arise. The tag functions not only to seek confirmation or disconfirmation from the hearer but more importantly to offer him an opportunity to deny the accusation and escape the guilt.

### 4.1.4　Epistemic Modals

Epistemic modals, sometimes referred to as downtoners in the mitigation literature, are linguistic devices that denote possibilities. They suggest that the content is dubious or uncertain (Holmes, 1984: 360), or they weaken the speaker's certainty of the truth value of the proposition (Caffi, 199: 893). They are used by the speaker to modulate the impact that his speech act is likely to have on the hearer (Blum-Kulka et al.1989: 284), or to reduce the illocutionary force of the speech act (Huo, 2004: 136).

In possible-world semantic terms, epistemic modals denote states of affairs that hold in some but not all of the possible worlds, or in a possible world that is different from the actual world. A distance is thus created between the possible world in which the proposition is true and the actual world in which it may not be true. This deictic distance corresponds with a cognitive distance, a psychological distance and an emotional distance (Haverkate, 1992). The cognitive distance indicates that the speaker's propositional attitude is less than certain. The psychological distance is related to the fact that the state of affairs bears no psychological reality in the hearer so that the hearer feels it has no immediate impact on him. The emotional distance is a mark of emotional withdrawal, noninvolvement or nonimmediacy (Haverkate, 1992; see also Caffi, 1999, 2007 and Fraser, 1980).

Epistemic modals in my data include "可能" "也许", and "好像", which are distributed in speech acts such as attributing and correcting. I'll examine these possibilities in turn in what follows.

（15）主持人：可能尤其是晚上这个心情不好，看着家家户户不光往回走，还提拉着香肠、火腿，看着人家家家团圆了我还要在这儿站着，情侣双双的，有的人还要违章，可能情绪就来了。(《说说警察》)

In this example, the host is attributing reasons to some policemen's rude behavior in law enforcement. The epistemic modal "可能" functions to denote a state of affairs that holds in a possible world different than the actual world and that bears no direct relevance to the actual world. From the speaker's perspective, he is not sure of the truth of the proposition and is appealing to little authority in making this attribution. From the hearer's perspective, he does not have to accept the attributed reasons and thus the range of imposition is reduced. From the perspective of those policemen concerned, the attribution amounts to an accusation and the modal functions to play down the guilt that the policemen might feel. As a result of this, the speaker is shifting some responsibility away from himself for causing feelings of guilt in the policemen and there is less reason for the policemen to hold a grudge against the speaker.

In the following example, the modal is used in making a correction:

（16）主持人：我们先听听小朋友的。
观　众：我可能不是小朋友，我今年上大学二年级。(《班干部管班干部》)

In this example, the audience member is claiming that she is not a child, as she was called by the host. At the primary level, mitigation derives from the fact that she is speaking far less forcefully than she is entitled to, considering that she certainly knows that she is not a child anymore. The audience member's claim is to correct the host's categorization, which is an FTA that threatens the host's positive face, according to Brown and Levinson's (1978, 1987) model. Thus the epistemic modal "可能" helps the audience member to avoid a direct confrontation with the host and reduces the threat to the host's face. Mitigation in this example, however, goes beyond that. Apparently, there is an element of humor in the host's playful miscategorization of the audience member and the use of the modal is in line with the humor, which would be lost if the audience member provided an unmodified, abrupt or serious correction of the host's misclassification. Seen in this light, the modal further functions to mitigate the threat to the conversational harmony.

In the following example, the modal is used in making a request.

（17）林新生：要是你有诚意的话，你给我送过来，我*可能*也欢迎，要
　　　　　　不过来我也算了。(《行千里路送万元钱》)

Since the modal denotes a state of affairs in a possible world that is different from the actual world where the interaction is situated, the requested action seems too far away to bear psychological reality. This psychological distance lifts up the imposition placed on the hearer by the request, thus reduces the threat to the hearer's negative face. On the other hand, the modal reduces the speaker's expectation of getting his request complied with and the disappointment derivable from the request being turned down. As made explicit in the context, the speaker does not believe that the hearer would really take the trouble to return the lost wallet to him and is testing the hearer's sincerity, so the epistemic modal also denotes the speaker's noninvolvement in the issue.

### 4.1.5   Subjectivizers

Subjectivizers are linguistic expressions explicitly indicating that what is asserted in the utterance is the speaker's subjective and personal opinion based on instinct rather than objective, solid evidence. On the one hand, the speaker is not fully committed to the truth of the proposition. In other words, the speaker is not sure of, or has doubts about, the proposition being true of the depicted state of affairs and, because of that, is assuming a nonassertive force in performing the speech act. On the other hand, they limit the scope of the validity of the proposition to the speaker himself, or put in another way, they indicate that the speaker is only speaking on behalf of himself rather than speaking for others. This leaves what is said open to negotiation, verification, challenge, or even rejection, thereby reducing the imposition of the speech act on the hearer. Additionally, if the speech act inherently produces some negative effects, subjectivizers contribute to minimizing them and to removing some of speaker's responsibility for having brought them about.

Subjectivizers in my data include "我认为","我个人认为" and their variants, and are used for an array of purposes. Consider example (18):

（18）主持人：为什么非法传销可以迷惑那么多人？

嘉　宾：*我个人认为这和人们的心态有很大的关系*……。(《细说传销》)

In answer to the host's question, the honored guest offers an explanation of the magic spell on people of what is called "pyramid selling". Without the subjectivizer the explanation would count as a bare assertion with a great assertive force. As it is, the subjectivizer explicitly indicates that the speaker does not guarantee that there is objective evidence for his assertion, therefore the assertive force of the speech act is greatly reduced. Moreover, the subjectivizer claims that the speaker is only speaking on his own behalf, which could be glossed as 'this is my own way of seeing things, you don't have to agree with me'. It is in this sense that the imposition of the speech act is reduced. At a more advanced level, it is possible that the speaker's explanation be interpreted as 'blaming the victim', and can then be seen as hurting the feelings of those innocent people who fell victim to the magic power of pyramid selling. If so, the subjectivizer functions to soften the blow since it admits that what the speaker has said may well be wrong and signals that the hearer does not have to accept the explanation. Lastly, should there arise a situation where the speaker is accused of being partial or unjust, the subjectivizer offers him an easy escape by playing down the weightiness of the explanation.

In following example, the subjectivizer is used to avoid a direct confrontation.

（19）嘉　宾：你说你爱人当时给你一篇文章，说做父亲的带小孩更聪明，为什么？

客　人：先声明，我没有看那篇文章，我只是接受这样一个观点，*我个人认为*。(《住家男人》)

With regard to a viewpoint expressed earlier by the guest, the honored guest is demanding a more detailed explanation, which the guest refuses to provide. It seems that the subjectivizer, while signaling nonimposition on the hearer, emphasizes noninterference with the speaker. In simpler terms, this means that if the speaker is speaking for himself, he should be left alone. It seems that, as a result of the reshuffling of rights and obligations caused by the subjectivizer, the speaker shoulders less obligation for providing a detailed explanation and the hearer has less right in demanding such an explanation.

## 4.2    Illocutionary Mitigation

Unlike propositional mitigation, illocutionary mitigation operates on the speaker's illocutionary nonendorsement or weak endorsement. When the speaker implicitly or explicitly expresses weak endorsement or nonendorsement to the ensuing illocution, the force of his speech act is reduced, and then mitigation is achieved.

The notion of illocutionary endorsement is borrowed from Caffi (1999, 2007). However, while Caffi refers by it to the speaker's choice of different illocutionary force indicators, I take it to mean the degree of determination or insistence with which the speaker sets out to perform his illocution. Thus, when the speaker is fully determined to perform an illocution, he strongly endorses it; when the speaker shows a sign of hesitation, he only weakly endorses it.

There are two factors that bear on the speaker's illocutionary endorsement, namely, illocutionary appropriateness and illocutionary justifiability. If a speech act is inappropriate in the sense of violating a social rule or norm, the speaker dissociates himself from performing it; if a speech act is inappropriate and thus not performable unless justified in a special way (e.g., by circumstantial needs), the speaker goes to great lengths to justify it. Both of these contribute to a weakening of the speaker's illocutionary endorsement, which leads to illocutionary mitigation.

Illocutionary mitigation includes four substrategies, or groups of linguistic devices that have mitigating potentials. These are disclaimers, deprecators, truth claimers, and hesitators. The following analysis will focus on the three dimensions, namely, the sense of mitigation in terms of weak illocutionary endorsement, the reshuffled rights and obligations of the interlocutors (the speaker and the hearer), the possible negative effects derivable from the illocution and why they end up being minimized. The analysis will be done by exploring the semantics and pragmatics of the mitigating strategies concerned.

### 4.2.1　Disclaimers

Disclaimers are linguistic devices that explicitly disclaim the speaker's illocutionary endorsement, or one of its prerequisites, by stating that the speaker does not entertain a certain intention or is not entitled to performing an illocution. Accordingly, disclaimers fall into three subcategories: intention disclaimers, entitlement disclaimers and knowledge disclaimers.

#### 4.2.1.1　Intention disclaimers

Intention disclaimers encode the strongest manifestations of illocutionary nonendorsement because they explicitly indicate that the speaker would not want to perform an illocution, regardless of whether he is actually or allegedly engaged in it. In my data, intention disclaimers include "不是说", "不想说" and their variants. Consider example (20) below:

（20）主持人：还有一个问题我也不想问，我觉得挺无聊的这个问题，但是我的同事非要我问。就是说当你看到孔令辉他们拿到世界冠军胸前挂上金牌的时候，他想知道你作为一个陪练心里是什么想法。(《勇敢的心》)

In example (20), the question which the host is posing to the guest is an embarrassing one, which is inappropriate from a social perspective because it is insensitive of the guest's pride. Therefore the host prefaces it with a disclaimer that disclaims his intention to perform the illocution. The intention disclaimer states that the speaker does not want to ask the question, or at least not for himself, thus clearly indicates his nonendorsement to the illocution. The embarrassing question is an FTA which threatens the guest's positive face, and is likely to stir up unhappy feelings in the guest. However, the use of the intention disclaimer reduces such a possibility to a minimum, as the disclaiming of illocutionary endorsement also symbolizes the disclaiming of intentionality of causing such unhappy feelings in the guest. If unhappy feelings actually arise in the guest, the host is held less responsible since he is only asking the question on behalf of others. In terms of rights and obligations, the disclaimer clearly indicates, theoretically at least, that the host has less right for posing such a question, that the guest has less obligation to provide an answer, and that the guest has less right to hold a grudge against the host for posing the question. At a communicative level, the intention disclaimer reduces the interactional disharmony and mitigates the possibility of a communicative breakdown.

The following example is another case of intention disclaiming.

（21）主持人：而且这里女生挺多的，我也*不好意思说*，他们说女生小心眼，争起来更要命。(《我是女生》)

In example (21), the host disclaims his intention of accusing girl students of being mean, which is an FTA threatening their positive face and is likely to produce a negative feeling (humiliation, hatred, etc.) in them. As is the case with example (20), mitigation consists in the direct disclaiming of illocutionary endorsement and a moral dissociation from what is perceived as inappropriate from a socio-cultural perspective.

With regard to the avoidance of unwelcome effects, negative feelings may be less likely to arise as a result of the use of the disclaimer. On the other hand, the host may be held less responsible for any residues of negative feeling, thanks to the lack of intentionality in bringing about such an effect. In terms of rights and obligations, the use of the intention disclaimer indicates that the speaker has no right to perform such an illocution if not for some circumstantial needs and that the hearer has less right to be antagonistic to the speaker.

In the following example, the speaker disclaims a malevolent intention.

（22）嘉　宾：小印，你年轻，我就以一个老大姐的角度来跟你说，说话虽然难听一点，但是我没有啥恶意，都是为了救孩子，为了救你的孩子。现在全社会都在关心你的孩子，社会上都能献出这份爱心，为啥你们夫妻两个就不能做出点牺牲，为了自己的孩子，来救救自己的孩子呢?(《想说爱你不容易》)

At the present stage of the interview, the speaker is taking the hearer to tasks for neglecting his paternal duties, which is an FTA that threatens both the hearer's positive and negative faces, and is likely to cause negative feelings in the hearer. Such negative feelings can be intensified if the hearer suspects the speaker of entertaining a malevolent intention. The disclaimer suppresses such intensifications by proclaiming the lack of such an intention on the part of the speaker. Another interesting feature about this example is that the disclaiming of the malevolent intention is done simultaneously with the clarification of the real, benevolent intention. These combine to justify the illocution and render negative responses to its performance unwarranted. The reduction of illocutionary force and the negotiation of rights and obligations between the interlocutors can be analyzed along similar lines to example (20) and (21).

### 4.2.1.2  Entitlement disclaimers

Entitlement disclaimers are linguistic devices which explicitly suspend the speaker's entitlement to performing the upcoming illocution, thereby weakening his illocutionary endorsement. Aspects of the speaker's entitlement that are often made explicit include preparatory conditions for performing a speech act, the speaker's qualifications for performing a speech act, and his knowledge status. These will be taken up in turn. First consider example (23):

（23）观　众：*如果易先生不嫌弃的话*，我也可以免费地把易先生的成果向我们一些企业界的同志们推荐一下。(《老吴无难事》)

In this example, speaker is making an offer to the hearer. One of the preparatory conditions for making an offer is that the recipient wants the offered thing to happen. The use of the disclaimer indicates that the speaker does not take it for granted that this condition holds, which weakens the speaker's illocutionary endorsement. In other words, the mitigating potential of the disclaimer consists in indicating to the hearer that the speaker is not sure whether his performing of the speech act is relevant or appropriate (Haverkate, 1992: 507). Additionally, the disclaimer reduces the speaker's imposition on the hearer, as the hearer does not have to accept the offer.

（24）主持人：我现在想听听你们两个人是不是对这种培养人才的方式——早发现、早培养的这种方式，基本上是采取了不认同的态度，是吗？*如果我没听错的话*。(《聪明的烦恼》)

In example (24), the speaker is drawing a conclusion from what the hearers have expressed. The disclaimer is an epistemic one embedded in a conditional which allows for the possibility that the speaker may be incorrect (Fraser, 1980). In speech-act-theoretic terms, one of the preparatory conditions for making a statement is that the speaker is right about what is to be stated. The use of the epistemic disclaimer indicates that this condition may not hold and the speech act may be infelicitous. The speaker's illocutionary endorsement is thus affected. On the other hand, the hearer does not have to accept the conclusion or can actually disregard it, which is equivalent to saying that the imposition is lifted. A further sense of mitigation is that the disclaimer gives the hearer a chance to deny the speaker's conclusion if he feels it might put him into an awkward situation.

Entitlement disclaimers may also disclaim the speaker's qualification involved in the performance of a speech act.

（25）嘉　宾：因为你花了那个时间下去所以它还是必须要挣钱的。
　　　主持人：*我不太懂这个事*，我就知道一句话叫一心不能二用，现在你在演唱会上花了这么多精力是不是意味着你写的东西不会比以前好了？（《再见罗大佑》）

In example (25) the host is voicing his disagreement with a point expressed by the honored guest, but he prefaces this with the disclaimer "我不太懂这个事", which disclaims the speaker's qualifications in raising the objection. Semantically, the disclaimer states a situation where the speaker does not comprehend the issue at hand. Pragmatically, the use of the disclaimer indicates that, since the speaker is not qualified in expressing opinions of the ensuing issue, what he is about to say carries little weight or bears nontransparent relevance to what is at the centre of the conversation, so that it demands little attention or effort of processing from the hearer. In terms of rights and obligations, the speaker has only limited right to voice the objection while the hearer has no obligation to take the objection very seriously or has the right to take it lightly. This lightens the imposition on the hearer of the expressed view and partly reduces the illocutionary force of the speech act. Disagreeing is an FTA that inherently threatens the hearer's positive face and may stir up negative emotions such as displeasure or even hatred in the hearer. Such effects, however, are greatly weakened due to the use of the disclaimer.

（26）客　人：这是第一回，完了就开始，派出所也送，谁想死他也去，我这人没什么文化，我要是说不对的地方大伙多多包涵。(《郭大姐救人》)

In example (26), the speaker is giving an account of her life-saving experiences, highlighting the number of suicide attempts that she witnessed and the variety of suicidal motivations. One risk with her account is that she might give the impression of being boastful about the number of lives she has saved. Another is that her crude wording of the account, especially in "谁想死他也去", may be offensive to good, refined tastes. These are perceived as possible negative effects derivable from the speech act, which the speaker struggles to control by means of the disclaimer. The disclaimer, while stating semantically that the speaker did not receive a fair education, pragmatically attributes the possible negative effects to her lack of education, accounts for them as having been unintentionally brought about by something out of her control, and dissociates her from responsibilities for the effects. As far as the hearer is concerned, it makes little sense to take offense at something out of the speaker's control, thus negative emotions can be suppressed. In more specific terms, the speaker's open acknowledgement of her lack of education, together with the implicitly inferred nonintentionality, renders her speech act excusable and the negative effects less likely. The illocutionary force of the speech act is also greatly reduced as a result of the inferable dissociation from what is perceived as morally inappropriate. There is also an element of apology associated with the disclaimer, which contributes to the suppression of negative feelings in the hearers.

### 4.2.1.3　Knowledge disclaimers

Knowledge disclaimers are linguistic devices which explicitly state that the speaker does not possess knowledge concerning one of the aspects of a speech act, and thereby reduces the illocutionary force of the speech act or the speaker's illocutionary endorsement in a particular way. The most salient aspects the speaker disclaims knowledge about include the truth value of a proposition, the appropriateness of a speech act and the scope of applicability of a statement or a judgment, etc. Knowledge disclaimers in my data are mainly represented by "不知道".

The following example can serve as a starter, where the speaker is speaking metaphorically of the essence of marriage.

（27）客　人：其实婚姻我觉得，我理解，*不知道对不对*，婚姻其实还像个房子，就是我们住的房子，就是说……。(《婚姻与法》)

In this example, the disclaimer semantically disclaims the speaker's knowledge about whether her understanding of marriage is sound or not. Pragmatically, it indicates that the speaker is handing over to the hearer the job of judging whether the statement is true of the state of affairs denoted in the proposition. This uncertainty or reservation largely reduces the assertive force of the speech act, as well as its range of imposition. In terms of rights and obligations, the speaker is speaking tentatively rather than authoritatively and the hearer does not have to accept the statement as true. Moreover, as a result of disclaiming, there is an increase in the hearer's obligation to engage in the meaning negotiation process and a corresponding decrease in the speaker's discursive responsibility. In case the hearer disagrees with the speaker's formulation, the disclaimer contributes to weakening the clash between the speaker and the hearer.

In example (28) below, the speaker is accusing mimic show performers of distorting his image.

（28）客　人：*我不知道别人，我感受到所有模仿我的人都是歪曲我的形象。*（《看上去很像》）

Literally, the disclaimer means '*I don't know about others, but…*', disclaiming knowledge about other people's situations. Pragmatically it limits the applicability of the speaker's assertion to his own situation. The speaker, by acting as his own 'spokesman', is expressing doubt about whether his assertion is extendable to other situations. The illocutionary force of the speech act is thus reduced in the sense that a general accusation is reduced to a local accusation, which may prove to be an exception to a general rule. In terms of rights and obligations, the speaker is appealing only to his personal experience as the point of reference for his assertion, and the hearer has the choice of whether to accept or to reject his point of view. As far as the avoidance of negative effects is concerned, there are several aspects to be explored. From the speaker's perspective, the disclaimer reduces the degree to which he exposes himself to others' counteraccusations. As for other mimic show performers, they are not directly accused and are spared the corresponding guilt. To a third, disinterested party, the disclaimer makes the depicted situation look less serious and worrisome.

（29）嘉　　宾：我倒想问一个问题，*不知道合适不合适？*

　　　客　　人：您问。

　　　嘉　　宾：就是说你们为什么在那儿办一个初中，而不办一个比如说中专，不办一个高中呢？（《村里来了新老师》）

In this extract, the honored guest asks the guest's permission before posing an embarrassing question. Semantically the disclaimer states that the honored guest does not know for sure that the upcoming question is appropriate. Pragmatically, it hands over to the hearer the responsibility of judging the appropriateness of the question and granting the permission. Mitigation, or the weakening of the speaker's illocutionary endorsement, lies in speaker's dissociation from the illocution. Mitigation also consists in the option which the hearer theoretically has to deny permission to the speaker. In other words, the disclaimer serves to reduce the imposition posed by the speaker on the hearer. From another perspective, the negative effects that are likely to arise are various owing to the problematic nature of the speaker's question. It can be misread as doubting the soundness of the hearer's decision and devaluating the educational campaign which the hearer initiated and is actively engaged in. If such misinterpretations occur, the question would be perceived as extremely unfair for the hearer, who has made great material sacrifices in return for the opportunity of setting up a school in this poor and isolated village. Thus the question could throw the hearer into the agony of being depreciated and present the speaker as an unjust person. However, such negative effects are less likely to arise as a result of the caution exercised by the speaker through his use of the disclaimer.

## 4.2.2    Deprecators

Deprecators are linguistic devices that refer to the inappropriateness of the ensuing illocution by giving a negative characterization of what the speaker is about to say. Negative characterizations are given with reference to some implicit social rule or norm. Thus, by showing that the upcoming illocution violates a social rule or norm, deprecators demonstrate why and how an illocution is socially and /or morally inappropriate.

Through the use of a deprecator, the speaker makes it clear that he is fully aware of the antisocial nature of the illocution, and implies that he dissociates from, or is otherwise reserved about, performing the illocution. This contributes to a weakening of the speaker's illocutionary endorsement. In other words, deprecators constitute mitigation in the sense that the degree to which the speaker's illocution is backed up by moral principles is decreased and its moral justifiability is suspended.

In terms of rights and obligations, it is clear that the speaker has no right to perform a morally inappropriate illocution, as shown above. It is also clear that the hearer has no obligation to take seriously what the speaker is about to say. He can choose to ignore it altogether, for instance. This reduction of imposition also contributes to the weakening of the speaker's illocutionary force.

The problematic nature of the illocution undoubtedly brings about an array of negative effects, depending on the type of social norms or rules violated and the context of the interaction. However, such negative effects can be kept to the minimum by the use of deprecators. Heisler et al.(2003: 1629), for example, point out that deprecators (or evaluative metadiscursive comments in their terminology) have the effect of downplaying the shocking nature of the talk presented to the interlocutor and in this way mitigate the tension that is introduced into the interaction by the target utterance. This is because the speaker not only warns the hearer of the unusual nature of the illocution through the use of a deprecator, but also, and more importantly, takes responsibility for performing the inappropriate illocution and apologizes for doing so. This assumption of responsibility and apologizing is the price paid by the speaker in exchange for the avoidance of possible negative effects.

To sum up, deprecators exhibit their mitigating potential because: (i) the speaker explicitly acknowledges that the speech act he is about to perform is inappropriate in some aspect because it violates some values that are generally adhered to, (ii) he would not normally violate the values and thus has reservations about presently performing the act, and (iii) he apologizes for performing this act and takes responsibility for any possible negative effects derivable from it.

Having spelled out the facets of deprecators, we are ready to examine them in specific contexts in details. Deprecators in my data mainly characterize the illocution in terms of unpleasantness, groundlessness, disrespect and bad moral taste related to what the speaker says. First consider example (30):

（30）嘉　　宾：我们天天生活确实挺单调的，就是每天训练，训练完了就是吃饭，完了就是睡觉。除了星期天以外，平时都必须呆在队里。
　　　　主持人：*我这一说就挺难听的，怎么有点像监狱呢？*（《勇敢的心》）

In this example, the host expresses his surprise at the boredom of the honored guest's life by likening it to life in a prison, but there is an insulting ring to the metaphor. The deprecator "我这一说就挺难听的" literally means that what the host is about to say is unpleasant to hear. Pragmatically, however, it indicates the problematic and inappropriate nature of the ensuing illocution. The weakening of the speaker's illocutionary endorsement is a function of the inappropriate illocution and the inferable dissociation from it. The lightening of imposition on the hearer is manifested in the fact that the hearer does not have to take seriously what is morally inappropriate, or even can afford to disregard it. In terms of rights and obligations, the speaker has no right to perform the illocution while the hearer has no obligation to give the illocution its due. The negative effect is that the insulting metaphor may lead to antagonism in the hearer. This effect, however, is downgraded to a considerable extent by the deprecator, which apologizes to the hearer for the inappropriate metaphor.

In the following example, the speaker is narrating the helplessness he experienced while looking for his lost mother.

（31）客　人：现在想起来觉得这一个人就消失了，消失在阳光空气中这种感觉似的，两个多月了仿佛家里就没有这个人，这感觉特别的怪异。人没了，*说句不好听的话*连追悼会都没法开，你见不到人，你什么都不知道。(《送我回家》)

The deprecator "说句不好听的" indicates that the upcoming utterance is inappropriate because it is immoral to assume one's own mother dead without evidence. Such inappropriateness, through a mechanism of tacit dissociation, contributes to the weakening of the speaker's illocutionary endorsement. In other words, the speaker would not have wanted to mention death of his own will. The illocution is likely to cause the negative effect of reflecting unfavorably of the speaker, in the sense that his filial love is seriously called into doubt. However, the speaker's illocutionary dissociation as indicated in the deprecator, in combination with the apology indirectly realized by the deprecator, counterbalances such an effect.

In the following two examples, the deprecation is formulated in terms of groundlessness.

（32）主持人：我这是*瞎猜*，我觉得可能她在聊她丈夫或者聊她孩子的时候，你心里不大痛快。

　　客　人：没有这一说，没有。但是这个事情，缘份嘛，不是你想要就要的，缘份要随缘的。(《不是我不明白》)

In example (32), the speaker is attributing to the hearer some jealousy over other people's happy marriage. This jealousy attribution exposes the delicacy of the hearer's mentality to public scrutiny and is inappropriate in a conventional sense. The inappropriateness also lies in the speaker's saying something he lacks evidence for. The deprecator, literally meaning that the speaker is blindly guessing at the hearer's mental states and the guesses are not well grounded, pragmatically acknowledges the illocutionary inappropriateness and declares the speaker's illocutionary dissociation. All these contribute to a reduction of the illocutionary force of the speech act. Since the speaker's opinion is not well-grounded, the hearer can deny, disregard or dismiss it more easily. Moreover, the possibility of being wrong, as admitted by the deprecator, helps remove the embarrassment that the hearer would otherwise be thrown into.

In the following extract, the speaker is expressing doubt about the soundness of the hearer's judgment, but he prefaces his utterance with a deprecator which literally means that his opinion is not well-grounded.

（33）主持人：那我这*瞎判断*，明明知道那里只有那么一点钱，可以偷了就偷了，骂两句也就算了，为什么还要跟他进行生死搏斗呢？（《该出手时就出手》）

In this example, the deprecator "瞎判断" indicates the speaker's illocutionary nonendorsement through a mechanism of tacit dissociation. It also reduces the imposition on the hearer since what is not well grounded can be taken lightly. In terms of negative effects, the speaker's doubt may throw the hearer into gloom or other negative emotions, which the deprecator functions to avoid by discrediting the speaker's opinion.

In the following two examples, the deprecation is formulated in terms of disrespect. Consider example (34):

（34）主持人：*这就不恭敬了这么说*，比如说他的学历只有小学或者中学，你在意吗？（《不是我不明白》）

The speaker is engaged in a *reductio ad absurdum*, in response to the hearer's earlier remark that she does not care about the level of education when choosing whom to marry. The deprecator indicates that the ensuing illocution is inappropriate in the sense of putting her into an embarrassing situation and that the speaker is dissociating himself from the illocution. In other words, the deprecator symbolizes the speaker's illocutionary nonendorsement, which in turn constitutes a reduction of the illocutionary force of the speech act. In terms of rights and obligations, the speaker has less right to perform an embarrassing illocution and the hearer has no obligation to seriously take what the speaker is about to say. From another perspective, the imposition of something embarrassing on the hearer is reduced since the hearer has the right to disregard what the speaker is about to say. All these contribute to the mitigating potential of the deprecator. As far as the negative perlocutionary sequel is concerned, the embarrassing illocution is likely to cause much displeasure in the hearer. This, however, diminishes considerably because the hearer gets compensated by the speaker's apology realized through the use of the deprecator.

（35）客　人：当你的想法没有被大家接受的时候，*我不客气了，你就要绕着走，慢慢攻，古人说攻心为上，你不要攻坟，要攻心。*（《硕士村官》）

In this extract, the speaker is pointing out the mistakes that the hearer made while he was an administrator in a village, which is an FTA that threatens the hearer's positive face. The deprecator, functioning indirectly as an apology, contributes to reducing the face threat. The weakening of the speaker's illocutionary endorsement and the reshuffling of rights and obligations can be analyzed along similar lines to example (34), which, for reasons of space, can not be dwelt on here.

The following two examples instantiate deprecation formulated in the form of a bad conscience.

（36）客　人：*当然我这话没良心啊！小时候我一看见沙子就高兴，在沙子上翻筋斗、打把式，那真是方显英雄本色。*（《走进沙漠》）

In example (36), the speaker is expressing his childhood fascination with sand which, considering the damage that deserts do to the development of economy, is morally inappropriate. This inappropriateness is reflected in the deprecator "没良心", which literally means conscienceless. The deprecator indicates, through a mechanism of tacit dissociation from what is morally inappropriate, a weakening of the speaker's endorsement to the ensuing illocution. To repeat the analysis given above, the use of the deprecator limits the speaker's right to perform the illocution and the hearer's obligation to accept what the speaker is going to say. In terms of negative effects, the illocution is disharmonious with the desert-fighting theme of the interview and thus is likely to invite protests or even attacks on his moral standards. However, this effect can be reduced by the deprecator because the negative evaluation embodied in it partly serves as the speaker's apology to the hearer and partly as the hearer's compensational revenge on the speaker.

In the following example, the speaker admits lying to his mother about surfing the internet in high school.

（37）客　人：我觉得我是把我妈哄得很好，包括高一一年上网，每天上好几个小时的网，这件事她都不知道，*这个说起来有道德问题*，回家编谎话哄她。(《家有顽童》)

The deprecator literally means that telling lies to one's own mother is morally questionable and pragmatically dissociates the speaker from the illocution, leading to a weakening of his illocutionary endorsement. Two negative effects are apparently derivable from the ensuing illocution. One the one hand, what the speaker is about to say will invite protests from the audience, on the other hand, it will cast much doubt on the speaker's moral worth. Both effects, however, are reduced by the use of the deprecator, which serves as an apology for what the speaker says and an assumption of responsibility for what he did.

### 4.2.3　Truth Claimers

Truth claimers are linguistic devices like "说实话", "实话实说" and their variants, which explicitly declare that the speaker is going to tell the truth. Truth claimers occur when the speaker is going to say something unpleasant or otherwise problematic, so they pragmatically indicate the inappropriateness of the upcoming illocution even though the content of the utterance is true. By extension, they indicate the speaker's dissociation from the ensuing illocution. In plain terms, the speaker would not want to say what he is about to say if it were not for the sake of telling the truth, nor in any contexts where truth telling is not urgent or salient. On the other hand, the fact that the speaker goes out of the way to justify his illocution indicates that the initial justifiability of the illocution is limited and that the speaker does not even take this limited justifiability for granted. Mitigation in the case of truth claimers firstly consists in this illocutionary reservation on the part of the speaker.

In terms of rights and obligations, the use of the truth claimers indicates that the speaker's right is limited, in the sense that he is justified in performing the upcoming illocution only in the current situation where truth telling is made salient by some circumstantial needs. In other words, the speaker would not normally perform such an illocution. Likewise, the hearer's obligation is limited to interpreting the illocution in the light of objective, impersonal truth revelation, not in any other manner. Mitigation also consists in this reshuffling of rights and obligations between the speaker and the hearer.

In the area of negative effects, since what the speaker is about to say is problematic, it has the potential of bringing about a cluster of these effects, depending on the contexts of use. However, the use of truth claimers carries the assumption that truth telling overrides everything else, be it face loss, pain or grief. This assumption foregrounds the truth interpretation and makes other interpretations irrelevant, so that any negative effects derivable from the illocution will be counterbalanced by the need for truth revelation. Another way for truth claimers to work out is that the speaker offers his apology to the hearer for being straightforward and possibly subjecting the hearer to the unpleasantness inherent in the truth. This implicates that the speaker would have been more sensitive of the hearer's vulnerabilities if it were not for the sake of truth telling. The dilemma thus depicted as facing the speaker makes the negative effects less likely to occur and, if they did occur, shifts some of the responsibility away from the speaker. Mitigation in the case of truth claimers thus further consists in the downsizing of the negative effects of the illocution on the hearer and the speaker's evasion of responsibility for the effects.

Truth claimers in my data are used in contexts of counteracting disbeliefs, making shameful revelations and performing FTAs. Now consider example (38) where a truth claimer is used in anticipation of the hearer's disbelief.

（38）客　人：在我们那个地方，*说句心里话*，不打麻将就有点奇怪
了。(《麻将声声》)

In this extract, the speaker is relating the popularity of mahjong games where she comes from, saying that it prevails to the extent that nonplayers are marginalized socially. However, what she is saying is so radical that it may not be readily credible, wherein lies the inappropriateness of the ensuing illocution. It can be assumed that one is socially and morally sanctioned against saying something incredible. Besides, the fact that the speaker takes the trouble to justify her illocution indicates that its appropriateness is limited. In both senses, the speaker's illocutionary endorsement is weakened. At a more explicit level, what the speaker is about to say has the potential to elicit disbelief in the hearer and the speaker might be suspected of exaggerating her case. Such negative effects are all directly deleted by the use of the truth claimer, which guarantees the credibility of what the speaker is about to say.

In the following two examples, the truth claimer is used in making shameful revelations.

（39）主持人：连考都没考，越来越神了！我再把沙发搬一搬，你对数学系的功课很有兴趣吗？

客　人：一般。*实话实说*我当时不对什么感兴趣。（《聪明的烦恼》）

In example (39), the speaker is relating his bewilderment at college life by referring to his lack of interest in any of the courses offered. The illocutionary inappropriateness lies in the shame caused by the speaker's not living up to the expectations placed on him as a young student who had been enrolled by a famous university and was expected to devote himself to his studies. The speaker is justified in relating something shameful only because he is telling the truth. It is in this sense that the use of the truth claimer weakens the speaker's illocutionary endorsement and reduces the force of the speech act. The ensuing illocution has the potential to reflect negatively of the speaker, i.e., the speaker would be viewed as shameless but for the use of the truth claimer. This negative effect is made irrelevant and erased by the use of the truth claimer, which urges the hearer to interpret the utterance in the light of truth to the exclusion of everything else.

（40）观　众：我当时，*说实在的*，我真有点动心。

主持人：可能一个是演的人太多，演得又太像。（《细说骗子》）

In example (40) the speaker is relating her experience of falling into a trap set by swindlers, which is normally unpresentable for the shame it would bring to her. The truth claimer indicates that what is upcoming is inappropriate and the speaker is justified in saying it only for the sake of revealing the truth. This partial dissociation from the illocution is what constitutes the weakening of the speaker's illocutionary endorsement. Besides, the mere fact that the speaker takes the trouble to justify his illocution is a symbol of a lesser degree of justifiability, which also contributes to the weakening of the speaker's illocutionary endorsement. In terms of negative effects, the illocution of making a shameful revelation is likely to make the speaker feel humiliated. However, the use of the truth claimer directs the hearer's attention to the truth dimension, thereby zooming out on the shameful aspect of the episode and minimizing the negative effect.

In the following two examples, the truth claimer is used in performing a speech act that threatens the hearer's face.

（41）嘉　宾：我坐在这儿，在这个场合应该实话实说，*说实话*我不同意今天听到的好多声音，对他们两个高学历的人到农村去做村官我不赞成这样的做法。(《硕士村官》)。

In example (41), the speaker is expressing disagreement with the viewpoints of many of those present at the interview. Disagreeing is an act that threatens the hearer's positive face and is inappropriate from a social perspective. The truth claimer indicates the limited justifiability of the illocution in the following ways. First, if an illocution is inappropriate, then one is not justified in performing it. Second, the fact the speaker goes out of the way to provide some justifiability for his illocution is a sign of its initial lack of justifiability. Third, even with the truth claimer, the illocution is justified only to a limited extent. This play on justifiability is clearly manifested in the speaker's appealing to a common agreement to 'tell it as it is' (实话实说), at the opening of his talk. Mitigation thus lies in this weakening of the speaker's illocutionary endorsement. In terms of illocutionary sequels, the FTA has the potential to elicit negative emotions like displeasure or even irritation in different hearers. However, the use of the truth claimer dilutes this potential on the strength of the assumption that truth outweighs everything else and should be given first priority. Besides, the use of the truth claimer symbolizes the speaker's apologizing to the hearer for being straightforward, which helps soften the negative effect. Another way of seeing this is that the truth claimer prompts the hearer to take the speaker's utterance exclusively in light of the truth revealed.

(42) 观　众：听了周先生的经历，我觉得他是金子，但是他不一定是做策划的金子。*现在就是实话实说嘛！*赶快回去改行，干什么都可以。但是做策划，你缺乏知识。(《一场策划一场梦》)

In example (42), the speaker is suggesting that the hearer go in other lines of business than professional devising by pointing out his lack of relevant knowledge. This is a face-to-face devaluation of the hearer and is inappropriate from the moral pinnacle. Note that the speaker limits, as well as justifies, his illocution by the use of the truth claimer. The weakening of the speaker's illocutionary endorsement can be implicitly inferred through dissociation from what is inappropriate, as suggested and illustrated in the previous examples. The illocution has the potential to brew hatred or similar sentiments in the hearer. However, the truth claimer serves to deintensify such a negative effect since truth-telling is impersonal.

### 4.2.4　Hesitators

Hesitators are linguistic devices such as "怎么说呢" which indicate that the speaker seems to be engaged in a word-searching or a thought-gathering process but is actually sizing up the situation, hesitating whether to perform a speech act, figuring out how to formulate an utterance in which to embed the illocution, or weighing the consequences of the illocution. As a gesture of caution, a hesitator reflects the inappropriate nature of what the speaker is about to say and the speaker's awareness of this inappropriateness.

The weakening of the speaker's illocutionary endorsement, in the case of hesitators, derives most interestingly from the speaker's illocutionary hesitation, in combination with an implicit dissociation from what is morally inappropriate. The hesitation displayed by the speaker reveals his uncertainty about the appropriateness and justifiability of the illocution, in addition to his unwillingness to perform the illocution. This constitutes mitigation by reducing the illocutionary force of the speech act.

In terms of rights and obligations, hesitators indicate that the speaker has less right to perform the upcoming illocution and the hearer has an obligation to interpret the utterance in the light of the hesitation displayed by the speaker. On the other hand, hesitators take away part of the obligation from the hearer of having to live with something unpleasant or otherwise inappropriate in a moral sense, thus reducing the imposition placed on the hearer. This is another sense of mitigation in the case of hesitators.

The illocutions prefaced by hesitators are, by their very nature, prone to negative effects, which may cover a wide range owing to the heterogeneity of the contexts in which they are used. Hesitators function to downgrade such negative effects through a deresponsibilizing mechanism which states that, since the speaker is unwilling to perform the illocution but is about to perform it out of some circumstantial needs, he should not be assigned the responsibility for any negative effects that the speech act can give rise to.

Hesitators in my data are used in a number of contexts for a number of purposes, which will be examined in the rest of this section.

（43）主持人：那时候有一种失落感，是吧？

客　人：特别有失落感！那时候怎么说呢，恨不得地上有一条缝，自己钻下去。(《强子》)

In example (43) the guest is relating the pitiful state he was reduced to by his failure in business. On the face of it, the hesitator means that the speaker is searching for the words to formulate an expression of the abyss of sadness and depression he was in. In addition, the hesitator indicates that the speaker is about to reveal something shameful and unpresentable. Furthermore, the hesitator indicates that the speaker is hesitating whether to perform the illocution or not, given the negative nature of the illocution. All of these contribute to a weakening of the speaker's illocutionary endorsement, directly or indirectly. In terms of negative effects, the refreshed memory of the extreme depression may expose the old wound and bring about pangs of pain and a sense of shame and regret in the speaker. The hesitator prepares the speaker by giving him the time to come to terms with the pain, the shame and their emotional impact.

In example (44) below, the speaker is offering his peculiar interpretation of going in for business.

（44）主持人：那时候你就决定要退下来，做策划指挥别人做生意，
　　　　　　　是吗?

　　　　客　人：*怎么说呢*，害自己不成试着害别人看看。(《相约星期
　　　　　　　二》)

The hesitator semantically means that the speaker is searching
for words or gathering his thoughts, but pragmatically it indicates that
the speaker is weighing the consequences of the upcoming illocution
and hesitating about performing it. What is problematic about the
illocution is that the speaker's formulation, although initially intended
to be a humorous interpretation of doing business, may be misread. The
hesitator acknowledges this and signals the speaker's reservation about
his illocutionary endorsement. In terms of negative effects, the speaker's
formulation is likely to lead the hearers to challenge the speaker's moral
worth if it is misread. The use of the hesitator counteracts this effect by
cautioning the hearer against such a misreading.

In example (45) below, the speaker compares his impressions of
country folks and city folks and concludes that the former are more kind-
hearted than the latter.

（45）主持人：好像都是远郊区或者农村。

　　　　客　人：所以给我一个特别大的感受，*怎么说呢*，就是农民比
　　　　　　　城里人善良，这是给我最大的感受，真的。(《送我回
　　　　　　　家》)

What is inappropriate about the speaker's conclusion is twofold:
that it may hurt the pride of the city folks present at the interview
or viewing the program on TV, and that it displays a high degree of
irrationality. The use of the hesitator reflects the speaker's awareness of

this inappropriateness and, through a mechanism of tacit dissociation, indicates the speaker's reservation about performing the illocution. In other words, the hesitator indicates that what the speaker is about to say is, in some respects, unutterable. Mitigation consists partly in this weakening of the speaker's illocutionary endorsement. With regard to the negative effects, the illocution is likely to give rise to resentment in the city folks, and invite protests or even counterattacks from them. However, the unwillingness of the speaker to perform the illocution as reflected in the use of the hesitator shifts part or all of the responsibility away from the speaker so that the hearer has no right to entertain the aforementioned negative emotion toward the speaker.

## 4.3 Perlocutionary Mitigation

Different from propositional mitigation and illocutionary mitigation, perlocutionary mitigation operates on the perlocutionary sequels that the ensuing illocution is likely to produce in the hearer. It works by explicitly referring to these sequels and aiming to soften them through a mechanism of anticipation and disarming.

Perlocutionary sequels are secondary effects of a speech act, which are related to, but different from, the main perlocutionary effect. While the main perlocutionary effect is conventionally associated with a particular speech act, perlocutionary sequels are the "side effects" of that act. In the case of a request, for instance, the main perlocutionary effect is the requestee's compliance with the request, and its perlocutionary sequels may include unwillingness or reluctance that goes with the compliance. In the case of an assertion, the main perlocutionary effect is to create belief in the hearer, and its perlocutionary sequels may include doubt or cynicism.

Perlocutionary sequels can theoretically be positive or negative, but those that fall into the domain of mitigation are inherently negative in the sense that they are detrimental to the well-being of the interlocutors and to the smooth running of the interaction. It is these negative sequels that perlocutionary mitigation aims to minimize by various means.

Perlocutionary mitigation highlights the softening of a negative effect of the speech act, leaving implicit the reduction of its illocutionary force. This latter sense of mitigation can be inferred as follows: since the perlocutionary sequels targeted at are negative, the corresponding illocutions are inappropriate from a social or moral perspective and, by a mechanism of tacit dissociation, the speaker should not be performing these illocutions. The speaker's illocutionary reservation and weak endorsement, then, constitute a reduction of the illocutionary force of the speech act.

According to how the sequels are operated on, perlocutionary mitigation can be classified into simple anticipation, concern showing, penalty taking and direct dissuasion.

### 4.3.1   Simple Anticipation

Simple anticipation is the mitigating strategy whereby the speaker, in explicitly referring to the perlocutionary sequel of an illocution, verbally predicts the hearer's negative response to the performing of the illocution and aims to disarm it. The underlying assumption is that since the speaker has given voice to the negative response, the hearer's mental state can be interpreted as having found expression or representation so that it is unnecessary or insensible for the hearer to entertain the negative response anymore.

Consider example (46) below, where the speaker is narrating how a married couple who were on the verge of divorce decided to make up thanks to a sweet potato.

(46) 客　人：*现在大家想起来可能不算什么*，可是在那个年代，那是64年吧，那块烤白薯，这个女的当时最后吃不下去，就哭了，最后这个案子就撤诉了。(《婚姻与法》)

One of the perlocutionary sequels is that the hearers, having had little experience of the 1960s when goods were extremely scarce, may think little of the potato and fail to appreciate its significance. This can have a bearing on the sensibility of what the speaker is about to say. Fully aware of this possibility, the speaker anticipates the hearers by directly voicing their mental state with "现在大家想起来可能不算什么", and attempts to discourage the hearers from actually entertaining this mental state.

The following is another example of disarming a negative response by simply anticipating it.

(47) 客　人：不过她接手之后，产品供不应求，*说出来也许你们不信*，预付款都交到六月份了。(《厂外来客》)

In example (47), the speaker is relating the big changes that have taken place since the takeover of his factory, stressing the magical increase in the market demand for their products. One of the negative perlocutionary sequels, as perceived by the speaker, is that the hearers may find it hard to believe what the speaker is about to say. This mental state finds expression in the speaker's use of "说出来也许你们不信", which represents the speaker's attempt to disarm the aforesaid mental state by anticipating the hearers. Put in simple terms, since the speaker is highly aware of the hearers' mental state of disbelief and has expressed it, the hearers have less reason to entertain it and definitely no need to express it.

### 4.3.2    Concern Showing

Concern showing is the strategy whereby the speaker, in making explicit reference to the perlocutionay sequel (which is the hearer's negative response to the illocution), shows concern with the hearer's mental and emotional well-beings, and indirectly expresses his lack of intention to disturb the hearer's mental and emotional equilibriums. The underlying assumption is that the speaker's concern, together with the apology implicitly conveyed in it, is compensation enough for the hearer not to entertain the negative response. The reduction of the speaker's illocutionary force is derivable from his illocutionary nonendorsement or dissociation, which is implicitly conveyed by the concern expressed.

（48）主持人：他到底是什么人，我们先弄清楚。

客　人：人民警察。人民警察看了要生气了。(《小巷总理》)

In example (48), the speaker is exposing the unlawful behaviors of a certain policeman. One of the negative perlocutionary sequels of this illocution, as perceived by the speaker, is that the other policemen may get mad at her for damaging their image. Aware of this, the speaker explicitly refers to this possibility with the mitigator "人民警察看了要生气了". This reference indicates the speaker's concern with the feelings of the policemen who happen to be viewing the program as well as her unwillingness to damage their image. It also represents her apology for having unintentionally caused anger in the police. The speaker's concern and apology are compensatory in nature, and they combine to keep the police's anger to a minimum. In plain words, since the speaker has shown concern and offered an apology, the hearer, theoretically at least, cannot bring himself to entertain the mental state of anger. On the other hand, the speaker's illocutionary nonendorsement can be inferred from a tacit dissociation from the inappropriate illocution of subjecting the police to humiliations.

The following is another example of concern showing.

（49）观　众：从各个方面，我总觉得好像不是，*怕周站长不爱听啊*，好像达不到县剧团的水平。(《开拍了》)

In example (49), the speaker is expressing his disapproval with the work that the hearer engages in in his spare time. One of the negative perlocutionary sequels of this is that it may give rise to displeasure in the hearer. The mitigator "怕周站长不爱听啊" explicitly refers to the hearer's displeasure and represents the speaker's attempt to control it. The use of the mitigator indicates that the speaker is concerned with the hearer, not wanting to hurt him or otherwise disturb his emotional equilibrium. It also conveys the speaker's implicit apology for accidentally subjecting the hearer to the negative emotion of anger. All these combine to reduce the possibility of the hearer actually displaying displeasure. On the other hand, the speaker's illocutionary force is weakened because the concern reflects the speaker's illocutionary nonendorsement or dissociation.

### 4.3.3　Penalty Taking

Penalty taking is the strategy whereby the speaker, in making explicit reference to a perlocutionary sequel, views the sequel as a penalty for his performing of the illocution and expresses his readiness to face up to it. The underlying assumption is that the speaker's readiness to take the penalty may discourage the hearer from actually inflicting the penalty.

（50）客　人：*我不怕大家笑话，我是在50岁以后智力处于高潮的时候。*(《老易不易》)

In this example, the speaker is narrating that he was at the peak of his intelligence in his 50s. However, there is an element of insensibility and incredibility to what he says from the conventional point of view. In other words, it violates the hearers' expectations based on conventions: people have generally reached their peak of intelligence before the age of 50. Thus one of the negative sequels of this illocution is that the hearers may ridicule the speaker for what he says. Fully aware of this possibility, the speaker sets out to discourage it with the mitigator "我不怕大家笑话", which literally means that " I don't fear inviting ridicule or sarcasm". The mitigator first indicates the speaker's acknowledgement that the hearers are justified in ridiculing him if they choose to view things from a conventional perspective. It further shows that the speaker is ready to take the blow of ridicule from the hearers, which gives the impression that he is offering to pay a price for what he is about to say and is putting himself at the mercy of the hearers. However, that the speaker is ready to face up to the penalty discourages the hearers from actually inflicting the penalty. Put in another way, since the speaker has anticipated the hearers' mental state, it makes little sense for the hearers to entertain it anymore.

The following is another example of penalty taking.

（51）观　众：谈到权力这个问题，我就说这个警察为什么老百姓反应那么大，　而且老百姓对他感到非常的怕，这个原因我觉得多多少少跟老百姓有关，*我不怕人家砸我家玻璃*，确实跟老百姓有点关系，这是一种老百姓对权力的放纵。(《说说警察》)

In example (51), the speaker is attributing to the civilians part of the responsibility of power abuse by the police. This is irrational as the civilians have little access to power and are often the victims of power abuse. One of the negative sequels of this illocution is that the speaker may be perceived as being unfair for "punishing the victim". Another is that what the speaker is about to say will cause indignation in the civilians and lead them to throw stones at his house windows. The mitigator "我不怕人家砸我家玻璃" explicitly refers to this negative sequel and represents the speaker's attempt to suppress it. Firstly, the mitigator indicates the speaker's acknowledgement of the hearers' justification in feeling indignant at him, which produces some comforting effect on the hearers. Secondly, the mitigator indicates that the speaker is ready to pay a high price and will say what he wants to say regardless of the serious penalty. This is compensation enough to make the hearers (mostly civilians) suspend their indignation and listen up to the speaker.

### 4.3.4 Direct Dissuasion

Direct dissuasion is the strategy whereby the speaker highlights the negative sequel of the speech act and attempts to disarm it by explicitly asking the hearer not to entertain the corresponding response or feeling. The underlying assumption is that since the speaker has made a request, he may have good reasons to justify it and the hearer had better wait up to see the reasons and comply with the requests.

（52）观　众：我觉得那位言畅叔叔吧，反正我觉得我挺看不起他的，真的，*你别不爱听*。我觉得，你看，他个儿也挺高的，我在这儿透过玻璃看过去也挺帅的长得，他不敢出来，我就是这么想。(《有话慢慢说》)

In this example, the speaker is expressing his contempt for the hearer. The most obvious perlocutionary sequel of such an illocution is that it may insult the hearer and hurt his pride. The mitigator "你别不

爱听" explicitly refers to this negative response and serves to disarm it by means of an explicit request. The use of the mitigator indicates to the hearer that, although it is natural for him to entertain a negative response, it is advisable not to do so because the speaker has good reasons to offer. Sure enough, the speaker proceeds to compliment the hearer on his good looks. Thus what looks like contempt turns out to be a well-meant encouragement in disguise. On the strength of the request and the compliment, the hearer will justifiably suppress his displeasure. The speaker's illocutionary nonendorsement is most clearly seen in the lack of genuineness in the contempt.

The following is another example of direct dissuasion.

（53）主持人：吕岛*你别生气*，我瞎猜一下，我猜猜为什么会选中王樱，因为她这个职业很诱惑人，作为电视观众可能很想看一个空中小姐在野外是怎么吃苦、怎么行走的。（《镜头前的生存体验》）

In example (53), the speaker is implicitly referring to the commercial orientation of the survival experiencing mission which the hearer initiated, saying that the airhostess was chosen as one of the participants for the purpose of attracting viewers when the videotape of the mission was played on TV. This may drown the originality of the program in a sea of commercial vulgarity and therefore discredit the hearer's work. The mitigator "你别生气" explicitly refers to the negative response that may arise out of the ensuing illocution and represents the speaker's attempt to disarm it by means of a request. By using the mitigator, the speaker expresses his awareness of the possibility that the hearer will get angry, announces his acknowledgement of the hearer's justification in entertaining such a negative response, indicates his lack of intention of offending the hearer, and urges the hearer not to take offense. Through such efforts, the speaker manages to dissuade the hearer from getting angry. On the other hand, the use of this strategy carries the assumption that the speaker will only perform the illocution on the condition that the hearer will not get angry, wherein lies the speaker's illocutionary nonendorsement.

## 4.4 Summary

In this chapter I have identified three supercategories of mitigating strategies, namely, propositional mitigation, illocutionary mitigation and perlocutionary mitigation, together with their subcategories.

According to the definition offered in chapter 3, mitigation involves the reduction of the illocutionary force of a speech act and the softening of a negative effect of the act. These definitional criteria have been used to qualify linguistic items as mitigators by testing their mitigating potential.

The criteria assume different degrees of explicitness in different mitigating strategies. Thus, in the case of propositional mitigation and illocutionary mitigation, what is made salient is the reduction of the illocutionary force of the speech act, while the softening of the negative effect has to be inferred from the context. In contrast, in the case of perlocutionary mitigation, what is highlighted is the softening of the negative effect of the speech act, while the reduction of its illocutionary force needs to be inferred.

# Chapter 5
# Contextual Constraints on Mitigation

## 5.0  Introduction

Verbal communication does not occur in a vacuum. Rather, it is anchored in contexts of various kinds. Indeed, as Verschueren (1999) proposes, language use is a process of constant making of linguistic choices, which is subject to the constraint of contextual factors along the social, mental and physical dimensions.

In my data, five categories of contextual constraints on mitigation can be isolated, namely, power, negative emotions, controversies, taboo topics and social values. In this chapter, I'll define these factors and describe the constraints they exert on verbal communication. In exploring and testing these factors, I will appeal to the following criteria: linguistic evidence, contextual inferability, cross-contextual consistency of correlation and communicative sense making. If a factor is linguistically made explicit with regard to the use of a certain mitigating strategy, this is taken as evidence that mitigation has resulted from the constraint of this factor. Likewise, if it can be inferred from the context that a factor is relevant to the use of a certain mitigating strategy, it is regarded as a constraint on mitigation. When there is a cross-contextual consistency of correlation between a factor and a certain mitigating strategy, that is, when the presence or absence of this factor is correlated with that of the mitigating strategy, it can be concluded that this factor has been exercising constraint on the use of mitigation. When there are communicative advantages to the use of mitigation with regard to a certain factor but social sanctions for the nonuse of mitigation, it can be assumed on the basis of human rationality that this factor is a contextual constraint on mitigation. Thus the first concern of this chapter is to establish the status of the contextual constraints on mitigation.

The second concern of this chapter is to account for mitigation in terms of the speaker's empathic adaptation to these contextual factors. It will be shown that adaptation to these constraints is a necessary condition for the speaker's employment of mitigation. That is, if the speaker did not care to adapt to a relevant contextual constraint, he would not have bothered to use mitigation as a communicative strategy. However, adaptation alone does not adequately explain the employment of mitigation, since if all the speaker cares about was simply to "approach points of satisfaction for his communicative needs", as proposed by Verschueren (1999), he would have opted for reinforcement. The speaker does not have to use mitigation in order to adapt to contextual constraints to achieve his communicative goal. It can thus be seen that adaptation is not the only motivation behind the use of mitigation. Besides, the semantic incongruence between a reduction of the speaker's illocutionary force and his illocutionary intention, as manifested in mitigated communication, also calls for a different interpretation from adaptation. A good candidate for this different interpretation is empathy. It will be demonstrated that empathy is also a necessary condition for the use of mitigation, i.e., only if the speaker feels empathy for the hearer does he adopt mitigation as a detour to achieve his communicative goal. In fact, it is also a sufficient condition for that. Thus empathic adaptation, combining elements of altruism and egoism, seems to offer a reasonably adequate explanation for the use of mitigation as a general strategy.

## 5.1   Mitigation as Empathic Adaptation to Power

### 5.1.1   Power

It is widely recognized that power plays an important role in defining interpersonal relationships and shaping human interactions. Brown and Levinson (1978, 1987), for example, postulate a positive correlation between the power differential between the interlocutors, the level of indirectness and the amount of facework rendered necessary. More specifically, the more power the hearer possesses over the speaker, the more indirect is the speech act strategy adopted and the more trouble the speaker needs to take to redress the face wants of the hearer. This bears direct relevance to the study of mitigation.

In the present study, power refers to those qualities or influences the possession of which puts one in a dominant position over those who lack them. Depending on its source, it includes experience-based power, expertise-based power and status-based power.

Power bears on verbal communication in the sense of determining turn allocation, the length of the speaking floor, the amount of contribution and the manner of speaking. Specifically, since power assigns a dominant role to the one who has it and a subordinate role to the one who lacks it, it is natural that the former takes more turns, speaks at greater lengths and speaks more assertively than the latter. Such is the 'rule' of speaking that governs human interaction. Any linguistic behavior that violates this rule is considered improper. Language users generally adhere to such rules in order for the communication to run smoothly, i.e., they modify their manner of speaking in accordance with these rules and the expectations thereby created.

The following section will exemplify that mitigation is the result of empathic adaptation to power in the areas of experience, expertise and status.

### 5.1.2  Empathic Adaptation to Power: An Analysis

The first type of power bearing on the use of mitigation is derived from personal experience. Empathic adaptation to experience-based power is typical of hearsays, tag questions and their combinations. Consider example (54) below:

（54）主持人：*我听说*有很长一段时间，这个大眼睛苏明娟，也处在
一个很尴尬的处境里。

嘉　宾：对，这孩子那些日子也跟我一样，烦得要命。(《掌声
响起来》)

In this example, the host uses the hearsay "我听说" due to the honored guest's experience-based power. This conclusion is supported by the following evidences. First, it can be inferred from the context that the honored guest has personally experienced some event relevant to the current topic and this hints at a possible relation of mitigation to this experience. Second, experience puts one in an authoritative position as regards what is experienced so that it would be natural and desirable for those who stand in a submissive position to seek an opinion or confirmation from him. Violation of this pattern of behavior would be deemed overdominant and damage the interaction flow. Thus the host can be viewed as speaking unassertively in order to adhere to this rule. In addition, in all the cases in which "我听说" is used the hearer enjoys a remarkable amount of experience-based power, so it can be assumed that this cross-contextual consistency of relatedness points to a strong correlation between experience-based power and the mitigating strategy of hearsay.

It can thus be established that the speaker uses mitigation because he needs to adapt to the hearer's power, otherwise he could have left his illocutionary force unmodified by making a bare assertion. However, he is not merely adapting to this power, for if that were the case, he would opt for reinforcement rather than mitigation. The reason for that is that adaptation, as interpreted by Verschueren (1999), is oriented to satisfying the speaker's own communicative needs, and reinforcement is the best strategy to bid for credits for what the speaker says in the face of the hearer's power. What the speaker is additionally doing in using mitigation, then, is being empathic with the hearer, in the sense that he is accommodating the hearer's speaking right by assigning him a dominant role. The hearsay semantically underrepresents the speaker's knowledge state because the speaker is certain of what he is seeking a confirmation about. This is meant to be altruistic to the hearer and to serve as a marker of the speaker's empathy for the hearer. Another line of arguing is to say that if he does not acknowledge or respect the hearer's power he would not bother to use the hearsay. It can thus be concluded that the use of the hearsay has resulted from the speaker's empathic adaptation to the hearer's power.

The second type of power bearing on the use of mitigation is expertise-based power, as illustrated in example (55).

（55）主持人：贺先生，*我们不太懂法律*，但是我总觉得，比如两个都是搞法律的人还在为消费者这个具体概念在争议，为什么没有一个单位、一个机构出面把它解释一下，认定一下呢？（《再看王海》）

Briefly, mitigation in this example consists in the speaker's weak endorsement to expressing dissatisfaction with the depicted situation. The disclaimer "我们不太懂法律" is used because of the hearer's expertise-based power and the speaker's lack of it. Linguistic evidence for this is provided by the disclaimer itself, which literally means "we know little about the law", and by the expression "两个都是搞法律的人", whose referents include the hearer. Expertise renders the possessor more authoritative and entitles him to more speaking floor. Conversely, the lack of it makes it necessary to yield the floor and hand over the right of making judgments, expressing viewpoints, etc., to others. This is an implicit rule which language users constantly adhere to. Violation of the rule would be viewed as social incompetence and invite social sanctions. Applied to the current example, this means that it is extremely proper for the speaker to adapt to the hearer's power by mitigating the expression of his dissatisfaction. But for the need to make this adaptation, the speaker would have directly expressed his dissatisfaction instead of prefacing it with a disclaimer.

However, mere adaptation would not necessarily have led the speaker to employ mitigation. Rather, it would more likely have resulted in the adoption of reinforcement, an obvious option at the speaker's disposal, given the speaker's desire to satisfy his communicative needs and the egoistic orientation of adaptation. He would more straightforwardly express his dissatisfaction. The true motivation behind the use of mitigation, therefore, is the speaker's empathy for the hearer. It is due to the need to empathize with the hearer that the speaker uses the disclaimer to show respect for his expertise and assign him a dominant role in the upcoming interaction. Moreover, the disclaimer semantically underrepresents the speaker's true knowledge state, in the sense that although he claims to know little about the law what he is saying (that there should be an agreement on a basic concept such as *consumer*) is commonsensically true. Thus the speaker's use of the disclaimer is more altruistic than egoistic. This can only be explained by assuming that he is being empathic to the hearer.

The third type of power bearing on the use of mitigation is status-based power, as can be seen in example (56):

（56）主持人：王先生我提个*冒昧*的请求，为了使谈话生动有趣，您考贾先生两道题。(《大学里来了个贾老师》)

In example (56), the speaker uses the deprecator "冒昧" to negatively characterize and indirectly apologize for his request, because of the need to adapt to status-based power in one of the honored guests, Mr. Jia. As is contextually made clear, Mr. Jia is a well-established novelist with a nation-wide fame. Thus the use of the deprecator is evidence of mitigational adaptation to status-based power, as it is with reference to Mr. Jia's status that the request is characterized as "冒昧". This relationship is more clearly seen if we consider that it would be verbose or even hypocritical to use the deprecator in cases where the hearer or addressee lacks such status-based power. Generally, the perception of the hearer's power inspires respect in the speaker, which is manifested in the way in which he formulates his utterances. In this example, the request made by the speaker constitutes an offense to the addressee, so it is necessary to signal and apologize for this offense. Failing this, the speaker would be deemed disrespectful and his request would possibly not be complied with. In light of such advantages and sanctions it can be concluded that the use of the deprecator has resulted from linguistic adaptation to status-based power. In other words, if the speaker did not adapt to the honored guest's status, he would not bother to signal his recognition of it.

The speaker is not only adapting to the Mr. Jia's status, but he is empathically doing so. For one thing, the negative characterization is formulated more from Mr. Jia's perspective than the speaker's own so that the use of the deprecator indicates that the speaker is converging to Mr. Jia's view on the request and his response to it. For another, the use of the deprecator keeps Mr. Jia's status intact and ensures his emotional well being. Such perspective taking and affective convergence point to the speaker's empathy for the honored guest. Nonadaptation or nonempathic adaptation would have led the speaker to overlook the challenge to Mr. Jia's status posed by his request or to ignore it even if he has perceived it, on account of the egoistic orientation of adaptation.

## 5.2 Mitigation as Empathic Adaptation to Negative Emotions

### 5.2.1 Negative Emotions

Language users do not engage in verbal communication emotion-free. Rather, they do so with emotions of various kinds, positive or negative. Emotions pervade verbal communication to such an extent as to constitute an indispensable part of it, and communicators are engaged in a constant process of monitoring the emotive distances in themselves or their interlocutors (Caffi, 1999, 2007; Verschueren, 1999). Negative emotions in the present study refer to the feelings that are likely to disturb one's peace of mind, and they include sorrow, grief, frustration, depression, sadness, disgust and hatred, etc. They can originate from refreshed memory of past sorrows or misfortunes, from losing face, or from being maltreated.

Negative emotions play an important role in directing verbal communication by exerting constraints on what can be said and how it should be said. They require the speaker to be more sensitive and gentle when dealing with them. This can be seen as an implicit rule of human interactions in general and verbal communications in particular, which language users adhere to. Failing to do this would be detrimental to the communication or even lead to a communication breakdown. Under the guidance of this rule, language users make linguistic choices and formulate their utterances according to their interlocutors' emotions. Specifically, language users downplay the information that is likely to give rise to a negative emotion, show understanding of an emotion that is already present in their hearer so that it is less likely to intensify. Failing on these measures would not only damage the communication but also harm the interpersonal relationship between the interlocutors.

If this reasoning is right, it can be assumed that mitigation, as a strategy of language use that concerns the reduction of illocutionary force and the softening of unwelcome effects, is a natural result of empathic adaptation to negative emotions.

### 5.2.2  Empathic Adaptation to Negative Emotions: An Analysis

The first category of negative emotions constraining the use of mitigation are those arising out of the memory of past sorrows. Consider example (57):

（57）主持人：李先生，我觉得在这个现场让你回忆1976年唐山地震那时候的情况，*可能有些不人道*，我知道你不大愿意回忆那时候的经历。

客　人：这是事实。

主持人：为什么呢？

客　人：唐山那次大地震以后，唐山的损失是相当惨重的，从我个人来讲，我的亲人牺牲了14位，所以有时候涉及到这方面的事尽量避免，有的时候要是一回忆，几天睡不好觉就是这样。(《心呼吸　新呼吸》)

Mitigation in this example consists in the speaker's illocutionary dissociation which can be inferred from the negative characterization and his unwillingness to subject the hearer to painful memories. The deprecator "可能有些不人道" is used in adaptation of the hearer's strong negative emotion based on past sorrows. The hearer's sorrow is over the loss of 14 of his family members and relatives in the catastrophic earthquake in 1976. A recall of them would subject him to nights of insomnia, as made explicit in the hearer's own explanation. Additional evidence of the negative emotion is the speaker's awareness of the hearer's unwillingness to engage in such a recall. The use of the deprecator is the result of linguistic adaptation to this negative emotion, in the sense that it is only with reference to the pains which the hearer would suffer that the speaker characterizes his request as inhumane. Besides, the use of the deprecator would be unimaginable in the absence of the strong negative emotion. From the social vantage point, failing to take the hearer's negative emotion into account would hurt him and damage the interpersonal relationship and the interaction alike, which is another motivation behind the speaker's adaptation to negative emotions by means of mitigation. It can thus be established that, but for the need to adapt to the hearer' negative emotion, the speaker would not have bothered to refer to the emotion and may have straightforwardly raised his question.

However, adaptation is not the only motivation behind the use of mitigation. Theoretically, mere adaptation would lead the speaker to downplay the hearer's negative emotion in order to score better at the communicative level, e.g., to push for cooperation, given that adaptation is egoistically oriented to satisfying the speaker's own communicative needs. So the speaker is extending his empathy to the hearer in the employment of mitigation. The use of the deprecator represents the speaker's attempt to converge to the hearer's response to the request, to show his understanding of the hearer's negative emotion and maintain the hearer's emotional well being. Besides, the semantic incongruence of the deprecator with the speaker's illocutionary intention, namely that the negative characterization makes it more difficult to perform the speaker's illocution, cannot be resolved unless it is assumed that the speaker is being empathic to the hearer. Moreover, the use of the deprecator is not strictly relevant to the performing of the speaker's illocution because it is verbose in the Gricean sense, which is more easily explained by empathic altruism than by adaptational egoism. It can be seen that empathic adaptation can explain the use of mitigation more adequately than adaptation.

The second category of negative emotions relevant to the use of mitigation are those which arise out of present misfortunes, as illustrated in example (58) below.

（58）主持人：小李我冒昧地问一个问题，你今年多大了？
　　　客　人：我今年25。(《共同面对艾滋病》)

In example (58), the host uses the deprecator "冒昧", which literally means "offensive", to negatively characterize his inquiry of the guest's age. It can be gathered from the context that the guest is an HIV carrier and is on the brink of an abyss of despair. It is also given in the context that, because of the disease, the guest has been subjected to various prejudices in his daily life. All these have cultivated a sensitive pride that is vulnerable to the slightest provocations, so that the host needs to be very cautious to be sure of his steps. Generally, language users take into consideration their interlocutor's misfortunes and the possible consequent emotions in the formulation of their utterances. Failing to do this is a symbol of social incompetence. On the other hand, failing to take account of the interlocutor's emotional states or needs will hurt the interlocutor and damage both the interaction and the interpersonal relationship. These lend support to the assumption of mitigational adaptation to misfortune-based emotions. One distraction of this reasoning is that age belongs to the domain of privacy and thus may have partly contributed to the use of the deprecator. This is not so, however, given the absence of the deprecator in other cases where the speaker asks the age of someone not suffering from AIDS. It can therefore be assumed that the use of the deprecator is the result of linguistic adaptation to negative emotions that arise out of a present misfortune.

However, the use of the deprecator is inconsistent with the speaker's illocutionary intention of inquiring of the guest's age, because the negative characterization makes it morally less justifiable and more difficult to carry out. This seeming irrationality is at odds with the egoistic nature of adaptation. What the speaker is additionally doing in the use of mitigation is being empathic to the hearer. The use of the deprecator is an expression of his understanding of, and identification with, the hearer's psychological vulnerability, as well as the speaker's sympathy for the hearer's sad experiences. The speaker's empathic adaptation to the hearer's negative emotion seems to be the necessary and sufficient condition for the use of the deprecator.

The third category of negative emotions mitigation adapted to are those resulting from feeling maltreated, misunderstood, depreciated or depressed. Take (59) for example:

（59）客人甲：要说最痛苦的时候，凭良心说平常日子不要紧，就这
　　　　　　　春节。朋友也好，同学也好，同事也好别提这事儿，
　　　　　　　一提这事儿，心想"哎呀，差不多是不小了！"
　　　客人乙：我觉得你怎么说得这么压抑呀？就这么回事。
　　　主持人：可能他心里就这样，看来问得的确有毛病，属于民间
　　　　　　　说的，叫"哪壶不开提哪壶"，对不起。
　　　客人甲：没事。(《不是我不明白》)

Prior to the current extract, the host has requested guest one to tell of his bachelorship-related agony, with which guest one, after much protesting and hesitation, complies by giving the narration at the beginning of the present extract. As is suggested in his own story and made explicit in guest two's metapragmatic comment, guest one sinks into a depression at the mention of the issue of marriage. Retrospectively, the host uses the deprecators "问得的确有毛病" and "哪壶不开提哪壶" to negatively characterize his earlier request. The negative characterization, together with the choice of the deprecators, is motivated by the host's adaptation to guest one's emotional state of depression. Linguistic evidence for this assumption is that the host's negative characterization is prompted by guest two's mention of depression. The assumption is also supported by the predicted disappearance of the deprecators in other cases where depression is irrelevant. Above all, it is most strongly supported by the observation that the host's mitigation has won over guest one whose cooperation is demonstrated in his forgiving response "没事" to the host's apology. It is clear that the use of the deprecators has resulted from linguistic adaptation to the guest one's negative emotion of depression.

Moreover, mitigation is the result of the host's empathy for the guest.

The deprecator is repetitive and echoic of an accusation made by guest one of the host's request, as indicated by "的确" in "问得的确有毛病". This means that the host is converging to guest one's perceptual, affective and judgmental perspectives. This convergence is taken one step further by the other deprecator "哪壶不开提哪壶", which is a clarification and justification of the previous accusation. But for the host's adoption and appreciation of guest one's perspective, he would not have used the deprecators. Mere adaptation would lead the host to concentrate on his own communicative needs regardless of the guests' emotional needs, but empathic adaptation certainly leads the host to address both types of needs by means of mitigation.

## 5.3 Mitigation as Empathic Adaptation to Controversies

### 5.3.1 Controversies

Controversy in the present study refers to the divergent, and sometimes diametrically opposed, views on the same issue held by different people engaging in verbal communication. It is realized as disagreements with an opinion expressed, objections to a formulation made, or as disbeliefs in the state of affairs described in the proposition of an utterance. Controversy is conflictive by its very nature in the sense that controversial views interfere with each other in finding their way to dominance or general acceptance.

Controversy figures prominently in human interactions. Firstly, due to the diversity in life backgrounds, cognitive idiosyncrasies and perceptual perspectives of language users, controversy pervades human verbal communication to a considerable extent. This is especially true of institutional interactions such as TV interviews, which focus on hotly debated topics. Secondly, the dissolution of controversies is often part of the goal of verbal communication, and perhaps one of the criteria for defining communicative success.

Controversy exercises great constraints on verbal communication. Generally speaking, the presence of controversy requires interactants to allow for the divergences and make more room for negotiation so that pragmatic monopoly can be avoided and a reasonable level of pragmatic balance secured. In fact, it is the awareness of omnipresent controversies that helps one navigate through the delicacies of human interactions.

Such is an implicit rule in human verbal communication. Adherence to this rule fits the pattern of linguistic behavior and is more likely to result in communication success. Conversely, violation of this rule risks communication breakdowns. Language users generally abide by such laws and correspondingly modify the formulation of their utterances, all the while being aware that there would otherwise arise conflicts or direct confrontations which would destroy the harmony of the interaction. To be more specific, language users typically understate their own cases, signal awareness of potential divergences, and acknowledges the credits of others' viewpoints, so as to reduce the risk of conflict and enhance the chance of communication success. Seen in this light, mitigation is a natural result of the constraining role of controversies in communication.

### 5.3.2 Empathic Adaptation to Controversies: An Analysis

The first type of controversy constraining the use of mitigation is disbelief, as illustrated in example (47), reproduced here as example (60).

（60）客　人：不过她接手之后，产品供不应求，*说出来也许你们不信*，预付款都交到六月份了。(《厂外来客》)

In this extract, the speaker uses the strategy of simple anticipation to preface his narration of the big changes that have taken place in his factory since a private investor took it over. As is made clear by the mitigator "说出来也许你们不信", mitigation is motivated by disbeliefs on the part of the audience in what the speaker is about to say. The disbelief originates from the near-magic quality of the speaker's story, which is not readily credible due to its divergence from the general states of affairs. More importantly, the disbelief constrains the interaction by requiring the speaker to take account of it in formulating his utterances. Unless the speaker takes the disbelief into consideration by signaling his awareness of it, his own viewpoints will be too strong to be accepted by the hearers, and the speaker would be accused of boasting because what he says is self-evidently false from a conventional perspective. However, if the speaker signals his recognition of the disbelief, he will be signaling his acknowledgement of the justifiability of the divergence and making some pragmatic concessions. This reduces the potential of conflicts and enhances the chance of harmony. Such communicative advantages are reason enough to assume that language users' employment of mitigation is reflective of linguistic adaptation to controversies. Moreover, in cases where disbelief is absent or irrelevant, it is hard to imagine the occurrence of such a mitigator as is used in this extract. Thus the cross-contextual consistency of their correlation is further evidence for the causal relationship of controversies with mitigation.

However, there are other ways to adapt to controversies, ways that would be more reasonable if the speaker egoistically concentrated on satisfying his communicative needs at the cost of others' needs, on voicing his own view regardless of others', for example. This alternative strategy is reinforcement. The reason why mitigation is favored over reinforcement in the face of controversies is that the speaker wants to be empathic with the hearer. In a general sense, the use of mitigation is equivalent to making pragmatic concessions to the hearer and represents the speaker's empathic altruism. Specifically, the mitigator "说出来也许你们不信", by predicting the hearer's response to the speaker's narration, symbolizes the speaker's adoption of the hearer's perspective and his respect for the hearer's viewpoint. Moreover, the mitigator is irrelevant to the performing of the speaker's illocution but is used for the sake of showing understanding for the hearer. All these point to the indispensability of empathic adaptation to an adequate account of mitigation.

The second type of controversy which mitigation is adapted to is disagreement, as shown in example (61):

（61）嘉　宾：我和范老师的意见截然相反。我认为沈阳市的规定很客观、很具体。

主持人：法律工作者也允许有不同意见，是吧？

嘉　宾：*个人观点嘛*。(《走自己的路》)

In this extract, the honored guest uses the subjectivizer "个人观点嘛" to mitigate his illocutionary force in adaptation of the controversy on the soundness of some traffic regulations in the city of Shenyang. This controversy requires the speaker to pay due respect to others' opinions while expressing his own, otherwise there would be serious clashes. The speaker, indeed, downgrades his assertion to a personal, subjective opinion, which is prone to inaccuracies and fallacies. The use of the subjectivizer indicates that the speaker does not intend to impose his view on the hearer, thus the hearer can have his own points of view. This greatly reduces the risk of conflicts and enhances the chance of communication success. Such benefits lend support to the assumption that mitigation is interadaptable with controversies such as disagreements. Linguistic evidence for mitigational adaptation to controversy is provided by the adjacency pair in which the host highlights the disagreement and the guest supplies the subjectivizer as an explanation and a justification of the disagreement.

More importantly, the use of the subjectivizer indicates that the speaker respects the hearer's viewpoints and accommodates his speaking right. In a word, it signals that the speaker is extending his empathy to the hearer. In addition, the subjectivizer is redundant in the sense that one generally expresses his own view without declaring it, so it can be assumed that the subjectivizer is allusive to the hearer's view, which the speaker is not to interfere with. This is further evidence for the speaker's empathy for the hearer. The conclusion to draw is that the speaker's empathic adaptation to divergent viewpoints naturally leads him to opt for mitigation in the form of the subjecitvizer.

The third type of controversy which mitigation is interadaptable with to is objection, as exemplified in example (62).

（62）嘉　宾：我一直有这样一个观点，*我也不怕大家可能反对*。从总体上来看在我们现在这样一个社会，处在社会这个发展阶段，从总体上说男性的工作效率要比女性高，个别的不一定。个别的……

主持人：已经有人举手了，咱们让潘老师说完待会儿批判更好批了。(《女人回家》)

In this extract, the speaker uses the mitigating strategy of penalty taking to preface his comment on the work efficiencies of men and women. The speaker's comment, which clearly favors men, will invite objections or even protests from women. The use of the mitigator "我也不怕大家可能反对" is a natural result of linguistic adaptation to controversy, as evidenced by the explicit reference to the perceived objection made in the mitigator itself. Moreover, the mitigator signals the speaker's awareness of the obviously controversial nature of his own comment and symbolizes his recognition of the justifiability of the hearers' objections. This makes it less likely for the hearers to accuse the speaker of having male chauvinist sentiments than would be the case in the absence of the mitigator. Such advantages must have motivated the rational speaker to adapt to the controversy by means of mitigation. In less confrontational situations where there is not as much controversy, the use of such a mitigating strategy is less likely to arise, which adds more weight to the assumption of mitigational adaptation to controversies.

More importantly, the use of the penalty taking strategy indicates the speaker's adoption of the hearer's perspective. That is, the speaker is viewing his own comment in terms of the hearers' response to it and is expressing his understanding of and identification with such a response. Besides, the speaker's willingness to take penalty from the hearer is reflective of his affective convergence to the hearers. Obviously, the speaker is being empathic with the hearers in the use of the strategy beyond adapting to their objections. Mere adaptation to controversies would not lead the speaker to use the strategy of penalty taking, but rather would lead him to feign ignorance of the potential objection. Given the egoistic orientation of adaptation, he would even opt for reinforcement in the face of objections in order to better satisfy his communicative needs. The reason why this has not happened is that the speaker is extending his empathy to the hearer. Finally, the use of the strategy is irrelevant and even detrimental to the performing of his illocution, which also points in the direction of the speaker's empathy for the hearer.

## 5.4  Mitigation as Empathic Adaptation to Taboo Topics

### 5.4.1  Taboo Topics

Taboo topics in the present study refer to those topics which are forbidden by social customs due to their bad, unpleasant or vulgar connotations. They include death, sex, and privacies such as age, income or marital status. Such topics are especially relevant to the *Tell It As It Is* interviews, which attempted to probe into the most sensitive and previously unexplored social and personal problems.

Taboo topics exercise constraints on human interactions in marking the areas that are off limits to the interactants. In verbal communications, language users evade taboos to the greatest extent. This is a rule that regulates linguistic actions: behaviors in agreement with this rule are deemed proper and socially desirable, while those which are not are deemed improper. Violations of this rule invites serious consequences: either the behavior would be despised or the speaker would be socially rejected.

Language users modify their utterances in accordance with such a rule. In cases where it is inevitable to touch upon the taboo topic, they signal the violation of the rule, apologize for it and disclaim intentionality behind it, so that the bad consequences specified above would not materialize. It is evident that language users greatly restricts their illocutionary endorsement in the face of taboo topics in order to avoid being socially cast out. Mitigation is therefore the natural result of empathic adaptation to taboo topics.

### 5.4.2   Empathic Adaptation to Taboo Topics: An Analysis

The first example of taboo that mitigation is interadaptable with is related to the Chinese custom of luck-talking in the Spring Festival season. Consider example (63) below:

（63）主持人：读书呢确实是个见仁见智的事情，可以容纳多种观点。过春节的时候大家都爱说好听的话，*我这句话可能就不太好听*，就是一个不看书的民族是没有希望的。（《读本好书过个年》）

In this example, the host uses the deprecator "我这句话可能就不太好听" to negatively characterize his comment, in adaptation of luck-talk-related taboos. The relevant social custom when the Chinese new year is drawing near is for people to engage in what is referred to as luck-talk: expressing wishes for each other's good health, good fortunes and success, and avoiding saying things or words that are thought to bring bad luck. The speaker's comment, which roughly means that people who don't do reading are hopeless, constitutes a violation of this custom as it is offensive to the merry atmosphere. Evidence for mitigational adaptation to this luck-talk-related taboo abounds. In terms of pragmatic progression, it is immediately after his description of the social custom of luck-talk that the host presents a negative characterization of his comment, so it can be assumed that the two are inherently related: the social custom provides a background against which to evaluate the speaker's comment, i.e., it is with reference to this custom that the comment is characterized in the light suggested by the deprecator. Cross-contextual consistency of correlation is clearly seen when we consider that the comment wouldn't be so deemed if made at some other time. From the perspective of social norm, given the anti-custom quality of the comment, the speaker would be deemed socially incompetent, ill-meant or at least linguistically awkward without the use of mitigation. Such sanctions must motivate the rational language user to adapt to taboo topics by means of mitigation. This further supports the hypothesis that mitigation results from linguistic adaptation to taboos. The deprecator serves a variety of purposes: it signals the violation of the custom, apologizes for the violation, and declares the lack of intentionality or malevolence behind the violation. It seems that the taboo calls for mitigation and mitigation redresses the disharmony caused by the violation of the taboo. This points to a close relationship between the taboo and the use of the deprecator.

However, adaptation to taboo topics is not the only motivation behind the use of mitigation. If the speaker were merely adapting to the taboo, he would more likely attempt to conceal his violation of it, for he would have been led to concentrate exclusively on his communicative goal. Thus the use of the deprecator indicates that the speaker is taking the hearer's perspective by viewing his own comment in identical lines with the hearer's and is converging to the hearer's affective needs by not subjecting him to the uncomfortable feelings associated with the violation of a taboo topic. This perspective taking is even more evident if we consider that the speaker will probably not use the deprecator when saying the same thing to people from another culture where this taboo does not exist. If this reasoning is right, the use of mitigation in this case can only be viewed as arising out of the speaker's empathic adaptation to the taboo.

The second type of taboo mitigation is interadaptable with is related to the cultural image of marriage, as seen in example (64).

（64）客　人：我觉得实际上婚姻呢，有一句话*听着好像挺不好听的*，就说婚姻像鞋一样。这个鞋合不合适只有你自己知道，只有你自己认为合适，这是挺紧要的。（《婚姻与法》）

In this extract, the speaker uses the deprecator "听着好像挺不好听的" to negatively characterize her metaphor, in adaptation of a marriage-related taboo. In the Chinese culture, marriage is taken seriously and regarded as something holy and pure. The speaker's metaphor, likening marriage to a shoe, has bad connotations because it is associative with a "worn-out shoe" (破鞋, an insulting term used to refer to a woman who is allegedly not careful with her sex life). Because of its bad connotations, the metaphor constitutes profanity of marriage and a violation of a taboo. Evidence for mitigational adaptation to the taboo is abundant. Firstly, it is with reference to the taboo that the metaphor is characterized in the light suggested in the deprecator. In the absence of the taboo, the speaker's metaphor would not be considered profane. Secondly, the violation of the taboo represented by the metaphor calls for, and depends on, mitigation to counteract possible consequent sanctions on the speaker. It is clear that mitigation is motivated by linguistic adaptation to the taboo.

However, this is not the whole story. The use of the deprecator is rendered necessary only by the sharing of the taboo between the speaker and the hearer: if the hearer is ignorant of such a taboo, or if the speaker does not care one way or another, it will not be used. Thus the use of the deprecator is an expression of the speaker's agreement with and appreciation of hearer's evaluations of the metaphor. It is also an expression of the speaker's convergence to the hearer's affect and aesthetic tastes and, in a word, an expression of the speaker's empathy for the hearer. Note that mere adaptation might have led the speaker to feign ignorance of the taboo and focus exclusively on his own communicative needs.

The third type of taboo with which mitigation is interadaptable is related to privacy. Consider example (65):

（65）主持人：卢先生，我发现了一个问题，这可能是您的个人隐私，如果我说得不对请您原谅。我发现您戴了一个戒指，其实我们在中国很少看到科学家戴戒指。(《和科学家谈心》)

In this example, the speaker uses the mitigator "这可能是您的个人隐私" to preface his comment on the hearer's wearing a ring. The relevant privacy here is one's marital status, which can not be freely talked about, especially if the relationship is not close between the interlocutors. It falls into a domain that is inaccessible to outsiders. It is a general rule that language users watch their steps so as not to step onto this territory, otherwise they will be viewed as trespassing upon others' privacy and deemed notoriously nosey. Such is the taboo. However, the speaker's mention of the ring may reveal the hearer's marital status, trespass on his privacy and constitute a violation of the taboo. The mitigator gives such a faithful representation of the taboo and its violation that it can be assumed that mitigation is the natural result of the speaker's linguistic adaptation to this privacy-related taboo. In other contexts which don't involve such a taboo, it is hard to imagine the presence of such a mitigator. The mitigator, by implicitly weakening the speaker's illocutionary endorsement, indicates that the speaker entertains no trespassing intention, which also supports the assumption that mitigation results from respect for others' privacy. It is thus clear that the use of mitigation is motivated by linguistic adaptation to privacies.

Mitigation is more importantly motivated by the speaker's empathy for the hearer, however. By marking off an area that is not to be trespassed upon by outsiders, the speaker is being linguistically altruistic to the hearer and taking the hearer's side either affectively or cognitively. Without taking the hearer's perspective, the speaker would not perceive his own question as violating others' privacies or would not verbalize the violation without caring for others' feelings. This reasoning points to the conclusion that the use of mitigation in this case has been motivated by the speaker's empathic adaptation to the hearer's privacy.

## 5.5   Mitigation as Empathic Adaptation to Social Values

### 5.5.1   Social Values

Social values in the present study refer to the moral or aesthetic principles that are commonly upheld in a speech community. They are behavioral standards and spiritual aspirations which members of the community attempt to measure up to.

Social values constrain human verbal communication by prescribing modes of linguistic behavior. As a general rule, those behaviors that are in line with value aspirations are held in high esteem while those that are at odds with the aspirations are despised. Following this rule, language users speak in ways that are consistent with the social values prevailing in their community.

The social values that pertain to my data include modesty, sincerity and restraint. These require the speaker to modify the formulation of their utterances in accordance with them. Modesty, for example, requires the speaker to claim less merit for his knowledge, ability, accomplishments, etc., than he deserves. The speaker will fulfill this requirement because he does not want to, and cannot afford to, sound arrogant. Restraint requires the speaker to exercise emotional control, especially when he has been subjected to unfair treatment or has been done wrong. As will be demonstrated, mitigation is the result of empathic adaptation to these social values.

### 5.5.2  Empathic Adaptation to Social Values: An Analysis

The most important value to which mitigation is adapted is modesty. First consider example (66):

（66）客　人：我承担过两项国家攻关项目，一项是"六五"，一项是"七五"。大概"六五"这个项目这个工艺路线是我提出来的。

主持人：这都是国家很重要的项目。

客　人：*自己不能说自己重要，反正是它整体的一部分吧*。(《老易不易》)

In this example, the speaker uses the disclaimer "自己不能说自己重要" and the understater "反正是它整体的一部分吧" to disclaim merits for the work he did, in accordance with the requirement of modesty. In the Chinese culture, great emphasis is placed on modesty: people expect to see it in others and strive to demonstrate it in their own behaviors. It is one of the basic qualities that is deemed desirable and to be cultivated in the individual. Modesty is highly relevant to the *Tell It As It Is* interviews, for the reason that the interviews will be broadcast and whatever the participants say will be exposed to public scrutiny. Modesty thus motivates the use of mitigation. As stated in the disclaimer, the speaker can not say that he ran important projects even though it was a fact, which is exactly what is prescribed by the principle of modesty. Another motivation behind the use of mitigation is social sanction in the event of a violation of modesty. If the speaker does not use mitigation to disclaim merit for himself when there is a chance to do so, he will present himself as an arrogant person and his moral worth will be cast into doubt. Mitigational adaptation to the value of modesty is further evidenced by the observation that in cases where modesty is not required mitigation of this kind is unnecessary.

However, in the use of mitigation the speaker is not only adapting to the social value of modesty, he is also being empathic with the hearer. The use of the disclaimer is motivated by the need for the speaker to converge to the hearer's value aspirations and to adopt the hearer's perspective of viewing things. Moreover, it is indicative of the speaker's affective convergence to the hearer, which is more explicit if we consider that the disclaimer is less likely to be used in confrontational encounters where the interlocutors do not care about each other's value aspirations. Thus the use of mitigation is motivated by the speaker's empathic adaptation to the hearer's value aspirations.

The following is another example:

（67）嘉　宾：但是话说回来，的确今天我们很多的年轻人有些不足的地方。*我个人觉得*不能够只怪他们，这是我们整个社会的问题，是整个教育体制上的问题。(《和大学校长品茶》)

In example (67), the speaker uses the subjectivizer "我个人觉得" to preface the expression of his view on who should take responsibility for the young students' problems. There are three things in operation in this extract: the speaker's power, the students' reputation and the requirement of modesty. As president of Beijing University and a well-known educator, the speaker could have spoken much more assertively than he does of an issue that clearly falls in his field. Besides, he should have spoken more assertively to defend the students' reputation. As it is, he mitigates the force of his illocution. It seems that, of the three major concerns, the requirement of modesty has won out. Modesty is relevant even though the speaker enjoys expertise-based and status-based powers. It requires the speaker to appeal to less authority than he is entitled to, which is exactly what he is doing in the use of the subjectivizer. This is linguistic evidence for the adaptation of mitigation to modesty. Additional evidence is provided by the observation that in other contexts where modesty is less relevant the use of the subjectivizer is rendered unnecessary. The subjectivizer limits the speaker's statement to a personal view, which implies nonimposition on the hearer. It also reduces the statement to a subjective opinion which may not be well-grounded. By using mitigation, the speaker presents himself as upholding the traditional value of modesty. Because of that, what is said by the speaker is given more credit so that the students' reputation does not suffer for the sake of the speaker's modesty. In other words, mitigation does not weaken his defense of the students' innocence. This double advantage makes it more attractive for the speaker to adapt to modesty by mitigating the force of his utterances. Another piece of evidence in favor of this reasoning is that, of the tokens of the subjectivizer "我个人觉得" found in my data, all except two are distributed with power. That is, 95% of its tokens are used by speakers with either expertise-based or status-based power. This means not only that modesty enhances credibility but also that modesty in powerful figures extremely enhances credibility. Put in other words, an authoritative figure does not have to assert himself in order to be heard and heeded; in fact, he is better heeded if he chooses not to assert himself, possibly for the reason that modesty in a powerful figure is more appreciated. This is further evidence that mitigation is the natural result of linguistic adaptation to the value of modesty.

More importantly, mitigation is motivated by the speaker's empathy for the hearer. The use of the subjectivizer signals the speaker's awareness, tolerance and even appreciation of the different views held by the hearer (or by the other participants in the interview, for that matter) and is in this sense being altruistic to the hearer. It also reflects the honored guest's considerateness for the hearer in the form of playing down his authority. More importantly perhaps, the speaker is converging to the hearer's value aspirations by being modest, too. But for these considerations, the speaker would not have bothered to use mitigation. The true motivation behind mitigation is, then, the speaker's empathic adaptation to social values.

The second value with which mitigation interadapts is sincerity, as exemplified in example (68) and (69) below:

（68）嘉　宾：我坐在这儿，这个场合应该实话实说，*说实话*我不同意今天听到的好多声音，对他们两个高学历的人到农村去做村官我不赞同这样的做法。(《硕士村官》)

（69）观　众：听了周先生的经历，我觉得他是金子，但是他不一定是做策划的金子。*现在就是实话实说嘛！*赶快回去改行，干什么都可以。但是做策划，你缺乏知识。(《一场策划一场梦》)

In both examples, the speaker uses the truth claimer "实话实说" or "说实话" to justify his illocution in adaptation of the requirement of sincerity. Sincerity is one of the qualities highly valued in the Chinese culture. It is especially relevant to the *Tell It As It Is* interviews, the thrust of which is to encourage participants to reveal their innermost secrets, to have no reservations in expressing their views and to hold no grudges against whatever unpleasant things could be said of them. Thus it is highly likely that sincerity is what the speaker is adapting to in using mitigation. Theoretically, the common agreement to "tell it as it is" may lead the interactants to perform FTAs, which typically call for the use of mitigation to redress the disturbed social equilibrium. On the other hand, but for that common agreement to be sincere and frank, the speaker would have held back from expressing disagreement in example (68) and from negatively evaluating the hearer's qualifications in example (69). In neither case, then, would he have used the truth claimer. Seen in this light, mitigation is the result of linguistic adaptation to the requirement of sincerity. Another way of seeing this is that the truth claimer "实话实说" or "说实话" mitigates the unwelcome perlocutionary effect of the speech act and describes the social value of sincerity, so that both mitigation and sincerity are embodied in it. This is further evidence that mitigation is the result of linguistic adaptation to sincerity.

This is only part of the story, nevertheless. The speaker is not only adapting to the value of sincerity but he is empathically doing so, that is, he is being empathic with the hearer. Generally, telling someone the truth is beneficial or advantageous to him, so the speaker's use of the truth claimer conveys his intention to be altruistic to the hearer by offering him the truth. Besides, the use of the truth claimer signals the speaker's and the hearer's common aspiration for the value of sincerity. This is made explicit in example (68) by the speaker's citation of a common agreement or obligation to tell the truth, as marked by "我坐在这儿，这个场合应该实话实说". In example (69), likewise, the speaker is appealing to truth telling as a common obligation (as explicitly marked by "现在就是") or as a justification for the performing of his illocution (as marked by "嘛").

It is in this sense that the speaker is offering his empathy to the hearer. The speaker's empathy for the hearer is more apparent when we consider that he would not use the truth claimer in cases where the hearer does not hold the value aspiration or the speaker does not care one way or another. Note that mere adaptation to the value of sincerity does not necessarily lead the speaker to use the truth claimer, for he does not have to declare telling the truth in order to do so.

## 5.6  Summary

In this chapter I have addressed the question of what contextual factors constrain the use of mitigation and have discovered five categories of these: power, negative emotions, controversies, taboo topics and social values. The criteria used to qualify these as contextual constraints on mitigation include linguistic evidence, contextual inferability, cross-contextual consistency of correlation and communicative sense making. Linguistic evidence abounds in most cases of mitigation. Contextual inferability and cross-contextual correlation are also obvious through observation and introspection. Most important of all, emphasis has been laid on the social sanctions connected with nonmitigation and the communicative advantages derivable from mitigation, which can be taken as less direct but weightier evidence for mitigational adaptation to these contextual factors.

Having established the adaptational relationship of mitigation to these factors, I pointed out the inadequacy of an adaptational account of mitigation. Specifically, it was demonstrated that, if the speaker merely adapted to the contextual constraint, he would have opted for reinforcement rather than mitigation in order to satisfy his communicative needs, given the egoistic orientation of adaptation. Besides, semantic incongruence between the meaning of the mitigator and the speaker's illocutionary intention, which clearly favors the hearer over the speaker, is resistant to an egoistic adaptational account. It was then suggested that, in using mitigation, the speaker is extending his empathy to the hearer by taking his perspective, converging to his affect or being altruistic to him. The notion of empathic adaptation seems to provide an adequate explanation for the use of mitigation.

The potential constraints on mitigation are far from having been exhausted, however. It is especially important to mention that I have left physical factors out of the exposition given above. Physical factors such as the video camera present at the interview, the venue of the interview and other factors can have a profound influence on the linguistic behavior in general and on the use of mitigating strategies in particular. Unfortunately, due to the limited access to the videotapes of the interviews, I could not observe the physical factors involved. Moreover, the relationship between mitigation and such physical factors is resistant to inference and so is more suitable to be studied with well-controlled experimental investigations. Besides, it is hard to linguistically track down such a relationship. Therefore, I have omitted an analysis of physical factors with much regret.

Anyway, the isolation of these constraints offers a partial explanation of the pragmatic phenomenon of mitigation. It directly addresses the relationship of language with the social and the mental worlds and reveals the extralinguistic factors that motivate the use of mitigation. However, this is only part of the picture. What effects are derivable from the interplay of mitigation with the constraining factors, i.e., what functions mitigation can perform in real-life interactions, has not been dealt with. This is the concern of the next chapter.

# Chapter 6
# Mitigating Functions

## 6.0 Introduction

This chapter explores the functions which mitigating strategies perform in specific communicative situations. Mitigating functions refer to what the speaker intends to do, and succeeds in doing, to the interpersonal relationship among the interlocutors or to the global organization of the communicative event. They are related to the contributions made by mitigation to the global dynamics of the communicative event. They result partly from the interplay between mitigating strategies and the contextual constraints that have motivated the use of these strategies.

Mitigating functions are different from the main perlocutionary effects of the speech acts in which mitigation occurs. While the main perlocutionary effects are conventional to a greater or lesser extent, mitigating functions are idiosyncratically designed by the speaker in a specific context. They are also divergent from perlocutionary sequels (which are very often unexpected) because they are the result of the speaker's pragmatic manipulations.

In identifying and describing mitigating functions, I'll fall back on three criteria: linguistic evidence, local coherence and pragmatic progression. If a hypothesized function is supported by linguistic evidence, it is partly qualified as a function of mitigation. Similarly, if it is consistent with the particular concerns of the speaker at the particular stage of the interview at which mitigation occurs, i.e., locally coherent, it is partly qualified as a function of mitigation. If it is beneficial to ensuring smooth pragmatic progression, i.e., moving effortlessly from one stage of the interaction to the next, it is partly qualified as a function of mitigation. This hypothesis making and confirmation is justified to the extent to which it enhances the validity of the exposition. Thus the first concern of this chapter is to establish the status of mitigating functions on the basis of my data in accordance with the criteria specified above.

The second concern of this chapter is to investigate how the speaker intends his mitigated utterance to be interpreted by the hearer. It will be hypothesized that through the use of mitigation the speaker metapragmatically conveys his empathic intention to the hearer, which he expects the hearer to recognize and accommodate in order to arrive at the desired interpretation of the utterance. The empathic intention is for the speaker to offer his empathy to the hearer in exchange for the hearer's empathy. As repeatedly demonstrated in the previous chapter, the speaker's use of the mitigating strategy marks his empathy for the hearer. On the other hand, the fact that the speaker goes on record performing his inappropriate illocution despite his wish to empathize with the hearer represents his attempt to get the hearer to empathize with him, on the basis of reciprocity. Thus the empathic intention is characterized by its reciprocity, i.e., the speaker metapragmatically constrains the hearer into taking his perspective and making an altruistic interpretation of his utterance.

The third concern of this chapter is to offer an account of how mitigation performs its functions. As the use of mitigation was accounted for in terms of the speaker's empathic adaptation to the contextual constraints on mitigation, so the realization of the mitigating functions will be explained in terms of the hearer's empathic adaptation to the speaker's mitigating strategy. Empathic adaptation means that the hearer empathizes with the speaker while adapting to his mitigating strategy to satisfy his (the hearer's) own communicative needs. It will be argued that the hearer's adaptation is a necessary condition, but not a sufficient one, for the realization of the mitigating functions, because nonadaptation to the strategy leads to nonrecognition of the speaker's empathic intention and mere adaptation does not guarantee the accommodation of the speaker's empathic intention. Empathy then is also a necessary condition for the realization of the mitigating functions in the sense that failing to take the speaker's perspective will lead the hearer to interpret the utterance in a way divergent from the one intended by the speaker. When confronted with the speaker's use of mitigation, the hearer has two options at his disposal, either to interpret the utterance from his own perspective or to do it from the speaker's perspective. Only the second choice contributes to the realization of the mitigating functions. In order for this to happen, the hearer must empathize with speaker. In other words, if mitigation performs any function at all it is because the hearer empathically interprets the speaker' mitigated utterance. Seen in this light, empathic adaptation is possibly the necessary and sufficient condition for the realization of the mitigating functions and offers an adequate account of the working mechanism of mitigation.

## 6.1  Interpersonal Functions

Verbal communication is a process that typically involves a speaker and a hearer. The relationship between them largely bears on the direction and the success of the communication. For this reason, interpersonal relationships are often given full considerations.

Interpersonal relationships are not established once and for all. In fact, they are subject to constant fine tuning and variations across contexts, so that they are redefined in each and every extract of verbal communication (Haley, 1959, quoted in Caffi, 1999: 902).

Interpersonal functions of mitigation refer to the effects that mitigation produces on the relationship between the speaker and the hearer. They are related to the changes (or the lack thereof) that are incurred by mitigation in the attitude the interlocutors hold towards each other or in the opinions they maintain of each other. Holmes (1984) observes that mitigation (attenuation in her terminology) expresses the speaker's attitude towards the hearer such that the mitigation of something negative expresses the speaker's positive attitude towards the hearer. Sbisà(2001) states that mitigation is consistent with variations in the 'core illocutionary effects' of a speech act, which concern the intersubjectively executed reshuffling of rights and obligations. Thus as a result of mitigation, the speaker stands in a different relationship with the hearer, the difference having been caused by the variation in the value of a parameter that pertains to the relationship. Caffi (1999, 2007) also holds that mitigation modifies interpersonal relationships between the interlocutors by decreasing or increasing the relational distance, and results in estrangement or solidarity between the interlocutors. Departing from and elaborating on these findings, I propose three interpersonal functions of mitigation on the basis of my data, namely image management, pacifications and solidarity building, which will be individually dealt with in the following subsections.

### 6.1.1　Image Management

Image in the present study refers to the positive light in which the individual views himself and wishes to be viewed by others. It consists of an individual's knowledge, cultural refinement, social common sense, moral standards, aesthetic tastes and value aspirations, amongst other things. It is a sign of the individual's social identity.

The individual's image is reflected in his behaviors, especially his linguistic behaviors. When people produce utterances in conversation, they do much more than impart information relating to the propositional content of their talk or the propositional inferences that can be drawn from what is explicitly uttered, they also say important things about themselves as communicating members of the social-cultural community to which they and their interlocutors belong (Overstreet and Yule, 2001; Heisler et al., 2003). Thus the discourse produced in verbal interactions is an important means by which language users present and represent themselves to those with whom they interact conversationally. Besides, shared assumptions of sense making lead to an exquisite sensitivity to the self-referential nature of talk. We are always aware that what we say tells as much about ourselves as about the external world. It is for this reason that conversational talk provides metaphorical information about the self and offers to others signs of who we are (Heisler et al, 2003: 1618).

An individual's image is not his private property. Rather, it is subject to the approval and confirmation of the speech community. Moreover, one's image is not constructed once for all, it is subject to assessments and reassessments in verbal communications. When an individual's actions (particularly verbal actions) do not seem characteristic of the type of person we assume he or she is, they may be treated as problematic actions, and we may reevaluate that individual's identity or retypify him. When what the speaker says violates a certain social norm and the expectations thereupon based either in content or in manner, he runs the risk of having his moral worth negatively judged (Heisler et al., 2003).

Being aware of such risks, language users often engage in the management of their image. When what they say violates a social norm and its corresponding expectations, language users may clarify their intentions, disclaim ill intentions, refute accusations, or express reservations about getting on record, hoping thereby to minimize the possibility of being negatively evaluated or retypified. From another perspective, as a result of such efforts of image management, the hearer would not give the speaker a negative evaluation that he would otherwise certainly have given. Thus the speaker's image is protected. It is evident that mitigation functions to maintain the good image of the speaker by counteracting the factors that are potentially detrimental to it. Consider example (70) as a starter:

（70）客　人：刚才那个老师说我比较小心眼，其实不然，*我不是说小心眼*，为什么那个时候我跟他们共同演了一个节目，正因为我那时候感觉到很新鲜，既然能给观众带去笑声我感觉非常新鲜。(《看上去很像》)

In this example, the speaker mentions an accusation previously leveled at him, denies it and continues to provide evidence to support his denial. The accusation was that the speaker is so narrow-minded and ungenerous as to be sore at those who mimic his performances. This can greatly damage his image. Fully aware of this, the speaker directly denies the accusation with the disclaimer "我不是说小心眼", which counteracts the potential of image damage by removing the ground for a negative evaluation on him. The speaker supplements his denial of the accusation with evidence of his tolerance with those in mimic shows. This makes his denial even weightier, and renders the accusation still more groundless.

As a result of this management effort, the speaker's image is protected. It is clear that the realization of the function of image management is dependent on the hearer's adaptation to the speaker's mitigating strategy in interpreting the utterance.

There is a lot to be tackled concerning how this function is realized. To repeat the analysis given to the examples in the previous chapter, the use of mitigation in the form of any strategy involves the speaker's empathy for the hearer. Thus the use of the disclaimer"我不是说小心眼"indicates that the speaker is adopting the hearer's perspective and converging to what he advocates: tolerance for those in the mimic show business. This explains why he supplies evidence for his appreciation of the entertaining value of mimic shows. From another point of view, the fact that he goes on record performing his illocution despite wanting to be empathic with the hearer indicates that he also wants to demonstrate his perspective (which is different from the hearer's) and expects the hearer to be empathic with him by stepping into his shoe. So far the speaker has communicated his empathic intention through the use of mitigation. The realization of the functions of image management is crucially dependent on the hearer's recognition and accommodation of this intention. More specifically, it depends on the hearer's refraining from interpreting the utterance from his own perspective and opting to do it from the speaker's perspective. This is rendered possible by the joint role of adaptation and empathy. Adaptation is necessary for the hearer's recognition of the speaker's empathic intention but is not sufficient for his accommodation of it, thus adaptation alone cannot guarantee the realization of the function of image management. If the hearer merely adapts to the disclaimer, he may stick with his own perspective and insist on a negative evaluation of the speaker although the speaker has tried to deny the accusation.

But if he empathizes with the speaker by taking his perspective, he will understand that the speaker was once tolerant of mimic show performers but has since then been unfairly taken advantage of by them. It is only on the basis of this understanding that the hearer is wholeheartedly willing to take back his accusation and the speaker's image is protected. It is only when the hearer empathically adapts to the speaker's use of the disclaimer can the function of image management be realized.

The following is another example of image management:

（71）主持人：我现在有个顾虑，我们这么讲不会有很大的副作用吧，别成了一堂非法电视传销课了。那么在这个听课的过程中，他就对非法传销有了一定的理解而且知道有可能能挣钱，那么就有可能要加入是吧。(《细说传销》)

In example (71), the speaker expresses his concern about the possible bad consequence of the interview before he proceeds with it. The interview was intended to expose the tricks involved in the pyramid selling which swept across China in the late 1990s. However, if not watched closely it could go off course and end up popularizing those tricks or arousing suspicions of the sort. If this happens, the image of the program will be seriously damaged. It will be accused of neglecting social responsibility and thus be negatively evaluated. The mitigator "我现在有个顾虑" explicitly states that the speaker is worried, while "我们这么讲不会有很大的副作用吧" refers to the possibility of the interview producing certain bad effects and "别成了一堂非法电视传销课了" specifies the bad effect that the speaker especially means to avoid. All these indicate the speaker's illocutionary dissociation and his readiness to cancel this part of the interview if it is necessary to do so. It is expected that these factors contribute to disallowing a negative evaluation to be made on the speaker and to the construction of his positive image of being conscientious and socially responsible. It is clear that the function of image management is realized because the hearer has adapted to the mitigating strategy.

In the use of the mitigators, the speaker is suspending his won perspective as host to the interview and taking the perspective of the general public or social critics by viewing the program in terms of its social consequences. The speaker's expression of concern is indicative of his affective convergence to the public's concern over the harm of pyramid selling, in the sense that it is voiced in anticipation of the public concern. In a word, the use of mitigation marks the speaker's empathy for the hearer. On the other hand, the fact the speaker goes on with the interview indicates that he attempts to get the hearer to take his perspective and understand that the interview program is worth running despite the risks involved in it. That is, the speaker intends to win the hearer's empathy in return for his empathy on the basis of fair exchange. Such is the speaker's empathic intention metapragmatically communicated to the hearer for him to recognize and accommodate in the interpretation process in order to realize the mitigating function of image management. The hearer's adaptation to the speaker's use of mitigation is necessary for the recognition of the speaker's empathic intention, and thereby contributes to protecting the image of the program. However, it does not ensure the hearer's accommodation of the speaker's empathic intention and is not a sufficient condition for the management of the image of the program. It is only through the hearer's empathy for the speaker that this function can be realized. In other words, it is only when the hearer is ready to take the speaker's perspective that he understands the speaker's dilemma of striking a balance between exploring something to the fullest and overdoing it or views the risky program in terms of its educational value. When the hearer is ready to empathize with the speaker he will interpret the mitigated illocution in the light proposed by the speaker. Thus the hearer's empathic adaptation to the speaker's mitigating strategy determines the realization of the mitigating function of image management.

### 6.1.2 Pacifications

As noted in section 5.2.1, language users do not engage in verbal communication emotion-free. Similarly, they do not leave it emotion-neutral. In fact, they cultivate and modify their emotions as it proceeds. One of the criteria of the success of human communication is whether the participants are emotionally positive when it closes. Thus language users spend a great deal of effort monitoring the emotional changes either in themselves or in their interlocutors, so as to ensure to a maximal extent that their interlocutors are emotionally undisturbed.

Some speech acts are likely to give rise to negative emotions or intensify those that already exist in the hearer. For example, if the hearer witnessed or experienced some misfortunes, talking about such misfortunes may cause sorrow, bitterness or antagonism in him (Fraser, 1980). Negative emotions are also likely to arise from the unusual nature of the talk (Heisler et al., 2003) or the problematic action that the speaker is about to perform (Overstreet and Yule, 2001). Negative emotions may even arise from privacy being trespassed, or from being accused, criticized, maltreated or depressed. Indeed, negative emotions pervade verbal communication to such an extent as to constitute an indispensable part of it. Therefore language users engage in a constant process of monitoring the emotive distances between themselves and their interlocutors (Caffi, 1999, 2007; Verschueren, 1999).

Negative emotions are inherently related to mitigation in the sense that they are a natural target of mitigation. In other words, they are so pervasive in verbal communication and have such an impact on it that they have to be removed or disposed of in order for the communication to stand any chance of achieving success. Thus one of the major functions of mitigation is that it pacifies negative emotions in the interlocutors.

Mitigation performs its pacifying functions by gently and tenderly treating the wounds, sensitive areas or vulnerability which are the source of negative emotions. It also achieves this goal by offering apologies and rewards. Consider example (52), reproduced here as example (72):

（72）观　众：我觉得那位言畅叔叔吧，反正我觉得我挺看不起他的，真的，*你别不爱听*。我觉得，你看，他个儿也挺高的，我在这儿透过玻璃看过去也挺帅的长得，他不敢出来，我就是这么想。(《有话慢慢说》)

In example (72), the speaker challenges the hearer's course of action by saying that he looks down upon him, asks the hearer not to take offense at this and then proceeds to offer an explanation. Showing contempt to the hearer is an FTA that largely threatens his positive face and thus is likely to stir up strong negative emotions in him. Anticipating this, the speaker adopts the strategy of direct dissuasion embodied in the mitigator "你别不爱听" to soothe out the negative emotions and pacify the hearer. Furthermore, the speaker makes heartfelt compliments on the hearer's looks so that the contempt turns out to be a well-meant encouragement. It is through the speaker's asking and reward offering that the hearer gets pacified.

The use of mitigation symbolizes the speaker's empathy for the hearer. The speaker takes the hearer's perspective in order to predict his response to the contempt, demonstrates his understanding and acknowledgement of the hearer's response, and attempts to be benevolent to the hearer (as evidenced by the making of the compliments). In return for this, he expects the hearer to empathize with him by accepting his suggestion. Such is the speaker's empathic intention, the recognition and accommodation of which is essential for the realization of the mitigating function of pacification. In order for mitigation to produce a pacifying effect, the hearer must empathically adapt to the speaker's mitigating strategy. If the hearer nonempathically adapts to it, he may fail to see the disguised encouragement behind the contempt and interpret the utterance in terms of its humiliating effects. But if he empathically adapts to it by taking the speaker's perspective he will understand the speaker's benevolent intention and truly gets pacified. Retrospectively, it was because the speaker was metapragmatically certain of the pacifying function of mitigation that so insulting an act as showing contempt could have been ventured in the first place.

（73）嘉　宾：三个方面我觉得特别麻烦，一个就是父母，父母望子成龙当然是好了，但是望子成龙别闹成，幸好我那两个孩子都不怎么出名，出了名别把孩子当摇钱树。我说难听点，别死乞白赖的。关爱是对的，这可好，我这孩子可出了名了。*我绝不是说你的父母*，我举个例子。

主持人：我们从现在开始统一说一下，*所有的都不是说你*，省得一句一解释了。

客　人：没事。(《掌声响起来》)

In this example, the honored guest severely criticizes those parents who unfairly take advantage of their children's premature fame to hoard money, denies targeting the criticism at the guest's parents, in which he is joined by the host, and elicits a calm response from the guest. Although the honored guest is criticizing a phenomenon in general, he can be mistaken as warning the guest because she has become famous at a young age. In that case, the guest would be thrown into deep antagonism. Anticipating this, the honored guest and the host use the intention disclaimer to pacify the guest. The pacification is evidenced by the guest's calm response "没事" which means she does not mind the criticism. It is clear that the guest gets pacified because she has adapted to the mitigating strategy.

By the use of mitigation, the speaker is not only empathically adapting to the hearer's negative emotions, but he is also attempting to get the hearer to empathically adapt to his mitigating strategy. Such is the speaker's empathic intention metapragamtically communicated to the hearer for her to recognize and accommodate so that the pacifying function could be performed. Mere adaptation to the mitigating strategy may not guarantee the hearer's accommodation of this intention, for the egoistic orientation of adaptation would leave her too preoccupied with her own emotional needs to see the speaker's concern over a general phenomenon. It is only through empathizing with the speaker that the hearer understands the speaker's horizon and truly gets pacified. Empathic adaptation is thus the key to revealing the working mechanism of mitigation.

### 6.1.3   Solidarity Building

Solidarity is related to the social distance between the two interlocutors, i.e., the closeness of their relationship. Solidarity building then refers to the establishment of a close or intimate relationship.

Solidarity building is relevant to the interview because most of the participants have not met each other before and are not yet on intimate terms. Another reason is that the guest, who is often troubled by something, is not accustomed to the atmosphere and may not be ready for full participation in the interview talk. In order to remove the psychological obstacles that impede free participation and ensure optimal involvement (both cognitive and emotive), the host sets out to build solidarity especially with the guest. Solidarity building helps to get the interview going smoothly.

Solidarity is built by the sharing and understanding of each other's views, interests, feelings, etc. One of the mitigating strategies that is used to build solidarity is the tag question. Huo(2004, 180) notes that in traditional Chinese medicine clinical interview talks the doctor uses tags not to seek confirmation of the patient's symptoms, but for affective purposes. In my data, it is the tag "是吧", not "是吗", that serves this purpose. Evidence for this assumption abounds. Firstly, the tag is most often used in the early part of the interview, which is characterized by history taking or other small talks. Secondly, the tag is frequently used by the host to the guest who does not feel comfortable with the interview. Thirdly, the tag often appears after the speaker's repetition, reformulation or summary of what the guest has been saying. Fourthly, there is no need of confirmation or disconfirmation in response to the tag, or, when there is a confirmation it is kept to a minimal *yes*. It is clear that the use of the tag functions to build solidarity between the interlocutors, especially between the host and the guest.

（74）主持人：我听说你干这件好事的时候，用的都不是您真的名字？
　　客　人：对。

主持人：用的哪个名字？

客　人：姓姜。

主持人：改了一个姓，是吧？

客　人：对。

主持人：就是怕别人知道说你傻，是吧？

客　人：对。（《行千里路送万元钱》）

In this example, the host uses the tag "是吧" twice to build solidarity with the guest. The first time the tag is embedded in a repetition of what the guest has just said, which is that he used a false name. The second time it occurs in a summary of what the guest has been saying several turns earlier, when he referred to his being called a fool for taking a long trip to return a lost wallet to its owner. In both cases the host is certain of the truth of his utterance, and knows that the guest's reply would be affirmative. In neither case, therefore, does the tag function to elicit a confirmation, much less an elaboration. This is why the reply in both cases is a minimal *yes*. It would make better sense to regard the tag as marking an attempt to build solidarity with the guest and take the guest's minimal *yes* as signaling that solidarity has been established. This reasoning is consistent with the background information that the guest's noble act has won him little but sarcasm and is now reserved about "exposing the old would". Solidarity building at this stage is beneficial to the unreserved participation of the guest in the interview. All these support the assumption that the tag questions are used here to build solidarity between the host and the guest.

Through the use of the tag questions, the speaker shows his understanding of what the hearer went through and indicates his empathy for the hearer. On the other hand, he expects the hearer to take his perspective and accommodate his intention of solidarity building. Thus the tags questions have resulted from the speaker's empathic adaptation to the hearer's experience and are meant to be empathically adapted to by the hearer in order to perform its functions. Nonadaptation or nonempathic adaptation would leave the hearer so paralyzed in his sorrows as to miss or fail to accommodate the speaker's solidarity building intention. Empathic adaptation, on the contrary, renders the hearer more ready to understand and accommodate the speaker's intention and contributes to the building of solidarity between the speaker and the hearer.

Apart from the tag "是吧", other mitigating strategies can function to build solidarity between the interlocutors. Consider example (75):

（75）嘉　宾：我觉得最大的问题，相声在艺术行列当中，人家看法还是低的。我*不瞒你说*，我就没让我孩子干这个。为什么？我就被人瞧不起。我妈死了我去买骨灰盒，那人说，说完了再买吧。我不能让我孩子再受这样。(《说相声》)

In this example, the honored guest first makes a comment on the low esteem in which his profession, the Chinese cross talk, is generally held, claims that he does not want his son to follow in his footsteps, and then offers an explanation for his decision. Prior to this extract, the other guests have been talking enthusiastically of the future of the art of cross talk, but the speaker has raised objections to all their views. In addition, his pessimistic view on his own trade runs in opposition to the optimistic expectations of the other guests. All these have created a social distance between them. In fact, the divergence is so big that the speaker seems to be on a different wavelength. This makes it necessary to reestablish solidarity with the other guests, especially when some of them are the speaker's friends and colleagues. The mitigator "不瞒你说", a variant of the truth claimer "实话实说", literally means truth telling but pragmatically implicates sincerity and honesty. More interestingly, it indicates that the speaker is putting the hearer on an equal footing and that he is ready to open up his heart and reveal his innermost secrets to the hearer. As evidence of this, the speaker follows up the mitigator with an account of the insult which he suffered for the sake of cross talk. On the assumption that people reveal their secrets (shameful ones particularly) only to those they know and trust, it can safely be said that the mitigator is intended to build solidarity between the interlocutors.

The use of the truth claimer symbolizes the speaker's empathy for the hearer in the sense of satisfying his emotional need of being trusted and treated as an intimate. On the other hand, it represents the speaker's attempt to get the hearer to treat him as an intimate and thereby build solidarity between them. This is possible on the basis of reciprocity. At a more advanced level, the speaker attempts to get the hearer to take his perspective and view the future of cross-talk in his light. This is essential for the building of solidarity. Not until the hearer is ready to step out of his own perspective and temporarily leave aside his own viewpoints is it possible for him to understand that the speaker's pessimism is not ill-grounded or ill-meant. Only when this happens can the solidarity be genuinely built. Mere adaptation would lead to the dominance of one's own perspective and brew prejudice instead of solidarity. It is clear that solidarity can only be built on the condition of the hearer's empathic adaptation to the speaker's use of the truth claimer.

## 6.2  Communicative Functions

The general purpose of communication is twofold. On the one hand, the interlocutors would want their partners to be fully engaged in the present event of communication so that it would bear fruits. On the other hand, they would want their opinions, attitudes, needs and feelings to be understood and accepted by their partners.

Communicative functions of mitigation refer to the purposes that mitigation serves in smoothing out the interactive process or in enhancing the effectiveness of the communication. Holmes (1983) observes that tag questions not only indicate the speaker's tentativeness but also represent the speaker's attempt to draw the hearer into the interaction. In this section, I want to extend this to other mitigating strategies and establish it as a general function of mitigation. Huo (2004) observes that mitigation regulates human interactions in general, and verbal communications in particular, by removing conflicts or obstacles along the physical, social and mental dimensions. Ran (2004) holds that the Chinese particle *ba* ("吧") mitigates the assertiveness and increases the tentativeness or negotiability of the speaker's tone and makes what the speaker says more acceptable. Inspired by such earlier researches and extending from their findings, I postulate three categories of communicative functions of mitigation, namely invitations, floor manipulations and persuasions. These will be dealt with in the following subsections.

### 6.2.1　Invitations

Invitations are those functions of mitigation that invite the hearer to engage in the interaction in ways suggested by the speaker. These include elaboration invitation, comment invitation, commitment invitation and negation invitation.

#### 6.2.1.1　Elaboration Invitation

At the beginning of the interview, the audience present and the TV viewers do not have the background information of the current topic, as the details of the event that gave rise to the topic have not been fully spelled out. In order for the interview to produce its desired result, it is necessary to make such background information known to the audience. Although the host has the details of the event, he would be overly predominant if he took over the job. It would be more appropriate for the guest to recount the event. However, the guest may not know where to start and how much detail to go into, so the host needs to invite the guest to elaborate on a certain aspect of the event.

A natural way to achieve this goal is to adopt mitigation. On the one hand, as far as experience-based power is concerned, the host stands in a subordinate position to the guest so that it is proportionate to his lack of power for him to speak unassertively. On the other hand, mitigation is characterized by negotiability, which performs an inviting function. Moreover, mitigation creates a gap in information which, given the guest's experience-based power, it is his obligation to fill up.

Holmes (1984: 357) notes that tags can be used to facilitate the interaction by encouraging hearers to contribute to the conversation. In this section I want to propose that other mitigating strategies can perform the same function.

（76）主持人：除了叫110，我*听说*你还自己采取过其他方法，类似解
　　　　　　放前咱们地下党和国民党斗争的这种方法，剪电线什
　　　　　　么的。
　　客　人：对，那天晚上，我的小孩吓坏了。因为经常这样子，
　　　　　　晚上小孩也睡不好，他害怕，就跑过来。因为我找他
　　　　　　们无数次，我也很气，我就一气之下跑下去，我就把
　　　　　　活动室的线剪了。(《麻将声声》)

In this example, the host uses a hearsay "听说" to invite the guest to elaborate on the relevant experience, and the guest responds by giving a detailed narration. What the guest is invited to elaborate on is her radical way of handling conflicts with her neighbors and this is valuable information for the interview. It would be appropriate and interesting for the guest to supply the missing information. The mitigator performs this inviting function because it highlights the guest's experience-based power which assigns her the obligation. In addition, the guest's solution to conflicts is so radical that a simple *yes* to the host's remark would not do; in fact, the guest needs to go to great lengths to justify it, as evidenced by her detailed account of the experience. Also, the host's humorous but serious characterization of the experience has created a suspense that deserves an elaborate resolution. All these mean that the hearsay has been designed to perform the function of elaboration invitation.

This function is realized by means of the hearer's empathic adaptation to the speaker's mitigating strategy. The use of the hearsay indicates that the speaker is offering his empathy to the hearer by showing respect for her power and, on the basis of reciprocity, expecting the hearer to extend her empathy to him by granting his wish. Such is the speaker's empathic intention underlying the use of the mitigating strategy, the recognition and accommodation of which is essential to the realization of the mitigating functions. Without empathizing with the speaker, the hearer would not give a response beyond a minimal *yes*, as from her point of view she has been sufficiently understood and there is no need for further communication. In other words, the hearer would be too busy with her own thoughts and needs to care about others' concerns. Empathic adaptation, in contrast, focuses the hearer on the speaker's intention and needs and ensures the realization of the inviting function by always being altruistic to the speaker.

Consider another example:

（77）主持人：您推广科技走得最远除了新疆还去了西藏，是吧？

客　人：去西藏了。

主持人：西藏*好像*更艰苦一点。

客　人：更艰苦一点，一个海拔高度高，一个高山反应，一个
交通困难，一个生活不方便，高山反应高压锅煮东
西煮不熟的，高压锅煮的开水基本上就是70度左右。
（《阿里木与特派员》）

In example (77), the host uses the epistemic modal "好像" to invite the guest to elaborate on the hardships involved in living in Tibet, in response to which the guest offers a detailed explanation. Retrospectively, the information concerning living in Tibet is so important to the interview that it would be desirable for the guest to supply the details. However, the guest would not do it automatically, which is why the host sets out to invite him to do so. Similar to the analysis given above, the mitigator creates an informational gap which it is the guest's obligation to fill up given his experience-based power. This is equivalent to saying that this function is not performable unless the hearer adapts to the speaker's use of the mitigating strategy.

What is interesting about this example is that the guest repeats the host's formulation instead of giving a minimal *yes* as a reply. Given that a repeated formulation is more emphatic than a simple confirmation and adds weight to the host's words, it must be warranted by more details than is provided by a mere confirmation, which partly explains why the guest proceeds to offer an elaboration. From the perspective of discourse analysis the repeated formulation is more likely a mark for turn extension than for turn termination.

Metapragmatically, the use of the epistemic modal signals that the speaker is being empathic with the hearer by highlighting his power and assigning him a dominant role in the upcoming interaction. It also symbolizes that the speaker expects the hearer to return empathy to him by granting his wish for an elaboration. Such is the speaker's empathic intention constraining the interpretation of the utterance and the realization of the mitigating functions. In order to make the functions performable, the hearer must recognize and accommodate this intention, i.e., he must empathically adapt to the speaker's use of mitigation. If he adapted to mitigation but not empathically, he would not provide an elaboration as requested by the speaker, for he would have been too preoccupied with his own thoughts or interests to have taken notice of the speaker's needs. It is only when the hearer takes the speaker's perspective that he understands the speaker's intention, and it is only when the hearer is willing to empathize with the speaker by granting his needs that mitigating functions such as elaboration invitation can be successfully performed.

### 6.2.1.2 Comment Invitation

As the interview talk proceeds, there frequently arise controversial points of view related to a phenomenon, which may confuse the general audience. In order for the interview to run smoothly and for the discussion to bear fruits, it is necessary to comment on the controversial points. But even though the host is capable of offering such a comment, he would be monotonously dominant if he did it. On the contrary, given the expertise-based power that the honored guest enjoys, it would be more appropriate and interesting for him to make the comment. Hence the need is created for the host to invite the honored guest to make a comment on a controversial point.

Comment invitations are achievable naturally through the host's use of mitigation. Firstly, it is proportionate to the host's lack of expertise-based power for him to speak unassertively and inconclusively. Secondly, in using mitigation the host appeals to little authority and highlights the honored guest's power. Moreover, mitigation creates a gap in information which it is the honored guest's obligation to fill up. It is clear that a comment invitation works in the same way as an elaboration invitation except that it is related to expertise-based power rather than experience-based power.

（78）主持人：我今天说了我一共有十万个为什么，那么现在刚开了个头，我想说的就是我说的这些问题您都能解答，但是如果您作为这个医院的院长您都能把它解决吗？

嘉　　宾：哎呀，这可是个大题目。

主持人：*据我了解*您做过医院的院长。

嘉　　宾：对。如果我们有这样一种现代化的管理体制，我觉得解决这些问题根本就不是问题，但是如果说按我们现在有些医院的这种管理体制的话，可以说比登天还难，就是非常难。（《医院里面有医生》）

In this example, the host attempts to elicit a comment from the honored guest, who hesitates about providing it. Then he uses an evidential "据我了解" to highlight the honored guest's expertise-based power and urges him once more. As a result of the repeated urge the honored guest finally complies with the host's comment invitation. This comment is vital for the interview to penetrate deeper into the issue under discussion and has properly been made by the honored guest. The function of comment invitation is performable through the use of the evidential because it elicits a confirmation of the host's authority highlighting statement"您做过医院的院长", which denotes a sufficient condition for the acceptance of the invitation. Therefore, if the honored guest admits ever being president of a hospital, he has no reason for noncompliance. In this case, comment invitation is performed indirectly by seeking confirmation of what seems to be a sufficient condition for compliance.

More importantly, the function of comment invitation is realized through the hearer's empathic adaptation to the speaker's use of mitigation. The speaker's empathy for the hearer in this case is firstly reflected in his respect for the hearer's power and the assignment of a dominant role to the hearer, as demonstrated in the making of the authority-highlighting statement. It is also reflected in his understanding of the hearer's delicate situation of having to answer a sensitive question. On the basis of reciprocity, he expects to receive the hearer's empathy in exchange for this understanding, which is for the hearer to accommodate his needs by providing a comment. This empathic intention metapragmatically constrains the working of mitigation. The realization of the mitigating functions is dependent on the recognition and accommodation of this empathic intention, which is in turn dependent on the hearer's empathic adaptation to the speaker's mitigating strategy. Thus empathic adaptation contributes to guaranteeing the realization of the mitigating functions and the success of the communication. The hearer's acceptance of the comment invitation in this example has resulted from his empathic adaptation to the speaker's use of the evidential.

（79）主持人：阎肃老师，您说*能不能*，我们从一个人的签名认不出
来，就能断定这个人毛了，心毛了，或者不好接触了。
嘉　宾：起码是。倪睿思目前的感觉还仅是个初步的，因为她

初露头角了。她慢慢还有几个飞跃，成了大名、大火，
那对于人生都是个巨大的考验，真的。马上心态就不
一样了，周围的眼神也不一样了，自个儿的眼神也不
一样了，会有的。(《掌声响起来》)

In example (79), the host uses the disclaimer "能不能" to invite the
honored guest to comment on the phenomenon of post-famous arrogance
in people, especially in the entertainment businesses. The honored guest
accepts the invitation by offering a long and convincing comment. The
host's invitation attempt is a combined result of the communicative needs
and the consideration of appropriateness. The comment is necessary
for the communication as it concerns warning the guest (the one being
talked about) of the dangers of premature fame, the theme of the present
interview. It should be made by the honored guest, who is a well-
established playwright and a senior scholar rich in life experience and
wits. The expertise of the honored guest is also reflected in the term of
address "老师", which literally means "master" but pragmatically signals
the host's respect for the honored guest's knowledge. Mitigation performs
the function of comment invitation in this case because the disclaimer
semantically marks optionality, pragmatically encodes negotiability,
and hands over the right of making judgments to the honored guest. The
honored guest, while adapting to the host's use of mitigation, actually
takes over the job. That is how the function is realized. Linguistic
evidence for the invitation function is also provided in "您说", which is a
more explicit way to invite the honored guest to make the comment.

The use of the disclaimer, together with the term of address, marks
the speaker's empathy for the hearer by highlighting his power and
assigning him a dominant role in the following interaction. Meanwhile,

it signals the speaker's expectation of empathy from the hearer in the form of granting his wish. This empathic intention of the speaker's must be recognized and accommodated in order for the mitigating strategy to realize its functions. That is, only if the hearer decides to repay empathy to the speaker does he provide a comment as intended by the speaker. From the vantage point of social norms, seeing that the speaker is conforming to the social convention of assigning more speaking floor to the powerful figure, the empathic hearer might adopt this frame of action by taking the floor. There is thus ample evidence to suggest that empathic adaptation is the working mechanism of mitigation.

### 6.2.1.3　Commitment Invitation

At a later stage of the interview, after the guest has given an account of his experience, the honored guests have commented on critical points and the host has examined every essential aspect of the issue under discussion, it is the audience's turn to raise questions or express their views. However, the audience may not venture to open up their hearts and fully express their views, because they are worried that their questions or views may touch upon the guest's vulnerabilities that have been exposed by the authoritative analyses of the honored guest(s). It is thus communicatively relevant to remove the audience's worry by checking on the guest's mental and emotional states and by getting him to promise not to take offense at what they say. Mitigation can successfully perform the function of commitment invitation mainly because it pacifies the guest by showing concern with his mental and emotional well-beings.

Consider the following example:

（80）主持人：赵先生，现场的观众把这个事情大概听清楚了，我想
他们会有更多的问题，我想可能很多问题还会很尖锐，
不知道你在不在乎？

客　人：我不在乎。

主持人：不在乎，现在大家就可以随意地提问，随意地发表自
　　　　己的观点。(《照相》)

In this example, the host warns the guest of the tough questions to be raised by the audience and asks the guest if he minds them. The guest replies that he does not, and the host sets out collecting questions and opinions from the audience. It has been contextually made clear that the guest is depressed because his work (tracking down the demoralization of what he calls "marginalized girls" by photographing their life) has been depreciated and even severely criticized. This depression is harmful to the communication either in discouraging audience participation or in brewing negative emotions. It is therefore necessary to remove these obstacles in order to ensure a desirable extent of audience participation. Mitigation can successfully elicit a commitment from the guest because the disclaimer "不知道你在不在乎" semantically entails optionality, pragmatically implicates the host's concern with the guest and interactively seeks a reply to the invitation. Although it is theoretically possible for the guest to turn down the invitation, he could not very well bring himself to do so, because of the need to repay the host's concern and because of the common agreement to "tell it as it is"("实话实说"). What is interesting about this example is the host's repetition and highlighting of the guest's commitment, which binds the guest to calmly taking the provocative questions from the audience and entitles the audience to expressing their opinions without reservations. This counts as linguistic evidence for the commitment invitation and its contribution to the communication proper.

The realization of the function of commitment invitation depends crucially on the hearer's empathic adaptation to the speaker's mitigating strategy. The speaker's empathy for the hearer, which is communicated by the use of the disclaimer, consists in his taking of the hearer's perspective to guess at the hearer's response to the upcoming questions, in viewing the questions in terms of the hurt derivable from them and in caring about the hearer's feelings. The empathy expected of the hearer, also communicated by the use of the disclaimer, lies in the hearer's taking the speaker's perspective by attaching great importance to securing audience participation. Only if the hearer empathically adapts to the speaker's use of mitigation can he ever view the program by the standard of audience participation. Otherwise the hearer would be so egocentric as to be ever preoccupied with his own wounds or overprotective with regard to his vulnerabilities. In such a case the hearer would not possibly commit himself to tolerating the audience's tough questions.

（81）主持人：我先声明，因为观众有各种各样的想法，也许他们的问题会很尖锐，*不知道你们姐弟俩能不能接受*？

客　人：可以。

主持人：可以吗？

客　人：可以。

主持人：哪位想说就请举手示意我。（《第三次生命》）

In this example, the guests (a sister and a brother who have had two kidney transplants in the past eight years and are living on borrowed time) may not be emotionally ready to face up to some of the questions to be raised by the audience, which may implicitly or explicitly refer to death. On the other hand, the audience may not want to grieve the guests through carelessness. Mitigation takes care of both questions. The disclaimer "不知道你们姐弟俩能不能接受" leaves options for the guests and indicates the host's concern with their emotional needs. This option is only theoretically existent, however; because in actuality the guest will act as is required if only to repay the host's kindness. The relevance of the commitment to audience participation is evident in the host's rechecking with it, which, if reconfirmed, produces much of a binding effect on the guest. That is why the host turns to the audience immediately after the second confirmation is given. It can be seen that the commitment can only be elicited if the hearer adapts to the speaker's mitigating strategy.

This is only part of the story, however. The use of the disclaimer indicates that the speaker is taking the hearers' perspective by viewing the questions in terms of their possible hurt to them and is converging to their affect by giving them the freedom not to answer the questions. For this considerateness or kindness, the speaker deserves to be rewarded with the hearers' empathy. When the hearers empathize with the speaker, they will take his perspective, understand the importance of hearing the audience's questions and be willing to commit themselves to taking the upcoming questions with much patience and tolerance. From another point of view, it is only when the hearers are ready to repay empathy to the speaker will they make the commitment, for without empathizing with the speaker the hearers' attention would be exclusively concentrated on their own sorrows. Empathic adaptation can thus be seen as the necessary and sufficient condition for the realization of the mitigating functions.

### 6.2.1.4   Negation Invitation

The interview does not always go smoothly. When the topic is depressingly serious and the interview gets dreary, it is necessary to light up the atmosphere with humor and relieve the gloom. When the discussion is just scratching the surface of matters, it is necessary to penetrate deeper into the matter and create a special effect. Humor and the pursuit of special effects are two features of the personal style of the host.

However, the humor must be closely related to the main theme of the interview, for digressive humor would lead the interview off track. The way that the host makes the interview both entertaining and instructive is to engage in negation invitation through mitigation. Negation invitation involves the speaker saying something obviously false or exaggerating something to the point of absurdity and inviting the hearer to negate it. Humor and instructiveness originate from the fact that what the speaker says, apart from being false and absurd, is socially relevant, that is, it is echoic of some people's mentality or logic. In this process, mitigation functions as a signal for the hearer to negate what the speaker has just said.

Consider example (82):

（82）主持人：有一个叫红君的网友一口气发了四五行，他说言畅不
　　　　　　　应该有什么压力，丘吉尔就是口吃你能说他不优秀
　　　　　　　吗？他说有资料表明，口吃患者的智商要高出正常人。
　　　　　　　这个我有点不高兴了，我觉得有点歧视我。
　　客　人：噢，不，不。
　　主持人：但是我觉得这是他鼓励你的一种方法。(《有话慢慢说》)

In this example, the host makes a false accusation and invites the guest to negate it, which the guest does. The guest suffers from a serious stammer and feels that he is prejudiced by people around him. In order to talk him out of such suspicions, the host engages in an implicit process of *reductio ad absurdum*. His false accusation echoes the guest's groundless suspicions. So through negating the accusation, the guest can see for himself the absurdity of his own suspicions. In the absence of the negation invitation, the humor and the special effect would be lost. Mitigation performs the function of negation invitation due to its negotiability:

nonassertiveness corresponds to a nonseriousness which helps reveal the host's humorous intention. Without mitigation, conversely, the host would be so assertive as to conceal his humorous intention. This would throw the hearer into bewilderment. It can be seen that the negation invitation is accepted because the hearer has adapted to the speaker's use of mitigation.

This is not the whole story, however. By performing his mitigated illocution, the speaker is expressing his empathy for the hearer by echoing his mentality, imitating his line of thinking and viewing things from his perspective, although all of these are done in a playful way. That is, the speaker is being suspicious in a way reminiscent of the hearer's. Meanwhile, the speaker is also trying to get the hearer to take his perspective and realize the falsity of the speaker's accusation. What's more, the speaker expects the hearer to see his intention of *reductio ad absurdum*. This empathic intention is what constrains the working of mitigation. The hearer must empathize with the speaker while adapting to his mitigating strategy in order to understand the speaker's intention and act as instructed or constrained by the speaker and thereby realize the mitigating functions. Note that it is impossible for the hearer to negate the speaker's accusation if it does not occur to him that prejudice against the host is very unlikely in this context. Also, the special effect is lost if the hearer does not see or accommodate the speaker's humorous intention. Thus the hearer's empathic adaptation to the speaker's use of mitigation determines the realization of the function of negation invitation.

Consider another example:

（83）嘉　宾：有个别造假的羽绒服造假最典型的呢就是把鸡杀了以后毛拔下来连洗都不洗，带着血就装进去了，然后放一段就都捂臭了。

主持人：*我听说*还有把整只鸡都塞进去的。

嘉　宾：整只鸡都塞进去还倒真赚了。结果弄得中国的商品在俄罗斯形象就特别坏。(《新鞋子旧鞋子》)

In this example, the honored guest has been talking about the low quality of the China-made products which were sold to Russia when the host cuts in on him with a funny statement and invites him to negate it. The invitation is accepted by the honored guest, who not only negates the statement but also joins the host in producing humor. The special effect is that the interlocutors can heartily ridicule the fake products and educate people about the cost of dishonesty. The contribution made by mitigation to this special effect is that it triggers off a negotiation process that leads to the negation of the host's statement and the making of the honored guest's humorous response. Without mitigation, the host would sound so assertive as to cause bewilderment in the honored guest. Needless to say, the honored guest's adaptation to the host's mitigating strategy has played a role in realizing the function of negation invitation. But there is more to the story.

In making his mitigated utterance, the host is expressing his empathy for the honored guest by converging to his mode of behavior, exposing the fake products, although in an exaggerated way. On the basis of this, he expects the honored guest to cooperate with his humorous intention by negating what he has said. This empathic intention is evidently recognized and accommodated by the honored guest, who does not only negate the host's utterance but also adopts the host's exaggerated style in doing the negating. The cooperation between the host and the honored guest is so perfect that a special effect is created which contains both seriousness and humor. Clearly the function of negation invitation has been performed because the hearer has taken the speaker's perspective and has arrived at an understanding and an accommodation of the speaker's empathic intention. In other word, the hearer has empathically adapted to the speaker's use of mitigation. Nonempathic adaptation would have led the hearer to continue his with his drearily serious style of speech.

## 6.2.2   Floor Manipulations

Floor manipulations are those functions of mitigation that concern the allocation of the speaking floor and floor length in the interview. During the interview, there is a lot of competition for the speaking floor due to the time limitation (half an hour for the whole interview and less than ten minutes for the audience). It thus makes sense to manage the speaking floor efficiently. Several possibilities come to mind: when someone wants to speak, he must announce his intention in order to catch and hold the others' attention; when there is the risk of being interrupted, the speaker needs to take measures to maintain the floor till he finishes speaking; when the speaker has finished speaking he must mark the termination so as to extend the floor to others; when the speaker has been talking at some length, yet is not coming to the point, the host needs to terminate the digression and make him yield the floor. Based on these possibilities, floor manipulations can be classified into floor taking, floor keeping and floor termination.

At an abstract level, mitigation can perform the functions of floor manipulations due to its metapragmatic features. We will go into more details in the following subsections.

### 6.2.2.1   Floor Taking

Mitigation helps one to secure the speaking floor through performativity, self-referentiality or a combination thereof.

（84）观　众：从我的感觉来说，*谈谈个人的想法，不一定对*。宋书记把个人的经历个人感觉运用到组织程序当中，作为一个领导者作为一个决策者在考虑这个问题的时候能不能更慎重，把个人的意志和个人的想法既融入组织当中成为组织的目标，同时把个人的感情也保留在其中，不能把个人的意志完全驾驭在组织之上，因为您一个人一声命令下去了187个人就抛家舍业去了深圳。

主持人：我觉得他这个问题是个重磅炸弹。

观　众：两年不让回家，都有妻儿老小，不知道怎么处理？

主持人：这个问题你不用再发挥就是个重磅炸弹了。（《我在南边挺好的》）

In this example, the audience member uses a subjectivizer "谈谈个人的想法" and a disclaimer "不一定对" to secure the speaking floor. The subjectivizer contains a verb of saying "谈谈" and a noun of thinking "想法", which in combination make the subjectivizer a hedged performative (Fraser, 1975). Performatives are illocutionary force indicators for whose sake saying constitutes doing (Austin, 1962; Searle, 1969). In other words, a performative is conventionally associated with a turn in which the propositional content of the performative sentence is spelled out. It is because of this conventionality that the subjecitvizer helps secure the speaking floor. In psychological terms, the mitigators have given rise to expectations that have to be satisfied by an account of why such a characterization as suggested by the mitigators is provided. In plain words, the hearer has to wait until the speaker closes his turn before he knows what this personal opinion is and judges whether it is right or not. In narrative terms, the mitigators have created a suspense that cannot be resolved until the speaker has a chance to finish talking. Moreover, the self-referentialality of the subjectivizer draws attention to itself, which is one prerequisite for taking the speaking floor. Linguistic evidence that mitigation can perform the function of floor taking is provided in the audience member's long-winded turn, which takes the host two metapragmatic comments to terminate. It is clear that mitigation has been designed to help one seize the speaking floor and that the function of floor taking is performed thanks to hearer's adaptation to the speaker's use of mitigation.

More importantly, the use of mitigation indicates that the speaker is taking the hearer's perspective by anticipating his negative response to the view to be expressed and is converging to his emotional needs by not being too aggressive or challenging. On the basis of this, he expects the hearer to empathize with him by hearing him out and giving his viewpoint serious consideration. Such reciprocal empathy is essential for the working of mitigation. If the hearer does not empathize with the speaker, he would not be patient enough to hear the whole story and would not give his viewpoint its due, especially if the viewpoint is critical of him.

Consider another example：

（85）嘉　宾：我觉得杨先生他这事以不成功而告终，有它的必然性。*怎么说呢*，他这举动本身不太符合常规，一个硕士生到农村当一个村官，有点感觉像什么？一个没文化的老农民当国家党领导人似的感觉，都是不符合常规的。（《硕士村官》）

In example (85), the speaker uses the hesitator "怎么说呢" to secure the speaking floor. Theoretically, the hesitator could mark word searching, thought gathering, consequence weighing, dissociation or floor taking. In the present case, it signals that the speaker is about to offer an explanation although he hesitates over its illocutionary appropriateness. Thus mitigation and floor taking are combined in one. In the absence of the hesitator, the floor could be seized by others as the current speaker has reached a transition relevant place.

The hesitation thus manifested is an indicator of the speaker's concern with the hearer's emotional well-being or of his empathy for the hearer. In other words, the speaker is viewing his explanation from the hearer's perspective in terms of the emotional disturbances which the hearer will be subjected to. On the other hand, the fact that he goes on record providing the explanation despite his concern symbolizes that he expects the hearer to step out of his won perspective and view the explanation in terms of its truth and originality. This is the speaker's empathic intention, which constrains the hearer to engage in empathic adaptation to the mitigating strategy. Empathic adaptation is necessary for the realization of the function of floor taking. It is only when the hearer wants to be altruistic to the speaker will he be willing to hear the speaker out. It is only when the hearer takes the speaker's perspective can he possibly understand and believe what is said. Without the influence of empathy, the hearer would not take the critical view so calmly. Rather, he would interrupt the speaker at the first opportunity because he could not wait to defend himself.

### 6.2.2.2   Floor Keeping

When there is the risk of being interrupted because of the strong competition for the speaking floor, the present speaker warns that he has a point to make so that the hearer will have to wait until he finishes expressing the view. When what the speaker is saying is absurd and provocative, it necessary to pacify the audience in order to keep the floor.

Mitigation can perform the floor keeping function. Metadiscursive comments (deprecators in my terminology), for example, have a proleptic dimension since they function as countering devices to potential negative reactions of the interlocutor. The use of these comments therefore constitutes an interactional strategy by which the speaker may keep the speaking floor in spite of the shocking or unusual nature of their talk, all the while giving the impression of relinquishing some (virtual) ground to the interlocutor ( Heisler et al., 2003).

Other strategies have the same potential. Consider example (62), reproduced here as example (86):

（86）嘉　宾：我一直有这样一个观点，*我也不怕大家可能反对*。从总体上来看在我们现在这样一个社会，处在社会这个发展阶段，从总体上说男性的工作效率要比女性高，个别的不一定。个别的……

主持人：已经有人举手了，咱们让潘老师说完待会儿批判更好批了。(《女人回家》)

In this example, the honored guest uses the mitigating strategy of penalty taking to maintain the speaking floor. What he is about to say can be taken as bias against women and he could be accused of having male chauvinist sentiments. Aware of this risk, he offers to take penalty and manages thereby to pacify the audience to some extent. Without the mitigating strategy, he could be too busy dealing with objections to finish his turn. Linguistic evidence for the floor keeping intention is provided in the host's comforting utterance "咱们让潘老师说完待会儿批判更好批了", which is used to help the honored guest to maintain the speaking floor by pacifying the audience. Thus it can be seen that the speaker can hold his floor because the hearers have adapted to his use of mitigation.

Moreover, the use of the mitigating strategy indicates that the speaker is adopting the hearers' perspective by viewing his statement in terms of the hearers' objections and converging to their emotional needs by offering to take penalty. That is, the speaker is offering his empathy to the hearer in the use of the mitigating strategy. On the other hand, the fact that he wants to offer his view although he is aware of the hearers' objections demonstrates that there is some truth to his view and he expects the hearers to take his perspective. Under the constraint of this empathic intention, the hearers will be patient and kind enough to at least hear him out. Otherwise, the speaker would more likely be interrupted in the middle of his speech than get a chance to finish speaking. Thus the hearers' empathic altruism for the speaker is essential for the realization of the function of floor keeping.

### 6.2.2.3   Floor Termination

Floor termination can be self termination and other termination. The following is an instance of self termination:

（87）嘉　宾：所以说我觉得要承认代沟。问题是每一代人生活的情况都不一样，要有一个相互的理解和尊重。*我不知道我讲得是不是准确。*(《儿子吸毒以后》)

In this example, the speaker uses a knowledge disclaimer "我不知道我讲得是不是准确" to terminate his turn. The negotiability of mitigation is consistent with turn termination in the sense that the current speaker has to extend the floor to others before they can possibly engage in negotiation. Further evidence is that the disclaimer occurs at the end of a conclusion (marked by the discourse marker "所以说"), which is a transition relevant place and facilitates floor termination. The realization of the function of floor termination is obviously related to the speaker's empathy for the hearer. As shown in this example, the use of the disclaimer indicates the speaker's respect for the hearer's authority and his attempt to hand over the right of making judgments to the hearer and to assign him a predominant role. This means that terminating one's speaking floor is one way to extend his empathy to the hearer or that the function of floor termination is a byproduct of the speaker's empathy for the hearer. If the speaker does not empathize with the hearer, he will not understand the hearer's need for the speaking floor, will not acknowledge the hearer's authority, nor will he so explicitly mark his turn termination.

The following is an instance of other termination.

（88）主持人：电话是留家里的电话吗？

观　众：留家里的或者服务中心的电话。

主持人：要是有一个机构的电话可能就更好，*是吧*？谢谢！还
　　　　有哪一位？（《送我回家》）

In this example, the host uses the tag "是吧" to terminate the floor for the audience member. The tag does not function to seek a confirmation of what the host has said, for he has merely repeated the audience member's words so there is no need for a confirmation. Rather, the tag functions to signal uptake or understanding, to highlight the point, and more importantly, to indicate to the audience member that he has contributed sufficiently to the discussion and might as well yield the floor to others. Linguistic evidence for the function of floor termination is provided by the host's thanking, which is a typical marker of turn closing. Evidence is also provided in the fact that the host turns to another audience member immediately after the tag and the thanking.

In the use of the tag question, the host is indicating his understanding and appreciation of the audience member's view. In addition, he is summarizing the gist of what the audience member has been saying for the benefit of highlighting his conversational contribution. All these represent the host's empathy for the audience member, in return for which the audience member is to empathize with the host. When the audience member takes the host's perspective, he will understand that the host wants to assign the speaking floor to as many people as possible and will be willing to terminate his floor. It can be seen that floor termination is motivated by the host's empathic adaptation to the audience member' need of the floor and is realized by the audience member's empathic adaptation to the host's allocation of the floor. Without empathizing with the host, the audience member would fail to accommodate the host's intention and tie up the speaking floor.

### 6.2.3  Persuasions

Persuasions are the functions of mitigation that concern the effectiveness of the communication, that is, whether the interlocutors have achieved their communicative goals or whether the speech act has released its main perlocutionary effect. Generally, someone who performs a directive speech act would want his directive complied with and someone who performs an assertive would want his interlocutor(s) convinced. Persuasions are the first and foremost criterion of communicative success.

However, there are always factors that impede the achievement of these goals. Controversies, negative emotions and taboos are among them. Mitigation serves to minimize the impact of these factors and facilitate the achievement of persuasions.

Persuasions include compliance enhancement and credibility enhancement, to which I now turn.

### 6.2.3.1  Compliance Enhancement

Compliance enhancement is often performed by Fraser's disclaimers, which mark common ground while leaving room for negotiation or which suspend a felicity condition that actually holds. It is also performed by deprecators, which function as implicit apologies and which, through a mechanism of fair exchange, prompt the hearer to do as required by the speaker. In fact, under the right conditions lots of mitigating strategies can perform the function of compliance enhancement.

Consider example (56), reproduced here as example (89):

（89）主持人：王先生我提个*冒昧*的请求，*为了使谈话生动有趣*，您考贾先生两道题。没事儿，您答不上来我们照买你的书不误。(《大学里来了个贾老师》）

In this example, the host is requesting one of the honored guests Mr. Wang to test the other honored guest Mr. Jia on his knowledge of literature history. This request is fraught with problems. First, Mr. Jia is a well-established writer who enjoys both expertise-based and status-based powers, so it would be disrespectful to test him on modern literature. Second, given such inappropriateness, the request would be too imposing on Mr. Wang, too. Third, should Mr. Jia fail to answer the questions, he would suffer a big loss of face. All these factors make it difficult to comply with the request. In order to solve these problems, the host resorts to mitigation. The deprecator "冒昧" characterizes the host's request negatively and functions to pacify Mr. Jia's negative emotions. The grounder "为了使谈话生动有趣" offers a reason and reduces imposition on both honored guests by not forcing them to do anything they don't fully understand (Blum-Kulka et al., 1989; Caffi, 1999). The two cost minimizers "没事儿" and "您答不上来我们照买你的书不误" remove Mr. Jia's reservations by assuring him that no damage will be done to his fame or popularity. In the absence of mitigation, the "testing" would not have gone as smoothly as it did.

The negative characterization represented by the deprecator is formulated in anticipation of the hearer's mental response to the performing of the speaker's illocution. It shows the speaker's understanding of identification with the response. It also demonstrates the speaker's attempt to maintain the hearer's emotional well-being. The use of the cost minimizers also indicates the speaker's convergence with the hearer's concern over his popularity. In a word, mitigation represents the speaker's empathy for the hearer. On the other hand, the fact that the speaker would still want to make such a request despite his wish to be empathic with the hearer symbolizes his attempt to get the hearer to see his perspective: that the test is needed to make the interaction more interesting. This is the speaker's empathic intention. The hearer's recognition and accommodation of this intention is essential for the enhancement of compliance. It is only when the hearer takes the speaker's perspective while suppressing his own, i.e., when Mr. Jia views the test in terms of its benefit to the interview rather than its damage to his popularity that he would comply with such a request. Nonempathic adaptation would not ensure a shift of perspective but would leave the hearer totally submerged in his own worries.

Consider the case of a disclaimer in example (90):

（90）主持人：王老师你看这样好不好，今天你们班的同学也到了现
　　　　　　　场，我想请他们当中的一个到台上来，我们坐在一起
　　　　　　　交流。不知道这样会不会对你有压力?
　　　　王老师：不会。
　　　　主持人：如果您没有压力我们大家用掌声欢迎她。
　　　　学　生：(在掌声中走上台)(《这个主任不好当》)

In this example, the host uses the felicity disclaimer "如果您没有压力" to secure the guest's compliance with his request. The disclaimer mitigates the illocutionary force of the speech act by assuming that one of the felicity conditions may not hold and by expressing uncertainty of the appropriateness of the speech act (Fraser, 1980; Holmes, 1984; Haverkate, 1992; Ran, 2004). In the present case, it keeps open the possibility of withdrawing the request in the event of the condition turning out invalid. However, the disclaimer does something more: if the condition actually holds, it binds the hearer to comply with the request, as the condition has been pragmaticalized into a necessary and sufficient condition. It is often the case that the nonassumption of felicity is strategic, i.e., the condition that is linguistically assumed not to hold actually holds somehow, as shown in the present example in which the guest explicitly states that she feels no pressure. This is a pseudo suspension of the felicity that strikes a balance between the speaker and the hearer: it gives the hearer one last chance to back out but, if the chance is not taken, binds the hearer to an obligation agreed upon. Thus it is more reasonable to view the disclaimer as urging the guest to comply with the host's request. Evidence for this function can be found in the fact that the host beckons the student to come onto stage immediately after the use of the disclaimer.

Thus the use of the felicity disclaimer indicates that the speaker is taking the hearer's perspective by viewing the request in terms of the pressure she will feel and is being altruistic to her by offering her one more chance to back out. Meanwhile, he is attempting to get the hearer to empathize with him by complying with his request. Such is the speaker's empathic intention which, on the basis of reciprocity, constrains the hearer into empathically adapting to the speaker's mitigating strategy. It is only when the hearer takes the speaker's perspective, i.e., when the hearer views the request in terms of its benefits to the interview, will she be willing to comply with it. Nonempathic adaptation would not necessarily lead to the hearer's accommodation of this intention and would make the compliance less likely.

### 6.2.3.2   Credibility Enhancement

Generally, mitigated statements are more acceptable and credible than bare assertions because they are more negotiable and less imposing. In cases where they are not readily acceptable, they are at least more difficult to refute, for the reason that to refute a weak statement would constitute making a strong counterstatement that may take more justifications and clarifications than the hearer is ready to offer. So, it often happens that as a result of mitigation the speaker is given the benefit of the doubt, that is, the hearer tends to believe what the speaker's mitigated utterance unless there is weighty counterevidence. Another way to achieve credibility enhancement is to use mitigation in combination with power and the assumption of responsibilities, as shown in example (91).

（91）主持人：刘先生，趁机给大家解释解释，很多百姓有想法，国家花这么多钱做这件事有什么意义？

　　嘉　宾：从两方面讲，南极是唯一没有国界的大陆了，相当于一个半中国那么大，它有那么多的自然资源，这关系到一个国家民族权益问题，这是一个方面；另一方面从科学研究的角度来讲，南极由于它特殊的自然地理环境，所以有些很重要的科学问题只能在南极来进行研究，所以我想从这两方面来讲，我们中华民族进入南极是完全必要的。而且现在说起来，*我个人觉得*我们去南极去晚了，因为像一些发达国家他们比我们早50年就去南极了。(《人在南极》)

In this example, the honored guest uses the subjectivizer "我个人觉得" to preface his assertion that China should have built a station in Antarctica earlier. Despite giving a nonimposing impression and presenting the speaker as being modest, the subjectivizer indicates the speaker's insistence on his view. The underlying logic can be glossed as "I don't impose on you, you don't interfere with me". However, since the speaker enjoys much expertise-based power (he has made many trips to Antarctica), is appealing to this power in highlighting his personal involvement, and is ready to take responsibility for what he says, his mitigated statement is more convincing than a bare assertion.

The credibility of what the speaker says is enhanced by the hearer's empathic adaptation to the speaker's mitigating strategy. The subjectivized formulation of the utterance indicates that the speaker is taking the hearer's perspective by giving full consideration to their view (which, as made explicit by the host, is that more fund should be channeled into creating jobs rather than building an exploratory station in Antarctica, especially when there were millions of people laid off their posts). Meanwhile, the speaker is attempting to get the hearer to take his perspective and judge the matter by the criterion of long-term benefits. This is the speaker's empathic intention, which constrains the hearer into empathically adapting to the speaker's mitigation in order to realize the function of credibility enhancement. When the hearer takes the speaker's perspective, he will realize that the words of such a powerful figure as the honored guest are weighty, especially if he offers to takes responsibility for them. It is only when the hearer is empathically disposed to the speaker that he is willing to believe what the speaker says.

In the course of empathically adapting to the speaker's mitigating strategy in order to realize the communicative function of credibility enhancement, the hearer has gone through an inferential process labeled analogical reasoning, which attributes to the speaker the hearer's own rationality-based feeling, response, or course of action on the ground of analogy. This process is generally left implicit and the hearer is unconscious of experiencing it, but in cases where the speaker's utterance is extremely problematic such an inference is easily retrievable. Thus, when the hearer is still troubled by uncertainty as to the soundness of the utterance even if he is ready to empathize with the speaker, he engages in this reasoning process to help him decide in favor of assigning credibility to speaker's utterance. This is shown in example (31), reproduced here as example (92).

（92）客　人：现在想起来觉得这一个人就消失了，消失在阳光空气中这种感觉似的，两个多月了仿佛家里就没有这个人，这感觉特别的怪异。人没了，*说句不好听的话*连追悼会都没法开，你见不到人，你什么都不知道。(《送我回家》)

The use of the deprecator "说句不好听的话", by metapragmatically conveying the speaker's empathic intention, constrains the hearer into empathizing with the speaker. However, the speaker's utterance is extremely inappropriate: it violates filial devotion and the taboo of talking about death in public and, more importantly, its crude wording is offensive to good, refined tastes. Thus the empathic hearer has to reason out how to take the utterance. The use of the deprecator indicates the speaker's awareness of the problematic nature of his utterance and this awareness is a sign of his rationality. As a rational being, the hearer reasons, the speaker would not say such a thing as violates the taboo, anymore than the hearer would, unless there is a special reason for doing so. So the speaker must have mentioned death for a special reason. Among the possibilities, the best candidate for the special reason is that the speaker is revealing his genuine feelings. Once the hearer arrives at this conclusion, he will be better able to appreciate the painful helplessness which the speaker has experienced and believe in what the speaker says regardless of the shocking nature of the utterance. This is how the communicative function of credibility enhancement is realized.

In the following example, the host's use of mitigation fails to enhance the credibility of what he says, contrary to what it was designed to do.

（93）主持人：你没有营业执照开始营业*可能是不行吧？*

客　人：可能是不行吧！

主持人：我们俩都很糊涂，这方面。(《回来以后》)

Here, the host uses an epistemic modal "可能" and the particle "吧" to attempt to convince the guest that opening a business without a license is illegal. The use of mitigation was intended to help the guest see the point for himself by drawing him into the meaning negotiation process. However, he echoes what the host says as if sharing his uncertainty, obviously a sign of his failure to comprehend the host's real intention. This noncomprehension is so conspicuous that the host gives a metacommunicative comment "我们俩都很糊涂，这方面" to humorously summarize the communicative failure. The metacommunicative comment is indirect evidence that mitigation was originally designed to perform the function of credibility enhancement. However, the function of credibility enhancement has not been performed because the hearer has not adapted to the speaker's use of mitigation.

The use of mitigation certainly underrepresents the speaker's knowledge state, as he knows for sure that the mitigated statement is true.

This indicates that the speaker is being considerate to the hearer by not imposing on him. Mitigation is also a sign of the speaker's convergence to the hearer's affect, for the hearer is still unhappy about being fined for running a business without a license. It is also a sign of the speaker's altruistic tenderness for the hearer's vulnerable pride as an ex-con. In exchange for this empathy, the speaker expects the hearer to take his perspective and come to terms with the facts. The success or failure of communication crucially depends on whether this empathic intention is recognized and accommodated. As revealed in his echoing of the host's mitigated statement, the guest obviously has failed to recognize the empathic intention or has failed to accommodate it if he has recognized it. That is why the function of credibility enhancement is not realized in this case. It is obvious that the hearer's nonempathic adaptation has left him paralyzed in his warped mentality, which is indicated in his inability or unwillingness to come to terms with the facts.

## 6.3  Summary

In this chapter, I have first been concerned with describing the mitigating functions and categorizing them into interpersonal functions and communicative functions. Interpersonal functions include image management, pacification and solidarity building. Communicative functions include invitations, floor manipulations and persuasions. These further include subfunctions. In identifying and qualifying these functions, I have appealed to the criteria of linguistic evidence, local coherence and pragmatic progression to establish their status as mitigating functions.

I have then been concerned with exploring the metapragmatic constraints exercised by mitigation on the interpretation of the utterance. It is hypothesized that the juxtaposition of mitigation and the performing of the mitigated illocution metapragmatically communicates the speaker's empathic intention. On the one hand, the mitigators exhibit a semantic incongruence, either in the form of underrepresentation, irrelevance, redundancy or even contradiction, with the speaker's illocutionary intention, which signals the speaker's empathy for the hearer. On the other hand, the fact the speaker goes on record performing his illocution indicates that he is attempting to get the hearer to take his perspective. The exchange of perspectives or the reciprocity of empathy is what is involved in the speaker's empathic intention. This intention constrains the hearer into empathically adapting to the speaker's mitigating strategy in the interpretation process.

I have finally been concerned with sketching an account of mitigation in terms of empathic adaptation in order to explain how the mitigating functions are realized. It is hypothesized that empathic adaptation is the necessary and sufficient condition for explaining the working of mitigation. That is, if and only if the hearer is ready to empathize with the speaker while adapting to his mitigating strategy will he act as intended by the speaker. More specifically, only when the hearer takes the speaker's perspective, converges to his affect and wants to be altruistic to him can the mitigating functions be realized. Mere adaptation or nonempathic adaptation does not ensure the hearer's taking of the speaker's perspective due to its egoistic orientation, and cannot explain the realization of the mitigating functions.

# Chapter 7
# Conclusion

## 7.0  Introduction

In chapter, I conclude the thesis by presenting its major findings, pointing out its implications and limitations, and suggesting directions for future studies.

## 7.1  Major Findings

Inspired by and drawing on earlier studies of mitigation, the present study has attempted to examine various aspects of the phenomenon, including its strategies, contextual constraints, functions and its working mechanism and has yielded the following findings.

### 7.1.1  Mitigating Strategies

It has been found that mitigating strategies can be well delimited on a strict definition that integrates two criteria: a reduction of the illocutionary force of the speech act and a softening of a negative effect of the speech act on the hearer. According to this definition, a linguistic element must simultaneously meet the two criteria in order to count as a mitigator, and those that involve only a reduction of the illocutionary force or only a softening of a negative effect, are disqualified as such. On the basis of this strict definition, marginal cases of mitigation such as the politeness marker *please* and deferential terms of address have been left out of the domain of mitigation while those core and typical cases have been happily embraced. This has led to a classification of mitigation into propositional mitigation, illocutionary mitigation and perlocutionary mitigation.

It has also been found that mitigation involves a means, a process and an end. The means refers to a reduction of the illocutionary force which comes in various modalities, and the end refers to a softening of a negative effect of different kinds. Thus the means triggers off a negotiation of rights and obligations between the speaker and the hearer which, through a mechanism of synchronic weakening, leads to the end of mitigation.

The illocutionary force of the speech act can be reduced in a number of ways. First, it can be reduced by illocutionary vagueness. This includes imprecision of the propositional content, attitudinal uncertainty regarding the truth of the proposition and limited applicability of the proposition, which all bear on the transparency with which the illocutionary point is presented. It can also be reduced by illocutionary nonendorsement, which takes the forms of illocutionary inappropriateness, circumstantial illocutionary justifiability and perlocutionary concern, all bearing on the determination with which the speaker gets on record performing the ensuing illocution.

According to the nature of the speech acts in which mitigation occurs, the effects to be softened range from arbitrariness, imposition, guilt, shame, humiliation, to embarrassment, displeasure, distaste, antagonism, among others, on a negativity scale. The softening of the negative effect can take the form of a deintensification of the effect proper or of a deresponsibilization for it. Mitigation is altruistic in the sense of cushioning the negative effect on the hearer and self-serving in the sense of shifting the responsibility for the negative effect away from the speaker.

Propositional mitigation as a superstrategy includes understaters, tag questions, evidentials, epistemic modals and subjectivizers, which all operate on epistemic modality or the proposition of the utterance, and, through a mechanism of synchronic weakening, lead to the softening of imposition, guilt, hurt, shame or sorrow, etc. Illocutionary mitigation subsumes disclaimers, deprecators, truth claimers and hesitators. These operate on deontic modality related to socio-cultural appropriateness and, through a deresponsibilization mechanism or a compensation mechanism, soften a cluster of negative effects on the hearer and minimize the speaker's responsibility for the negative effects. Perlocutionary mitigation comprises simple anticipation, concern showing, penalty taking and direct dissuasion, which all operate on the speaker's perlocutionary concern and an illocutionary dissociation implicitly derived from the concern. Through a mechanism of responsibility assumption and of anticipatory disarming, these soften negative effects of various kinds.

Thus, the tripartite classification of mitigation has gone beyond earlier studies in bringing into focus illocutionary mitigation and perlocutionary mitigation, which have barely received any attention from earlier studies.

### 7.1.2   Contextual Constraints on Mitigation

Mitigation has been found to be interadaptable with such contextual factors as power, negative emotions, controversies, taboo topics, social values, and more importantly, the social norms related to these factors.

Power comes in the forms of experience, expertise and status. Mitigation adapts to power because the powerful hearer has more authority with regard to the state of affairs depicted in the proposition or because the hearer inspires respect in the speaker. In this case, it is consistent with the norm for the speaker to adopt a tentative or unassertive manner of speaking.

Mitigation adapts to negative emotions because these are detrimental to the emotive and cognitive involvement of the conversationalists in the interaction and constitute a target of mitigation in themselves. It is also because the norm requires the speaker to handle the negative emotions in the hearer sensitively and gently, by downplaying the information that is likely to intensify the negative emotion or speaking in a considerate and sympathetic manner that pacifies the negative emotion.

Mitigation adapts to controversies in the sense of making pragmatic concessions to the hearers. This can be done by signaling awareness of divergent views, acknowledging their merits and showing appreciation of them. Such mitigation is motivated by the need to minimize the possibility of conflicts and maximize that of communicative success.

Mitigation adapts to taboo topics because, when the speaker violates a taboo in his speech, the social norm requires him to signal the violation, disclaim intentionality behind the violation, assume responsibility for the violation and apologize for it. The speaker would be socially rejected if he did not mitigate his violation of a taboo topic.

Mitigation adapts to social values such as modesty, sincerity and restraint because these values are strictly adhered to in the community. By mitigating his utterance, the speaker presents himself as upholding or reinforcing these values.

By analyzing examples extensively, the present study has found that different contextual factors constrain language use in their unique ways and are correlated with specific mitigating strategies. Thus, power in the hearer entitles him to more speaking rights and obligations and constrains the speaker into using tag questions and disclaimers typically to limit his own speaking rights and obligations. Negative emotions in the hearer call for the speaker's understanding and sympathy and constrain him into using deprecators, disclaimers and the strategy of concern showing predominantly. Controversies require the speaker to respect and acknowledge others' different views and lead the speaker to employ subjectivizers, epistemic modals more frequently than other strategies. Taboos motivate the speaker to use disclaimers to avoid violating them or to use deprecators to apologize for an inevitable violation. Social values such as modesty, sincerity and restraint require the speaker to present themselves as upholding these values by means of subjectivizers and disclaimers. It has also been found that these contextual factors are especially relevant to specific participants in the interview and lead to the clustering of different strategies of mitigation around different participants. The host, for example, has to constantly adapt to the power in the guest or the honored guest and to the negative emotions in the guest, therefore his mitigating style is characterized by a combination of tag questions, deprecators and disclaimers. Controversy and modesty are especially relevant to the honored guest, who overwhelmingly uses subjectivizers to adapt to the different views held by other honored guests and to present themselves in a positive light. The guest has little to adapt to, his concern being to recount his experience or feelings as accurately as possible. The audience have only to adapt to the competition for the speaking floor and guest's negative emotions, so they mostly use subjectivizers to take and keep the floor and use the truth claimer "实话实说" to pacify the guest.

These findings are well-supported by evidence from a few sources. First, there is the linguistic evidence. In the context of the use of mitigation, there is often a linguistic description of, or mere reference to, a contextual factor and/or the social norm related to this factor. This juxtaposition indicates that it is with reference to this social norm that the ensuing illocution is characterized in the light suggested in the mitigator. For example, if it is only with reference to a cultural taboo that the illocution is negatively characterized by a deprecator, then we can safely conclude that mitigation through the use of the deprecator has resulted from linguistic adaptation to the taboo. Second, it makes good social and communicative sense to regard mitigation as interadaptable with these factors. When an inappropriate illocution is being performed, mitigating its force and negative effects brings social and communicative rewards (avoiding interpersonal conflicts, image management and achieving the communicative goal) while nonmitigation constitutes disrespect for the hearer and profanity for the social norm, which invites serious sanctions on the speaker and the communication. Seen in this light, mitigation is motivated by linguistic adaptation to these factors. Intuitively, these findings are also supported by a cross-contextual consistency of correlation because in other contexts where these factors are absent mitigation disappears.

To sum up, these factors are highly relevant to the interview talks and mitigational adaptation to them is an instance of linguistic adaptation to the social and mental worlds of language users.

### 7.1.3   Mitigating Functions

The present study has found that mitigation performs various functions at the interpersonal and the communicative levels.

At the interpersonal level, it contributes to managing the speaker's image either by preventing him from being negatively evaluated or by presenting him as upholding social values. When what the speaker says violates a social norm and its corresponding expectations, he may clarify his intentions, refute accusations, or express reservations about getting on record, hoping thereby to minimize the possibility of being negatively evaluated. From another perspective, as a result of such efforts of image management, the hearer would not give the speaker the negative evaluation that he would otherwise naturally give. Thus the speaker's image is protected. Mitigation also contributes to pacifying the hearer's negative emotions by gently treating the sensitive areas or vulnerabilities, which are the sources of the negative emotions. Mitigation further helps to build solidarity between the speaker and the hearer by signaling understanding and appreciation of the hearer's feelings and viewpoints.

At the communicative level, mitigation performs inviting functions by creating an informational gap and assigning to the hearer the obligation to fill up the gap. It performs floor manipulations by means of its performativity, negotiability, or more interestingly, by creating psychological expectations in the hearer. Expectations concerning why the illocution is characterized in the light suggested by the mitigator cannot be satisfied unless the speaker is given a chance to state his case, thus the function of floor keeping is realized. Mitigation further performs persuasions by a mechanism of fair exchange. For example, the speaker offers an apology or shows concern with the hearer in return for the hearer's compliance with the speaker's request.

Through a detailed analysis, the present study has found that these functions are regularly associated with specific participants who use different strategies to adapt to specific contextual constraints. Thus, image management is especially relevant to the host and the honored guests, who use deprecators and disclaimers to adapt to social values and taboo topics to avoid being negatively evaluated. Pacifications are the result of the host's adaptation to the guest's negative emotions by means of concern showing and disclaimers. Solidarity building occurs between the host and the guest who feels ill at ease at the beginning of the interview. The inviting functions result from the host's adaptation to the guest's experience or negative emotions or to the honored guest's expertise by means of tag questions, disclaimers, and concern showing. Floor manipulations are realized by means of its performativity, negotiability and by creating psychological expectations in the hearer, mostly through the use of subjectivizers by the audience. Persuasions are the ultimate goal of communication aimed to be reached through all forms of mitigation.

Such functions are supported by linguistic evidence. For example, mitigation often occurs in a transition relevance place to release a floor termination function. In the case of tag questions, there is often no need on the part of the hearer to confirm the question as the speaker is only repeating or reformulating what the hearer has said in a previous turn and the hearer's response to this is predictably a minimal *yes*. Thus the tag question represents the speaker's attempt to build solidarity with the hearer and the hearer's minimal *yes* is a signal that solidarity has been established. What's more, mitigation goes naturally with the provision of evidence for what the speaker says, which is further evidence that mitigation is designed to enhance the credibility of the content of the utterance.

These functions are also consistent with the speaker's concerns at the particular stage of the interview at which mitigation occurs. Thus, invitations are consistent with the host's concern throughout the interview to involve the participants fully into the interview and to get the right person to speak at the right time. They are also consistent with his desire to fully explore the previously unexplored terrains. Negation invitation is particularly consistent with his concern of addressing humor and instructiveness simultaneously. Floor manipulations are consistent with his pursuit of an orderly and efficient running of the interview and of an optimal degree of audience involvement. Interpersonal functions are consistent with the speaker's concern with his own image, with the hearer's emotions and with the relational harmony between them. Persuasions are consistent with the speaker's ultimate concern of being complied with and being able to convince the hearer.

### 7.1.4  General Findings

Four patterns emerge from a summary of the findings concerning the mitigating strategies, the contextual constraints on mitigation and the mitigating functions. Firstly, tag questions are almost exclusively used by the host, who adapts to the power in the guest or the honored guest in order to perform inviting functions. This is consistent with the observation that the host is mainly concerned with securing a maximal degree of participation in the interview to make it run smoothly. Secondly, the subjectivizer "个人认为" is surprisingly monopolized by the honored guests whose power entitles them to speak more assertively. This is explained by their empathic adaptation to the controversial views held among themselves in order not to impose and not to be imposed upon. Thirdly, subjectivizers such as "我认为" and "我有个观点" are favored by the audience, who adapt to the strong competition for the speaking floor in order to seize and keep the floor. Fourthly, the truth claimer "实话实说" is favored by all participants partly because it justifies unreserved outpourings while mitigating resentment and partly because it has come into vogue due to the popularity of the TV program.

### 7.1.5   Empathic Adaptation and Mitigation

It has also been found that mitigation is inherently related to empathy. On the one hand, it involves an incongruence, such as underrepresentation, irrelevance, redundancy or contradiction, between the semantic meaning of the mitigator and the speaker's illocutionary intention. That is, the semantic meaning of the mitigator is often contradictory to the speaker's illocutionary intention, irrelevant to the propositional development or the pragmatic progression, redundant, or illogical from a commonsensical point of view. This semantic incongruence can only be reconciled by assuming that in the use of mitigation the speaker is taking the hearer's perspective, showing affective convergence to the hearer and being altruistic to him. On the other hand, despite being aware of the problematic nature of his illocution and despite his wish to empathize with the hearer, the speaker goes on record performing the illocution. This irrationality can only be explained by assuming that the speaker is bidding for the hearer's empathy on the ground of reciprocity. In other words, by the use of mitigation the speaker is also attempting to get the hearer to take his perspective, converge to his affect and make an altruistic interpretation of his utterance. These constitute the speaker's empathic intention in engaging in mitigated communication. Metapragmatically speaking, through the use of mitigation the speaker explicitly communicates his empathic intention to the hearer and hopes thereby to realize various functions of mitigation. More specifically, mitigation conveys the metapragmatic message that in general or in other contexts the speaker would agree with the hearer, but in the present context he would expect the hearer to agree with him. In terms of interpretation, the speaker discourages the hearer from making a conventional interpretation of the utterance but constrains him into making a novel and altruistic interpretation based on the adoption of the speaker's perspective. Such is the speaker's empathic intention involved in the use of mitigation which exerts great constraints on the interpretation of the mitigated utterance or illocution.

In order to account for mitigation, the present study proposes the notion of empathic adaptation. Adaptation is egoistically oriented, empathy is altruistically oriented while mitigation is both altruistic and egoistic. Thus empathic adaptation captures the very nature of mitigation, which is that it is egoistic via being altruistic. Empathic adaptation means that the language user empathizes with his interlocutor while adapting to a contextual constraint or a mitigating strategy and the speaker's empathic intention constrains both the speaker and the hearer into engaging in empathic adaptation. Thus, the general account of mitigation in terms of empathic adaptation runs as follows. First, in the face a contextual factor, the speaker's empathic intention constrains him into empathically adapting to this factor, resulting in the use of mitigation. This symbolizes the speaker's full consideration of the hearer's cognitive, psychological and emotional needs at the expense of the his own communicative needs or, in other words, the upper limit of the hearer's welfare and the lower limit of the speaker's communicative needs. Then, on the basis of reciprocity, the speaker's empathic intention constrains the hearer into empathically adapting to the speaker's mitigating strategy, which the hearer does. The hearer's empathic adaptation includes an empathic/altruistic inferential process of analogical reasoning which leads him to defend and justify the speaker's inappropriate illocution to the best of his ability as if defending and justifying his own. This justifying removes the ground for making negative evaluations on the speaker or entertaining negative emotions against him, and is responsible for realizing the interpersonal functions of image management and pacification. It highlights the speaker's rationality by stressing that he would not say something whose inappropriateness he is aware of unless there is a special reason, and this leads the hearer to attribute credibility to the content of the speaker's utterance. This is how the communicative function of credibility enhancement is realized. The explanatory power of this notion is manifested in its account of the motivation of mitigating strategies and the realization of mitigating functions. On the one hand, the use of mitigation can be viewed as resulting from the speaker's empathic adaptation to various contextual constraints. That is, the speaker does not only have to take his communicative goal into account, but also has to adopt the hearer's perspective and affect with regard to the corresponding constraint. In a sense, the mitigated utterance denotes what the hearer would want to say regarding a contextual factor. Given the egoistic orientation of adaptation, the speaker would probably opt for reinforcement rather than mitigation if he were not empathic with the hearer. Conversely, if the speaker empathizes with the hearer while adapting to the contextual constraint to reach his communicative goal, he will naturally choose mitigation as it takes care of both needs. On the other hand, the realization of mitigating functions can be viewed as resulting from the hearer's empathic adaptation to the speaker's mitigating strategy. If the hearer adapted to the speaker's use of mitigation, but were not empathic with the speaker, he would be stuck in his own perspective or preoccupied with his own affect, so much so that he would fail to see the speaker's perspective and mitigation would fail to realize its functions. But if he empathizes with the speaker and wants to be altruistic to him, the hearer will interpret the utterance in a way that is advantageous to him. If and only if this happens can the mitigating functions be realized.

## 7.2 Implications

A number of implications can be drawn from the present study and its findings. First, the present study has introduced an element of empathy to capture the essence of mitigation and to explain why mitigation is used and how its interpersonal and communicative functions are realized. This is one step in the direction of establishing a pragmatics that integrates emotive communication, as advocated by Caffi and Janney (1994).

Second, mitigation integrates elements of semantics, pragmatics and metapragmatics. The present study has found that semantics hands over to pragmatics when there is semantic incongruence encoded in the mitigator, which is resolved when pragmatics takes over. Similarly, pragmatics hands over to metapragmatics when there is a conflict between the speaker's communicative needs and his illocutionary concern. This conflict is resolved by metapragmatics by means of the empathic constraints on the interpretation process of the hearer. Such a finding bears direct evidence of the interplay among semantics, pragmatics and metapragmatics.

Third, the metapragmatics of mitigation includes not only metapragmatic awareness as conceptualized by Verschueren (1995, 1999, 2000), but also self reflexivity in the form of reference as captured by Lucy (1993). It further includes self-naming, self-description, self-characterization. Most important of all, it includes the speaker's constraint on the interpretation of the utterance, as highlighted by Caffi (1984), Blum-Kulka (1992), Jacobs (1999), Overstreet and Yule (2002). This has an important implication for the delimitation of metapragmatics.

Fourth, the ability to use and comprehend mitigation is part of the pragmatic competence of the language user. The present study, with its findings, has marked an area that merits extensive attention in language teaching and language acquisition. By drawing the teacher's and the student's attention to the pragmatic phenomenon of mitigation, the present study has an implication for applied pragmatics

Moreover, since mitigation is closely related to the social values and cultural taboos, the present study warns against hasty and uninformed cultural prejudices. This in turn helps avoid cross-cultural communication breakdowns.

## 7.3 Limitations of the Present Study

The most serious limitation of the present study is its subjectivity. As the research methodology is qualitative, much of the reasoning, exposition and generalizing is based on introspection and my intuition as a native speaker of the Chinese language. Because of this the findings are inevitably subjective to a certain degree. Especially relevant in this aspect is my use of the criterion of cross-contextual consistency of correlation in isolating and qualifying contextual motivators of mitigation, which is solely based on my subjective imagining.

The next limitation concerns the data used. Although the interview talks were improvised, the data are still partly artificial due to the participants' concerns with self-presentations. In other words, it is possible that in ordinary language use mitigation is not as highly employed and its functions are not as readily observable. So the findings of the present study need much testing before they can be generalized to other communication activities.

The third limitation is that in exploring the contextual constraints on the use of mitigation I have left out the physical factors. This has distorted the picture and rendered the present study incomplete.

Last, even though the notion of empathy has been borrowed from psychology and adapted for its use in pragmatics, it has not been carefully defined and delimited, so the account of mitigation in terms of empathic adaptation may lose part of its explanatory power.

## 7.4  Suggestions for Future Research

Given the limitations of the present study, it is suggested that future studies be designed so as to overcome them and contribute more to the understanding of mitigation.

As the naturalness of data bears directly on the reliability of research findings, it is advisable to use other data sources than television interview talks, such as naturally-occurring data, which have greater validity.

In addition, future qualitative studies should be complemented by quantitative studies in order to obtain empirical evidence for the hypotheses generated through introspection.

It is also worthwhile investigating physical constraints on the use of mitigation in real-life communication. It is my firm belief that this will be a fruit-bearing undertaking.

# Bibliography

[ 1 ]  Austin, A., M. Salehi and A. Leffler. Gender and developmental differences in children's conversations [J]. *Sex Roles* 16: 497-510. 1987.

[ 2 ]  Bargiela-Chiappini, F. Face and politeness: new (insights) for old (concepts) [J]. *Journal of Pragmatics* 35: 1453-1469. 2003.

[ 3 ]  Barron, A. Acquisition in interlanguage pragmatics: Learning how to do things with words in a study abroad context[M]. Amsterdam/ Philadelphia: John Benjamins. 2003.

[ 4 ]  Basso, K. and H. Selby (eds). *Meaning in anthropology* [C]. Albuquerque: University of Mexico Press. 1976.

[ 5 ]  Batson, D. *The altruism question: Toward a social-psychological answer* [M]. Hillsdale, New Jersey: Lawrence Erlbaum Associates. 1991.

[ 6 ]  Berman, J. *Empathic teaching: Education for life* [M]. Amherst/ Boston: University of Massachusetts Press. 2004.

[ 7 ]  Blum-Kulka, S. Learning to say what you mean in a second language: A study of the speech act performance of learners of Hebrew as a second language [J]. *Applied Linguistics* 3: 29-60. 1982.

[ 8 ]  Blum-Kulka, S. Interpreting and performing speech acts in a second language: A cross-cultural study of Hebrew and English [A]. In: N. Wolfson and E. Judd (eds). 36-55. 1983.

[ 9 ]  Blum-Kulka, S. Indirectness and politeness in requests: same or

different? [J]. *Journal of Pragmatics* 11:131-146. 1987.

[ 10 ] Blum-Kulka, S. You don't touch lettuce with your fingers: Parental politeness in family discourse [J]. *Journal of Pragmatics* 14: 259-288. 1990.

[ 11 ] Blum-Kulka, S. The metapragmatics of politeness in Israeli society [A]. In: Watts et al. (eds). 225-279. 1992.

[ 12 ] Blum-Kulka and House. Cross-cultural and situational variations in requesting behavior [A]. In: Blum-Kulka et al. (eds). 123-154. 1989.

[ 13 ] Blum-Kulka, S., J. House and G. Kasper (eds). *Cross-cultural pragmatics: Requests and apologies* [C]. Norwood, New Jersey: Ablex. 1989.

[ 14 ] Brown, P. and S. Levinson. Universals in language use: Politeness phenomena [A]. In: E. Goody (ed). 56-289. 1978.

[ 15 ] Brown, P and S. Levinson. *Politeness: Some universals in language use* [M]. Cambridge: Cambridge University Press. 1987.

[ 16 ] Bylund, C. and G. Makoul. Empathic communication and gender in the physician-patient encounter [J]. *Patient Education and Counseling* 48: 207-216. 2002.

[ 17 ] Caffi, C. (ed). Metapragmatics. *Special issue of Journal of Pragmatics* 8: 433-592. 1984.

[ 18 ] Caffi, C. Metapragmatics [A]. In: J. Mey (ed). 581-586. 1998.

[ 19 ] Caffi, C. On mitigation [J]. *Journal of Pragmatics* 31: 881-909. 1999.

[ 20 ] Caffi, C. *Mitigation*[M]. Amsterdam: Elsevier. 2007.

[ 21 ] Caffi, C. and R. Janney. Toward a pragmatics of emotive communication [J]. *Journal of Pragmatics* 22: 325-373. 1994.

[ 22 ] Cameron, D., M. Fiona and K. O'leary. Lakoff in context: The

social and linguistic functions of tag questions [A]. In: J. Coates and D. Cameron (eds). 74-93. 1988.

[ 23 ] Chen, R. Responding to compliments: A contrastive study of politeness strategies between American English and Chinese speakers [J]. *Journal of Pragmatics* 20: 49-75. 1993.

[ 24 ] Chen, R. Self-politeness: A proposal [J]. *Journal of Pragmatics* 33:87-106. 2001.

[ 25 ] Chen, Y. and A. He. *Dui bu dui* as a pragmatic marker: Evidence from Chinese classroom discourse [J]. *Journal of Pragmatics* 33: 1441-1465. 2001.

[ 26 ] Chin, J., J. Liem, M. Ham and G. Hong. Transference and empathy in Asian American psychology: Cultural values and treatment needs [M]. Westport: Praeger Publishers. 1993.

[ 27 ] Ching, M. 'Ma'am' and 'Sir': Modes of mitigation and politeness in the Southern United States. Abstract in *Newsletter of the American Dialect Society* 19:10. 1987.

[ 28 ] Clark, R. and J. Della. Cognitive complexity, social perspective-taking, and functional persuasive skills in second-to-ninth grade children [J]. *Winter* 3: 128-134. 1977.

[ 29 ] Coates, J. and D. Cameron (eds). *Women in their speech communities* [C]. London/New York: Longman. 1988.

[ 30 ] Cole, P. and J. Morgan (eds). *Syntax and semantics, Vol.3: Speech acts* [C]. New York: Academic Press. 1975.

[ 31 ] Coplan, A. Empathic engagement with narrative fictions [J]. *The Journal of Aesthetics and Art Criticism* 62: 143-152. 2004.

[ 32 ] Coulmas, F (ed). *Conversational routine* [C]. Mouton: The Hague. 1981.

[ 33 ] Culpeper, J. Towards an anatomy of impoliteness [J]. *Journal of*

*Pragmatics* 25: 349-367. 1996.

[ 34 ] Culpeper, J., D. Bousfield and A. Wichmann. Impoliteness revisited: with special reference to dynamic and prosodic aspects [J]. *Journal of Pragmatics* 35: 1545-1579. 2003.

[ 35 ] Daneš, F. Involvement with language and in language [J]. *Journal of Pragmatics* 22: 251-264. 1994.

[ 36 ] Davis, M. *Empathy: A social psychological approach* [M]. Oxford: Westview Press. 1996.

[ 37 ] Eckert, P. The whole women: Sex and gender differences in variation [J]. *Language Variation and Change* 1: 245-267. 1989.

[ 38 ] Eisenberg, N. and J. Strayer (eds). *Empathy and its development* [C]. Cambridge: Cambridge University Press. 1987.

[ 39 ] Erman, B. Female and male usage of pragmatic expressions in same-sex and mixed-sex interactions [J]. *Language Variation and Change* 4: 217-234. 1992.

[ 40 ] Erman, B. Pragmatic markers revisited with a focus on *you know* in adult and adolescent talk [J]. *Journal of Pragmatics* 33: 1337-1359. 2001.

[ 41 ] Faerch, C. and G. Kasper. Internal and external modification in interlanguage request realizations [A]. In Blum-Kulka et al. (eds). 222-247. 1989.

[ 42 ] Farris, C. The gender of child discourse: same-sex peer socialization through language use in a Taiwanese pre-school [J]. *Journal of Linguistic Anthropology* 2: 198-224. 1991.

[ 43 ] Farris, C. Cross-sex peer conflict and the discursive production of gender in a Chinese pre-school in Taiwan [J]. *Journal of Pragmatics* 32: 539-568. 2000.

[ 44 ] Fasulo, A. and C. Zucchermaglio. My selves and I: Identity markers

in work meeting talk [J]. *Journal of Pragmatics* 34, 1119-1144. 2002.

[ 45 ] Félix-Brasdefer, J. Interlanguage refusals: Linguistic politeness and length of residence in the target community [J]. *Language Learning* 54: 587-653. 2004.

[ 46 ] Filipi, A. and R. Wales. Perspective-taking and perspective shifting as socially situated and collaborative actions [J]. *Journal of Pragmatics* 36: 1851-1884. 2004.

[ 47 ] Fishman, P. Interaction: The work women do [A]. In: B. Thorne, C. Kramerae, and N.Henley (eds). 89-101. 1983.

[ 48 ] Flowerdew, J. Pragmatic modifications on the 'representative' speech act of defining [J]. *Journal of Pragmatics* 15: 253-264. 1991.

[ 49 ] Fox Tree, J. and J. Schrock. Basic meaning of *You know* and *I mean* [J]. *Journal of Pragmatics* 34: 727-747. 2002.

[ 50 ] Fraser, B. Hedged performatives [A]. In P. Cole and J. Morgan (eds.). 187-210. 1975.

[ 51 ] Fraser, B. Conversational mitigation [J]. *Journal of Pragmatics* 4: 341-350. 1980.

[ 52 ] Fraser, B. Perspectives on politeness [J]. *Journal of Pragmatics* 14:219-236. 1990.

[ 53 ] Gass, S. and J. Neu (eds). Speech acts across cultures: Challenges to communication in a second language [C]. Berlin: Mouton de Gruyter. 1996.

[ 54 ] Gillotti, C., T. Thompson and K. Mcneilis. Communicative competence in the delivery of bad news [J]. *Social Science and Medicine* 54: 1011-1023. 2002.

[ 55 ] Giora, R., O. Fein, J. Ganzi, N. Levi and H. Sabah. On negation as

mitigation: The case of negative irony [J]. *Discourse Processes* 39: 81-100. 2005.

[ 56 ] Goffman, E. *The presentation of self in everyday life* [M]. New York: Doubleday Anchor. 1959.

[ 57 ] Goffman, E. Interactional ritual essays on face to face behavior[M]. Garden City: Anchor Books. 1967.

[ 58 ] Goldstein, A. and G. Michaels. *Empathy: development, training and consequences* [M]. Hillsdale, New Jersey: Lawrence Erlbaum Associates. 1985.

[ 59 ] Goodwin, M. He-Said-She-Said: Talk as social organization among black children [M]. Bloomington: Indiana University Press. 1990.

[ 60 ] Goodwin, M. Games of stance: conflict and footing in hopscotch [A]. In: S. Hoype and C. Adger (eds). 23-46. 1998.

[ 61 ] Goody, E(ed). *Questions and politeness: Strategies in social interaction* [C]. Cambridge: Cambridge University Press. 1978.

[ 62 ] Grice, P. Logic and conversation [A]. In: P. Cole and J. Morgan (eds). 41-58. 1975.

[ 63 ] Gu, Y. Politeness phenomena in modern Chinese. *Journal of Pragmatics* 14: 237-258. 1990.

[ 64 ] Haley, J. An interactional description of schizophrenia [J]. *Psychiatry* 22:321-332. 1959.

[ 65 ] Hassall, T. Modifying requests in a second language [J]. *International Journal of Applied Linguistics* 39: 259-283. 2001.

[ 66 ] Haugh, M. and C. Hinze. A metalinguistic approach to deconstructing the concepts of 'face' and 'politeness' in Chinese, English and Japanese [J]. *Journal of Pragmatics* 35: 1581-1611. 2003.

[ 67 ] Haverkate, H. Deictic categories as mitigating devices. *Pragmatics*

2: 505-522. 1992.

[ 68 ] Heisler, T., D. Vincent and A. Bergeron. Evaluative metadiscursive comments and face-work in conversational discourse. [M] *Journal of Pragmatics* 35:1613-1631. 2003.

[ 69 ] Hewitt, J. and R. Stokes. Disclaimers [J]. *American Psychological Review* 40: 1-11. 1975.

[ 70 ] Hoffman, M. Empathy and moral development: implications for caring and justice [M]. Cambridge: Cambridge University Press. 2000.

[ 71 ] Holmes, J. The function of tag questions [J]. *English Language Research Journal* 3: 40-65. 1983.

[ 72 ] Holmes, J. Modifying illocutionary force [J]. *Journal of pragmatics* 8:345-365. 1984.

[ 73 ] Holmes, J. Sex differences and miscommunication: Some data from New Zealand [A]. In: B. John (ed). 24-43. 1985.

[ 74 ] Holmes, J. Functions of *you know* in women's and men's speech [J]. *Language in Society* 15: 1-22. 1986.

[ 75 ] Holmes, J. *Women, men and politeness* [M]. London: Longman. 1995.

[ 76 ] Holmes, J. Women, language and identity [J]. *Journal of sociolinguistics* 1: 195-223. 1997.

[ 77 ] House, J. Politeness in English and German: The functions of *please* and *bitte* [A]. In: Blum-Kulka et al.(eds). 96-119. 1989.

[ 78 ] House, J. and G. Kasper. Politeness markers in English and German [A]. In: F. Coulmas (ed). 157-185. 1981.

[ 79 ] Hoype, S. and C. Adger (eds). *Kids' talk: strategic language use in later childhood* [C]. New York: Oxford University Press. 1998.

[ 80 ] Huo, Y. *Mitigation and pragmatics as a linguistic regulation*

*theory: The case of TCM clinical interviews* [M]. Kunming: Yunnan University Press. 2004.

[ 81 ] Hymes, D. On communicative competence [A]. In: J. Pride and J. Holmes (eds). 269-293. 1972.

[ 82 ] Jacobs, G. Preformulating the news: An analysis of the metapragmatics of press releases[M]. Amsterdam/Philadelphia: John Benjamins. 1999.

[ 83 ] James, A. Compromisers in English: A cross-disciplinary approach to their interpersonal significance [J]. *Journal of Pragmatics* 7: 191-206. 1983.

[ 84 ] Ji, S. 'Face' and politeness in Chinese culture [J]. *Journal of Pragmatics* 32: 1059-1062. 2000.

[ 85 ] John, B (ed). Cross-cultural encounters: Communication and miscommunication [C]. Melbourne: River Seine. 1985.

[ 86 ] Johnson, N (ed). *Current topics in language: Introductory readings* [C]. Cambridge, Massachusetts: Winthrop Publishers. 1976.

[ 87 ] Kakava, C. Opposition in Modern Greek discourse: cultural and contextual constraints [J]. *Journal of Pragmatics* 34: 1537-1568. 2002.

[ 88 ] Kang, A. Negotiating conflicts within the constraints of social hierarchies in Korean American discourse [J]. *Journal of Sociolinguistics* 7: 299-320. 2003.

[ 89 ] Kasper, G. Linguistic politeness: Current research issues [J]. *Journal of Pragmatics* 14:193-218. 1990.

[ 90 ] Kasper, G. and S. Blum-Kulka (eds). *Interlanguage pragmatics* [C]. New York/Oxford: Oxford University Press. 1993.

[ 91 ] Kasper, G. and K. Rose. *Pragmatic development in a second language* [M]. Massachusetts: Blackwell. 2002.

[ 92 ] Kasper, G. and Y. Zhang. *Pragmatics of Chinese as a second and target language* [M]. Hawaii: Hawaii University Press. 1995.

[ 93 ] Kellett, J., R. Humphrey and R. Sleeth. Empathy and complex task performance: two routes to leadership [J]. *The Leadership Quarterly* 13: 523-544. 2002.

[ 94 ] Kiesling, S. Men's identities and sociolinguistic variation [J]. *Journal of sociolinguistics* 2: 69-99. 1998.

[ 95 ] Koike, D. Negation in Spanish and English questions and requests: Mitigating effects? [J]. *Journal of Pragmatics* 21: 513-526. 1994.

[ 96 ] Kunyk, D. and J. Olson. Clarification of conceptualizations of empathy [J]. *Journal of Advanced Nursing* 35: 317-325. 2001.

[ 97 ] Kurzon, D. The politeness of judges: American and British judicial behavior [J]. *Journal of Pragmatics* 33: 61-85. 2001.

[ 98 ] Kyratzis, A. and J. Guo. Pre-school girls' and boys' verbal strategies in the United States and China [J]. *Research on Language and Social Interaction* 34: 45-74. 2001.

[ 99 ] Kyratzis, A. and S. Ervin-Tripp. The development of discourse markers in peer interaction [J]. *Journal of Pragmatics* 31: 1321-1338. 1999.

[ 100 ] Labov, W. Mitigation and questioning in a verbal repertoire [A]. In: Johnson, N. (ed). 81-90. 1976

[ 101 ] Ladegarrd, H. Politeness in young children's speech: context, peer group influence and pragmatic competence [J]. *Journal of Pragmatics* 36: 2003-2022. 2004.

[ 102 ] Lakoff, G. Hedges: A study in meaning criteria and the logic of fuzzy concepts [A]. In: Peranteau et al. (eds). 183-228. 1972.

[ 103 ] Lakoff, R. *Language and women's place* [M]. New York: Harper Colophon. 1975.

[ 104 ] Leaper, C. Influence and involvement: age, gender and partner effects [J]. *Child Development* 62: 797-811. 1991.

[ 105 ] Leech, G. *Principles of pragmatics*[M]. London: Longman. 1983.

[ 106 ] Lucy, J(ed). *Reflexive language : Reported speech and metapragmatics* [C]. Cambridge: Cambridge University Press. 1993.

[ 107 ] Macaulay, R. You know, it depends [J]. *Journal of Pragmatics* 34: 749-767. 2002.

[ 108 ] Malone, M. *Worlds of talk—The presentation of self in everyday conversation* [M]. Cambridge, Oxford and Malden: Polity Press. 1997.

[ 109 ] Mao, L. Beyond politeness theory: 'Face' revisited and renewed [J]. *Journal of Pragmatics* 21: 451-486. 1994.

[ 110 ] Markkanen, R. and H. Schröder (eds). Hedging and discourse: Approaches to the analysis of a pragmatic phenomenon in academic texts [C]. Berlin: Walter de Gruyter. 1997.

[ 111 ] Martinovski, B. A framework for the analysis of mitigation in courts: Toward a theory of mitigation [J]. *Journal of Pragmatics* 38: 2065-2086. 2006.

[ 112 ] Matsugu, Y. Japanese epistemic sentence-final particle *kana*: Its functions as a 'mitigation' marker in discourse data [J]. *Pragmatics* 15: 423-436. 2005.

[ 113 ] Maynard, S. Mitigation in disguise: *Te-yuu-ka* as preface to self-revelation in Japanese dramatic discourse [J]. *Poetics* 29: 317-329. 2001.

[ 114 ] Meier, A. Passages of politeness [J]. *Journal of Pragmatics* 24: 381-392. 1995.

[ 115 ] Mey, J. *Pragmatics* [M]. Oxford: Basil Blackwell. 1993.

[ 116 ] Mey, J(ed). *Concise encyclopedia of pragmatics* [C]. Amsterdam: Elsevier. 1998.

[ 117 ] Miller, P., D. Danaher and D. Forbes. Sex-related strategies for coping with interpersonal conflict in children aged five and seven [J]. *Developmental Psychology* 22: 543-548. 1986.

[ 118 ] Nagano, H. Empathic understanding: Constructing an evaluation scale from the microcounseling approach [J]. *Nursing and Health Sciences* 2: 17-27. 2000

[ 119 ] Nichols, S. Mindreading and the cognitive architecture underlying altruistic motivation [J]. *Mind & Language* 16: 425-455. 2001.

[ 120 ] Nordenstam, K. Tag questions and gender in Swedish conversations [J]. *Working Papers on Language, Gender and Sexism* 2: 75-86. 1992.

[ 121 ] Norrick, N. Involvement and joking in conversation [J]. *Journal of Pragmatics* 22: 409-430. 1994.

[ 122 ] O'Driscoll, J. About face: A defense and elaboration of universal dualism [J]. *Journal of Pragmatics* 25: 1-32. 1996.

[ 123 ] Overstreet, M. and G. Yule. Formulaic disclaimers [J]. *Journal of Pragmatics* 33: 45-60. 2001.

[ 124 ] Overstreet, M. and G. Yule. The metapragmatics of *and everything* [J]. *Journal of pragmatics* 34:769-784. 2002.

[ 125 ] Peranteu, P., J. Levi and G. Phares(ed). *Papers from the 8the regional meeting* [C]. Chicago Linguistic Society. 1972.

[ 126 ] Pissiconi, B. Re-examining politeness, face and the Japanese language [J]. *Journal of Pragmatics* 35: 1471-1506. 2003.

[ 127 ] Pride, J. and J. Holmes (eds). *Sociolinguistics*[C]. London: Penguin. 1972.

[ 128 ] Ran, Y. *The pragmatics of discourse markers in conversation* [D].

Unpublished Ph.D Dissertation. Guangdong University of Foreign Studies, Guangzhou. 2000.

[ 129 ] Redmond, M. A multidimensional theory and measure of social decentering [J]. *Journal of Research in Personality* 29: 35-58. 1995.

[ 130 ] Reynolds, M. *The measurement and development of empathy in nursing* [M]. Hants/Burlington: Ashgate Publishing Ltd. 2000.

[ 131 ] Reynolds, W. and B. Scott. Empathy: a crucial component of the helping relationship [J]. *Journal of Psychiatric and Mental Health Nursing* 6: 363-370. 1999.

[ 132 ] Richmond, S. Being in others: Empathy from a psychoanalytical perspective [J]. *European Journal of Philosophy* 12: 244-264. 2004.

[ 133 ] Rose, K. and G. Kasper (eds). *Pragmatics in language teaching* [C]. Cambridge: Cambridge University Press. 2001

[ 134 ] Sbisà, M. On illocutionary types. *Journal of Pragmatics* 8: 93-114. 1984.

[ 135 ] Sbisà, M. Illocutionary force and degrees of strength in language use [J]. *Journal of pragmatics* 33: 1791-1814. 2001.

[ 136 ] Searle, J. *Speech acts*[M]. Cambridge: Cambridge University Press. 1969.

[ 137 ] Searle, J. Indirect speech acts [A]. In: P. Cole and J. Morgan(eds). 59-82. 1975.

[ 138 ] Searle, J. A classification of illocutionary acts [J]. *Language in society* 5:1-23. 1976.

[ 139 ] Sheldon, A. Pickle fights: gendered talk in pre-school disputes [J]. *Discourse Processes* 13: 5-31. 1990.

[ 140 ] Sheldon, A. Conflict talk: sociolinguistic challenges to self-

assertion and how young girls meet them [J]. *Merrill-Palmer Quarterly* 38: 95-117. 1992.

[ 141 ] Sheldon, A. You can be the baby brother but you aren't born yet: pre-school girls' negotiation for power and access in pretend play [J]. *Research on Language and Social Interaction* 29: 57-80. 1996.

[ 142 ] Shiffrin, D. Discourse Markers [M]. Cambridge: Cambridge University Press. 1987.

[ 143 ] Silverstein, M. Shifters, linguistic categories, and cultural descriptions [A]. In K. Basso and H. Selby (eds). 11-55. 1976.

[ 144 ] Silverstein, M. Metapragmatic discourse and metapragmatic function [A]. In J. Lucy(ed). 33-58. 1993.

[ 145 ] Skewis, M. Mitigated directness in *Honglou meng*: Directive speech acts and politeness in eighteenth century Chinese [J]. *Journal of Pragmatics* 35:161-189. 2003.

[ 146 ] Smith-Heffner, N. Women and politeness: The Javanese example [J]. *Language in Society* 17: 535-554. 1988.

[ 147 ] Sollitt-Morris, L. *Language, gender and power relationships* [D]. Unpublished PhD Dissertation. Wellington: Victoria University of Wellington. 1997.

[ 148 ] Spiro, H., M. Curnen, E. Peschel and D. James (eds). *Empathy and the practice of medicine* [C]. New Haven/London: Yale University Press. 1993.

[ 149 ] Stubbs, M. Discourse analysis. The sociolinguistic analysis of natural language [M]. Oxford: Blackwell. 1983.

[ 150 ] Tannen, D. Indirectness in discourse: Ethnicity as a conversational style [J]. *Discourse Processes* 4: 221-238. 1981.

[ 151 ] Thomas, J. Meaning in interaction: An introduction to pragmatics

[M]. London/New York: Longman. 1995.

[ 152 ] Thonus, T. Tutor and student assessment of academic writing tutorials: What is "success"? [J]. *Assessing Writing* 8: 110-134. 2002.

[ 153 ] Thornborrow, J. and D. Morris. Gossip as strategy: The management of talk about others on reality TV show 'Big brother'. *Journal of Sociolinguistics* 8: 246-271. 2004.

[ 154 ] Thorne, B., C. Kramerae, and N. Henley (eds). *Language, gender and society* [C]. Massachusetts: Newbury House. 1983.

[ 155 ] Trosborg, A. Interlanguage pragmatics: Requests, complaints and apologies [M]. Berlin: Walter de Gruyter. 1995.

[ 156 ] Verducci, S. A conceptual history of empathy and a question it raises for moral education [J]. *Educational Theory* 50:3-80. 2000.

[ 157 ] Verschueren, J. *International news reporting: Metapragmatic metaphors and the U-2* [M]. Amsterdam/Philadelphia: John Benjamins. 1985.

[ 158 ] Verschueren, J. Metapragmatics [A]. In J. Verschueren et al. (eds). 367-371. 1995.

[ 159 ] Verschueren, J. *Understanding Pragmatics*[M]. London/New York: Edward Arnold. 1999.

[ 160 ] Verschueren, J. Notes on the role of metapragmatic awareness in language use [J]. *Pragmatics* 10: 439-456. 2000.

[ 161 ] Verschueren, J, J.-O. Ostman and J. Bloommaeret (eds). *Handbook of pragmatics: A manual* [C]. Amsterdam/Philadelphia: John Benjamins. 1995.

[ 162 ] Watts, R., S. Ide and K. Ehlich (eds). *Politeness in language* [C]. Berlin: Mouton. 1992.

[ 163 ] Wee, L. 'Extreme communicative acts' and the boosting of

illocutionary force [J]. *Journal of Pragmatics* 36: 2161-2178. 2004.

[ 164 ] West, C. and D. Zimmerman. Small insults: A study of interruptions in cross-sex conversations between unacquainted persons [A]. In: Thorneet et al.(eds). 102-117. 1983.

[ 165 ] Wetzel, P. Are 'powerless' communication strategies the Japanese norm? [J] *Language in Society* 17: 102-117. 1988.

[ 166 ] White, S. Empathy: a literature review and concept analysis [J]. *Journal of Clinical Nursing* 6: 253-257. 1997.

[ 167 ] Wierzbicka, A. Different cultures, different languages, different speech acts: Polish vs. English [J]. *Journal of Pragmatics* 9: 145-178. 1985.

[ 168 ] Wilkinson, M. How do we understand empathy systematically? [J] *Journal of Family Therapy* 14: 193-205. 1992.

[ 169 ] Wiseman, T. A concept analysis of empathy [J]. *Journal of Advanced Nursing* 23:1162-1167. 1996.

[ 170 ] Wolfson, N. and E. Judd (eds). *Sociolinguistics and language acquisition* [C]. Rowley, Massachusetts: Newbury House. 1983.

[ 171 ] Woods, N. Talking shop: sex and status as determinants of floor apportionment in a work setting [A]. In: J. Coates and D. Cameron (eds). 141-157. 1988.

[ 172 ] Wouk, F. Gender and the use of pragmatic particles in Indonesian [J]. *Journal of Sociolinguistics* 3: 194-219. 1999.

[ 173 ] Wynn, R. and M. Wynn. Empathy as an interactionally achieved phenomenon in psychotherapy: Characteristics of some conversational resources [J]. *Journal of Pragmatics* 38: 1385-1397. 2006.

[ 174 ] 何自然. 言语交际中的语用移情 [J]. 外语教学与研究,

1991(4)：11-15.

［175］何自然，冉永平（编著）. 语用学概论（第二版）[M]. 长沙：湖南教育出版社,2002.

［176］冉永平. 言语交际中"吧"的语用功能及其语境顺应性特征[J]. 现代外语2004(4)：340-349.

［177］冉永平. 指示语选择的语用视点、语用移情与离情 [J]. 外语教学与研究,2007(5)：331-337.

# Acknowledgements

In the process of writing the present dissertation, I have received much help from a number of people, who deserve a word of thank from me.

I am grateful to Professor He Ziran for enrolling me into the Ph.D program and for always showing confidence in me and giving me guidance.

I am hugely indebted to Professor Ran Yongping, who first suggested mitigation to me as a topic of research, and then guided me through the writing process step by step, all the while making insightful comments on my work which became my inspirations. I owe him a special debt.

I want to extend my thanks to Professor Huo Yongshou for being so generous as to forward to me some of the references I needed. They turned out to be highly valuable for writing the literature review.

I also want to thank Liao Kaihong, my colleague and friend, for proof-reading the whole text before it was finalized. His proof-reading contributed largely to improving the quality of my dissertation by eliminating many spelling mistakes and grammatical mistakes.

Last but not least, I am thankful to my wife Xietian and my daughter Li Xiaoyu, for lending me their moral support and for tolerating my procrastination. Much of the time spent in writing this dissertation was theirs.